D1480378

FROM WILDERNESS TO WASTELAND

Kennikat Press
National University Publications
Literary Criticism Series

General Editor
John E. Becker
Fairleigh Dickinson University

FROM WILDERNESS TO WASTELAND

The Trial of the Puritan God in the American Imagination

CHARLES BERRYMAN

National University Publications
KENNIKAT PRESS // 1979
Port Washington, N. Y. // London

Manufactured in the United States of America

Published by
Kennikat Press Corp.
Port Washington, N.Y. / London

Library of Congress Cataloging in Publication Data

Berryman, Charles, 1939–
    From wilderness to wasteland.

    (Literary criticism series) (National university publications)
    Bibliography: p.
    Includes index.
    1. American literature—History and criticism.
    2. Authors, American—Religion and ethics.
    3. God in literature. 4. Puritans—United States.
    I. Title.
PS166.B4   810'.9'31   79-1177
ISBN 0-8046-9235-1

CONTENTS

for
JO
KENNETH
and
CHRISTOPHER

PREFACE

The story of the religious imagination in America has long been a battle-field for historians, theologians, and literary critics. The present book is designed to outrage and attract all three. It follows the rise and fall of the Puritan image of God from the arrival of the English settlers in the seventeenth century to the return voyage of T. S. Eliot three hundred years later. Although this book is based on the scholarship and teaching of American literature, it is neither a monograph for historians and critics nor exclusively a textbook for students. Instead it is an essay on the design and adaptation of religious ideas in the American imagination. It is written for a general audience willing to ask why various gods have been invented, worshipped, and abandoned.

The first chapter describes the sovereign God accepted by the early Puritans in America. The theology of the Puritans is defined in terms of the psychological and political demands inherent in starting a new life at the edge of the wilderness. Adapting the theology of John Calvin to the dangers of the New World was the first challenge of the American imagination.

The next chapter recalls the compromises of doctrine and experience worked out by the second and third generations in New England. The life of Cotton Mather is used to illustrate the consequences of loyalty to a fading cause. Mather inherited the responsibility of the Puritan vision at a time when the practical authority for enforcing it was diminishing

The third chapter turns to the Great Awakening and the extraordinary career of Jonathan Edwards. Both are seen as examples of a basic contra-diction in the religious imagination: the Great Awakening compromised the faith that it wanted to advance, and Jonathan Edwards wrote the final theology for a religion which his own congregation had already rejected.

The fourth chapter records the challenges to Puritan dogma represented by the philosophy of the Enlightenment. The success of Benjamin Franklin is described as an example of the new respectability and power commanded by empirical science, and Thomas Jefferson is used to illustrate the anti-Puritan thrust of democratic expectations.

The fifth chapter describes the alternatives to Christianity suggested by Emerson in the nineteenth century. He challenged the theology of his Puritan ancestors by recommending a substitute faith in nature and self-reliance. In the campaign to alter the direction of the religious imagination in New England, the voice of Emerson was often more decisive than he himself anticipated.

The sixth and seventh chapters analyze the tragic literature of Hawthorne and Melville against their heritage of Puritan theology. Both authors responded to their religious backgrounds with uncertainty and criticism. Hawthorne probed the psychological motives of his Puritan characters, and Melville dramatized the heroic assault against divine power.

In the last chapter the career of T. S. Eliot is described as a reactionary challenge to a world of infidels. The remains of the old God were planted by Eliot in the spiritual desert of the twentieth century and a few dry tears shed over the grave. With the migration of Eliot to the English setting of his Puritan ancestors, the theme of this study is brought full circle.

The aim of this book is to follow the historical progress from the idea of a sovereign God shared by the early Puritans in New England to the skeptical vision of scientific and democratic humanism in the twentieth century. While historians have told parts of the story in detail, they often neglect the study of literature which records the fundamental change in imaginative patterns. While theologians have argued at length about the decline of religious dogma, they seldom consider the psychological and literary forces which cause men to create various gods according to their own shifting images. While literary critics have written many volumes about the religious imagery of Hawthorne, Melville, and Eliot, they often ignore the stages of Puritan decline which help to locate these authors in history. This book is a step toward bringing the three fields together.

It is expected that parts of this book will appear controversial. Christian readers may be disturbed to find the assumptions of their faith challenged by a chronicle of its decline and failure. Historical scholars may ask why so much space is given to the critical analysis of literary fiction. And conversely the literary critics may wonder about the chapters of historical reporting. Such are the problems of an interdisciplinary study. The central interest is the American imagination itself; its patterns are the doctrines of faith, the narratives of fiction, and the design of history. But does that abstraction—the American imagination—have any substance? If coherent patterns of thought and belief are described in the following pages, they represent the common fiction that we call art, religion, and history. The early Puritans in America understood their history in biblical terms, and literally believed in a supernatural origin for their religious images. In the present study, however, all inventions of the human imagination are considered to be the product of psychological motives, political or social forces, and literary customs. Unless it is encouraged to change, the imagination repeats its own artistic and religious designs. The most important change in three centuries of American experience—the change from obedience to skepticism—is the subject of this study.

FROM WILDERNESS TO WASTELAND

ABOUT THE AUTHOR

Charles Berryman is an Associate Professor of English at the University of Southern California in Los Angeles. His essays on Arnold, Chaucer, Emerson, Thoreau, and W. B. Yeats have appeared in many scholarly and literary journals. His television programs on modern American literature have been broadcast in Los Angeles by KNXT-TV.

1

SOVEREIGN IN AMERICA:
The Puritan God

The English Puritans who sailed across the Atlantic in the seventeenth century to build the Massachusetts Bay Colony believed themselves to be in direct contact with the terror and grace of their God. A storm at sea was recognized by the company of Governor Winthrop as a token of divine punishment. Fair winds and a calm ocean were omens indicating God's approval of their voyage to the New World. But how did these Puritans define their image of supernatural power? And how did their feelings of ambition, fear, love, and guilt help to shape the idea of God in their imaginations?

The first great spiritual leader of New England was John Cotton. He served as minister of the First Church of Boston from his arrival in the Massachusetts Bay Colony in 1633 until his death almost twenty years later. What the early Puritans in America thought about the nature of their God is well revealed in a collection of his sermons entitled *The Way of Life*. John Cotton was a scholar thoroughly familiar with the literature of the Protestant Reformation. He accepted the definition of God set forth in the writings of John Calvin, and applied it to the experience of his congregation in the New World. God is presented in *The Way of Life* as a sovereign Judge, often jealous and wrathful, yet capable of granting unexpected and undeserved mercy. All genuine worship of this God, according to the theology of John Cotton, must involve an experience of mystical piety. Each member of the Puritan congregation was required to obey the absolute rule of the Lord, and be ready for the possible reception of divine grace.

Why did the first generation of Puritans in America feel such a particular need to affirm the sovereign power of their God? And why did the confession of piety achieve a central position in defining the nature of their worship? The Protestant Reformation had been largely responsible for renewing the power of the jealous and wrathful God known to the Hebrew prophets in the Old Testament. Martin Luther and John Calvin both directed their followers to a God endowed with the sovereign authority to grant either damnation or grace. The Protestant Reformation was also the occasion for a renewed emphasis upon mystical piety. Although the leaders of the Reformation in the sixteenth century often looked back to Saint Augustine to find their chief model for the experience of piety, the Reformation itself represented a new tide of evangelical faith powerful enough to split the Christian world. The Puritans, who came to Massachusetts a century later with Governor Winthrop, still believed themselves to be in the vanguard of that revolution. They expected to build in the wilderness the "holy City of God" envisioned by Saint Augustine and set forth in Protestant theology by John Calvin.

The rededication to Jehovah encouraged by the Protestant Reformation may be explained in both political and psychological terms. The discounting of papal supremacy by the followers of Luther and Calvin demanded a shift of power to other figures of authority both divine and secular. To justify turning the pope into the image of Antichrist, the Protestant imagination strengthened the idea of God as sovereign Judge. The Protestant rejection of the church in Rome was thus given the apparent sanction of divine approval. The jealous God of the Old Testament was called upon by the reformers to punish the idolators who continued to pledge their faith to Rome. Corrupt and oppressive rule by the hierarchy of the church was replaced in theory by the single authority of Holy Scripture. In practice, the civil and religious power long exercised by the pope was seized and divided among the independent political rulers of northern Europe. The separation of the English church from Rome, and the strengthening of the English monarchy under Henry VIII, were simultaneous expressions of the demand for new forms and figures of authority.

New ways of embodying power were also necessary to control and direct the energies of exploration, trade, art, science, and philosophy that were appearing as part of the English Renaissance. During the second half of the sixteenth century, Queen Elizabeth skillfully used her authority as ruler of church and state to increase greatly the power of England. The generation of Francis Drake, William Shakespeare, and Francis Bacon confirmed the far-reaching independence of English military strength, art, and philosophy. Queen Elizabeth was not seriously threatened when the pope excommunicated her in 1570. Although he accused her of being a bastard and a heretic, the charges meant little to her Protestant subjects who were prepared to celebrate her rule over England as the sovereign reign of "Gloriana."

Elizabeth's success with the government of both state and church was not continued by the Stuart monarchs who inherited her throne. Elizabeth had always followed a middle course between the reactionary Catholic forces, who desired to see the work of the Reformation undone, and the Puritans, who demanded an acceleration of the reform movement. After the death of Elizabeth at the beginning of the seventeenth century, the growing strength of the Puritans brought England within two generations to open civil war. The disenchantment of the Puritans with the authority of King James and King Charles only served to strengthen their faith in a sovereign God. The great migration to the New World began in this mood of rebellion. Thousands of English Puritans crossed the Atlantic in the 1630s convinced that they were embarked on "a special work of God's providence." The Puritans coming to the New World thought of themselves as completing the process begun a century earlier with the first escape from the supremacy of the pope. In the wilderness of America there would be neither pope nor king; only the sovereign and merciful God. It is true that some of the immigrants to New England still kept up the pretense of loyalty to the English crown, but King Charles was three thousand miles away and soon would be executed. John Cotton could thus address his congregation at the First Church of Boston as if they were ruled in the wilderness directly by God and must answer only to His commands. The recent experience of these new American Puritans had taught them how to define power in terms of an absolute hierarchy and how to exalt their God as the all-powerful Sovereign.

The revival of the jealous and wrathful God of the Old Testament may also be explained psychologically. Assuming that all gods are inventions of the human imagination, Freud argued that the image of a very powerful God may be understood as the projection of an insecure conscience. If a child's behavior is controlled by the commands of parents—"Do not do that!"—which the child gradually learns to anticipate, in time the voice of denial and restriction becomes a part of the individual psyche. The conscience may later respond to the commands of political authority, the fatherland, and the religious commandments—"Thou shalt not!"—of God the Father. The Protestant rebellion against such traditional father figures as pope and king may have released feelings of guilt and fear, which in turn could be controlled only by strengthening the power of conscience and submitting individual will to the strict authority of a sovereign God. The sermons of John Cotton repeatedly call upon his congregation to surrender their ambition and pleasure to the commands of the heavenly Father.

The strengthening of conscience at the expense of other forces in the psyche created a remarkable tension in the Puritan mind that could not be indefinitely sustained. Even the heroic efforts of the early Puritans in America to uphold the image of the all-powerful God soon proved to be in vain.

The power of conscience is psychologically controlled by threats of punishment and promises of reward. The child who fears the will of his father is likely to obey the father's commands. When the child learns to think well of himself by acting obediently, his desire for self-satisfaction will also prompt him to obey his father's wishes. In both ways the conscience is strengthened. It was the task of the Puritan minister to preach the fear of God and to remind his congregation of divine grace. The alternatives of punishment and reward thus played an important role in the Puritan worship of an absolute Judge.

The ordinary power of fear was compounded by the many unknown dangers confronting the first generation of Puritans in America. In his history *Of Plymouth Plantation* William Bradford recalled the terrors of the first settlers:

> Being thus passed the vast ocean, . . . they had now no friends to welcome them nor inns to entertain or refresh their weather-beaten bodies; no houses or much less towns to repair to, to seek for succour. . . . And for the season it was winter, and they that know the winters of that country know them to be sharp and violent, and subject to cruel and fierce storms, dangerous to travel to known places, much more to search an unknown coast. Besides, what could they see but a hideous and desolate wilderness, full of wild beasts and wild men—and what multitudes there might be of them they knew not.[1]

Subject to extreme fear and uncertainty, the early Puritans felt totally dependent upon divine providence. As William Bradford concluded, "What could now sustain them but the Spirit of God and His grace?" But after a few generations in the New World, the original fear and uncertainty were moderated by a growing commonwealth, and the power of the Lord no longer appeared so terrible.

The unknown danger of being among the first settlers in the Massachusetts Bay Colony was balanced by the satisfaction of being in the vanguard of a divine mission. Believing that England had been a nation especially chosen to carry forward the Protestant Reformation, the

English immigrants to the New World expected to complete the task of building the city of God in the wilderness. The early Puritans in America thought of themselves as enjoying the reward of a special covenant with God, and they expected their colony in the New World to serve as a model for the continued reform of Christianity. "For we must consider," said Governor Winthrop in 1630, "that we shall be as a city upon a hill, the eyes of all people are upon us."[2] If the sovereignty of God was exalted by the early Puritans because they wanted to think well of their own faithful adventure, the power of God was questioned after a few generations when the initial self-satisfaction was threatened by doubt, backsliding, and a "Half-Way Covenant."

PURITAN DOCTRINE IN THE NEW WORLD

Although the description of a sovereign God preached in the early days of the Massachusetts Bay Colony was reinforced by the experience of the congregation—the fears and rewards of facing a new continent—the theology of the first Puritans in America had been defined a century before in the *Institutes of the Christian Religion* by John Calvin. In the Protestant theology outlined by Calvin, the sovereignty of God is supported by four essential doctrines: the guilt of original sin, the rule of predestined election, the doctrine of limited atonement, and the confession of irresistible grace. The Puritans who came to Massachusetts with Governor Winthrop were informed by countless sermons about the way each Calvinist doctrine should be directly experienced in the New World.

1. The Guilt of Original Sin. If absolute sovereignty is attributed to God, then man is denied all initiative and power. How can such an abject position be explained without accusing God of wanton tyranny? The standard Christian answer is to credit God with a benevolent creation, and then to blame man for a primal act of disobedience. All sin and suffering is thus interpreted as a consequence of Adam and Eve disobeying God in the Garden of Eden. The early Puritans in Massachusetts not only accepted the biblical story of the Fall of Man as literal truth, they consequently tormented themselves with the idea of inherited guilt. The story of original sin was told repeatedly in the sermons heard by the congregation of the First Church of Boston. If man is inherently burdened with guilt, then God must always be exalted as Judge. The Puritans lived in dread apprehension of the Last Judgment, and to maintain a vigilant search for any symptoms of guilt. They were forced to enlarge the power and scope of introspection. It may not be a coincidence that psychoanalysis later came into being in the two countries with very strong Protestant traditions. In searching the depths of the human psyche, Freud and Jung are the modern counterparts of Luther and Calvin. The remarkable development of psychoanalysis on this side of the Atlantic likewise owes much to the tradition of Puritan introspection in America.

Although the doctrine of original sin implicates all men in the guilt of Adam and Eve, the leaders of the Massachusetts Bay Colony took upon themselves the task of enforcing the commandments of the sovereign Judge. The relentless campaign to expose and punish any appearance of sin was conducted with the sanction of divine justice. The Puritan attempt to whip the offending Adam visible in any sinner often required the stocks, the pillory, and even the gallows. Civil and religious authority were technically separate in the Bay Colony, but the ultimate law was Holy Scripture, and all crimes could be seen as a religious offense. Any form of conduct disliked by the magistrates could be interpreted as the work of the Devil. No person was totally secure against the possible charge of witchcraft. In his history of the Plymouth settlement, Governor Bradford felt obliged to explain "how some kind of wickedness did grow and break forth here, in a land where the same was so much witnessed against and so narrowly looked into, and severely punished when it was known, as in no other place."[3] Besides acknowledging "our corrupt natures" as the cause of the evil, Governor Bradford explained how "the Devil may carry a greater spite against the churches of Christ and the gospel here, by how much the more they endeavour to preserve holiness and purity amongst them and strictly punisheth the contrary when it ariseth either in church or commonwealth." Thus a vicious cycle of guilt and punishment was reinforced. Blaming the Devil served to excuse and encourage the continual increase in repression. The routine of inquisition and punishment was hardly new in the history of Christianity, but among the Puritans in Massachusetts there were few restraints to check the zealous prosecution.

The feeling of guilt imposed by the doctrine of original sin was exaggerated in Puritan minds already dominated by the strict voice of conscience. If the primal sin is disobedience of the Father, it follows psychologically that the guilt will be kept alive with punishment designed by the parental voice of conscience. The self-destructive effects of extreme guilt are dramatized in Hawthorne's *The Scarlet Letter*. Although the novel is a romantic fiction created two centuries after the pretended fact, Hawthorne's picture of the guilt and anxiety of the Puritan mind is a tour de force of psychological analysis. Hawthorne shows how the conscience of the anguished sinner drives him to self-flagellation and finally to death. Dimmesdale's sin, of course, is more specific than just the common guilt derived from Adam and Eve, but even Governor Bradford was quick to explain that "incontinency between persons unmarried . . . and some married persons also" is the inheritance of original sin. One rehearsal of the primal guilt was enough to inflame the conscience and break the independent will of the Puritan minister.

The experience of the early Puritans in New England reinforced their belief in the doctrine of original sin. The physical danger of the wilderness and the constant fear of its savage inhabitants both served to remind the first settlers of Calvin's emphasis upon the corrupt nature of the fallen world. Belief in original sin began to decline only in the next century when the colonies had achieved a degree of comfort and stability. When the doctrine was compromised by a growing sense of human achievement, the sovereignty of the Puritan God was also challenged.

2. The Rule of Predestined Election. As long as man is still viewed as an abject sinner "trembling in the hands of an angry God," his only hope rests in God's mercy and grace. The congregation of the First Church of Boston was told repeatedly that salvation depends entirely on God's will. In the *Institutes of the Christian Religion* the doctrine of predestined election is stressed by Calvin in order to guarantee the absolute sovereignty of God. If salvation or damnation has already been determined, then all men are powerless to influence the decision. No one can obtain grace for himself by the power of his faith or the devotion of his good works.

Two forms of heresy, the Antinomian and the Arminian, were prepared to challenge the doctrine of predestined election. The Antinomians felt that God's will could be discovered by intuitive faith, independent of Scripture and the established church. When Anne Hutchinson professed this kind of visionary faith among the first generation of Puritans in the Massachusetts Bay Colony, she was accused of heresy and exiled to the wilderness of Rhode Island. The second form of heresy, the Arminian, was more difficult to suppress. It was a Dutch Protestant, Jacobus Arminius, who maintained that the will of God could be influenced by faithful piety and the good conduct of a moral life. Arminians therefore refused to accept the idea of predestination. Theological conflict on this matter raged throughout the first century of the Puritan experience in the New World.

Many of the thousands of sermons that survive from the early years of the Massachusetts Bay Colony were directed against any challenge to the doctrine of predestination. But the heretics could not be exiled and silenced forever. The futility of attempting to suppress all forms of the Antinomian heresy was illustrated by the long and bitter struggle in Massachusetts between the Puritans and the Quakers. With their belief in an "inner voice," the Quakers claimed to be in direct contact with God. The Puritan ministers of the Bay Colony were not prepared to tolerate any Christian sect which professed a faith independent of Puritan doctrine. When the first ship arrived in Boston Harbor in 1656 carrying two Quaker women, the heretics were immediately taken to jail and searched for signs of witchcraft. A law was then enacted in the colony to provide for the arrest, punishment, and exile of any similar heretics. When that measure did not stop the intrusion of Quakers into Massachusetts, the magistrates of the Bay Colony felt obliged to punish a few members of the "cursed sect" with execution on the gallows. Only in the next century were the suppressive measures gradually abandoned. And then the heresy of believing in man's own ability to discover and influence the will of God ironically became a popular faith.

John Cotton's sermons on the rule of predestined election were reinforced by the experience of the first Puritan settlers. The will of God must have seemed mysterious and arbitrary to those English men and women who sailed across the Atlantic and confronted a strange wilderness. What else could explain the indiscriminate suffering of the ocean crossing? What else could sustain their precarious hold upon the margin of the new land? What else protected them from the savages and wild animals of the unknown forest? More than half the original settlers at Plymouth died during the first winter ashore. Under such extreme conditions it is hardly surprising that men should feel incapable of either predicting or influencing their salvation. The doctrine of arbitrary and predestined election was thus firmly anchored in the experience of the early Puritans. But in time the danger and strangeness of the New World would diminish, and then the mystery and power of God would also decline. When it became rather common to attribute survival to steady and productive work, the credit shifted from God to man.

3. The Doctrine of Limited Atonement. The congregation of John Cotton was also taught that Christ's sacrifice was not an atonement for the sins of all men. Only the "chosen few" would be saved. Only the "invisible saints" would be accepted by God. The doctrine of limited atonement was a corollary of Calvin's first two principles: man is guilty of original sin; election by God is arbitrary and predetermined. Christ's sacrifice is therefore merely a sign of His promise to those already selected for redemption. If atonement through Christ is limited, the hopes of men are apt to be denied, and the sovereign power of God is magnified even further.

The doctrine of limited atonement added to the uncertainty and tension of Puritan experience. The fear and anxiety created by not knowing for certain whether you were destined for eternal bliss or damnation was often more than individual Puritans could tolerate. One young Boston woman, who was tormented by a sinful conscience, threw her infant child down a well just to be sure of her own damnation. The anticipation of God's punishment was easier to bear than the anxiety and suspense of unknown Judgment. One member of Jonathan Edwards's congregation cut his own throat because his terrified conscience demanded immediate Judgment. The "severity in punishments" mentioned by Governor Bradford was slight in comparison to the psychological torment created by the belief that atonement through Christ was limited and unpredictable.

In the next century the doctrine of limited atonement was gradually abandoned. In the wake of the Great Awakening, the standards for church membership were often relaxed, and the promise of salvation was made to seem available to more people. When the doctrine of limited atonement declined in importance, the exclusive God feared and worshipped by the first settlers lost much of His power and sovereignty.

4. The Confession of Irresistible Grace. The negative points of Calvin's theology—original sin, predestination, and limited atonement—were all balanced against the positive confession of irresistible grace. Although it was maintained by Calvin that man is both sinful and powerless, Calvin also believed in the divine gift of undeserved mercy. The jealous and wrathful God may unexpectedly extend His grace even to the lowest sinner. The miracle of divine blessing was described by Calvin in the traditional Christian language of regeneration. To receive the gift of divine grace was to be born again into the spirit of God. The moment of regeneration was described by Calvin as an expression of irresistible joy and fulfillment. The fear and anxiety in the mind of the Puritan sinner were thus offset by the hope of divine election. Although salvation could not be achieved by any human effort, or predicted with any certainty, the wonderful mercy of the sovereign God might at any moment fill the darkness with light. The congregation of the First Church of Boston received constant reminders of their sinful condition, and at the same time they were told to live in hope of receiving divine grace.

The sovereign God worshipped by the early settlers in Massachusetts was a dynamic paradox. Two conflicting forces were held together with considerable tension in the Puritan definition of supernatural power. Exerting pressure in one direction was the wrathful Judge of the Old Testament, demanding strict obedience and threatening eternal punishment. The opposing force was the mercy of a benevolent Father, capable of forgiving his sinful children and offering a chance of salvation. Both the forces attributed to God were strongly reflected in the experience of the early Puritans crossing the Atlantic and clearing settlements at the edge of the wilderness. Life was full of unexpected terrors. A storm at sea or a savage Indian raid might suddenly be witnessed as a sign of God's wrath. Mary Rowlandson's famous account of her capture by the Indians is filled with the terrible recognition that God was testing her faith. But at sea a mild-looking sky might betoken God's approval, and on land a good harvest would be an indication of God's blessing. Without hesitation Mary Rowlandson attributed her miraculous survival to the mercy of divine providence. The two forces of the God worshipped by the early Puritans represented the deepest instincts of human nature: fear and love. But the Puritan theology made extraordinary demands upon each instinct. Fear was intensified until it became the terror of "sinners trembling in the hands of an angry God." And love was increased until it became the irresistible grace of God.

John Cotton preached the central doctrines of Calvin's theology to the congregation of the First Church of Boston at the same time that Puritans in England were attending the Westminister Assembly to work out the design of their Protestant theology in what became known as the Westminister Confession. The Puritans in America, however, were convinced that they represented the vanguard of the Protestant Reformation. Listening to the sermons of John Cotton in the 1640s, the men and women of the Massachusetts Bay Colony could recognize the terror and grace of God in their direct encounter with the New World. Doctrine and experience were then in remarkable harmony. John Cotton fortunately did not live long enough to see them splitting apart. As the leading Puritan minister in the first decades of the American experience, he received without question the honor and respect that would never be so readily available to those who came after him. During his own lifetime John Cotton was hailed as "the patriarch of New England." The first biography ever written about an American is the record of his devout and scholarly life. After working for almost twenty years to plant the roots of Calvinism in the New World, John Cotton died in 1652 when the Massachusetts Bay Colony was just transferring power to its second generation. He could not have foreseen the impossibility of holding fast to the Puritan faith, or the troubled shadow that the loss would impose upon the American imagination.

PURITAN PIETY IN THE NEW WORLD

Although the doctrines of Calvinism were fundamental to the religious piety recommended and practiced by the early congregations in New England, it is easier to describe the abstract statements of theology than it is to account for the religious experience shared by the Puritans. One famous summary of the Puritan imagination, drawn from a study of sermons, diaries, and other historical records, is the synthesis offered by Perry Miller in *The New England Mind: The Seventeenth Century*. Miller locates the religious experience of the Puritans in the tradition of piety dramatized in the writings of Saint Augustine. The hallmarks of this experience are a heightened sense of human guilt and a transforming confession of what is believed to be God's undeserved grace.

The acknowledgment of guilt was a crucial stage in the spiritual progress of Puritan worship. Following the emphasis of Calvin upon the doctrine of original sin, the Puritan awareness of man's fallen nature became an inquisition of fear and anxiety. The spotlight of conscience was turned relentlessly upon the shadows of the human psyche to reveal the signs of temptation, sin, and guilt. Only in our own century has depth analysis become once again such an earnest pursuit.

How was the doctrine of original sin expressed in terms of the religious piety of the early Puritans in America? Considered as a psychological experience, and not just as an abstract doctrine, the conviction of sin shared by the Puritans was a radical expression of humility and a total surrender of individual purpose to the authority of a supernatural and sovereign Judge. The masochism inherent in the experience was illustrated by the several forms of self-abuse practiced by the Puritans. Fasting and scourging were common means of self-chastisement. The mental drama was a paradox—a passionate fear of passion. The sense of extreme guilt was rooted in sexual fear and inhibition. Hawthorne's study of the sinful Puritan minister shows the deep connection of passion and conscience. The experience of original sin also involved another paradox: it was a proud expression of self-abasement. Puritan ministers competed with one another to paint the darkest picture of man's sinful nature. It was not uncommon for a Puritan to boast of his humility. Jonathan Edwards seemed to derive a terrible pleasure from envisioning man as a venomous spider waiting to be crushed by an angry God. The Puritan experience of guilt was a dynamic assault upon the self, a death wish accompanied by the terror and thrill of self-loathing. The radical humility encouraged by the Puritans was believed to be the prerequisite for the experience of supernatural grace. Only by emptying themselves of all sinful concerns could they hope to become vessels of divine love. The two main components of the Puritan experience were thus extensions of the basic Christian paradox. Only the person who "loseth his life for my sake shall find it."

The experience of divine grace was described by the Puritans as a force of regeneration, which might come as an unexpected wave of emotion and serve as a release from the anxiety and fear of guilt. The transforming rapture of grace lifted the Puritan above his worldly cares and gave him the chance to feel in communion with his God. Puritans looked upon the experience as a foretaste of the happiness that would be enjoyed by the chosen few in Paradise. Implicit in the reception of grace was the surrender of individual ego necessary for the self to merge into a higher spiritual communion. The sinner, burdened with fear and guilt, felt reborn among the Puritan saints.

Although humility and surrender of self were necessary stages in the expectation of divine grace, the experience itself often led to spiritual pride. By interpreting the experience as a sign of God's favor, the Puritan saints often exchanged their humility for self-righteousness, and the rhetoric of guilt might then yield to complacency. When the Puritan aspiration for divine approval was mixed with common ambition, the experience of grace could be confused with mere self-satisfaction.

In the early days of the Massachusetts Bay Colony some confession of grace was often held as a requirement for church membership. The congregation would then in theory consist only of the visible communion of saints. But that exclusive method of determining church membership soon led to insoluble problems: how can it be determined if the confession of grace is genuine, and how can the young children of the saints be included in the communion? A remarkable amount of time and energy was spent by the Puritans in designing the Half-Way Covenant in a futile attempt to solve the impossible questions.

The religious experience of the Puritans at times included such extreme events as mystical visions, seizures, fainting spells, and bursts of uncontrollable weeping. But the exaggerated display of emotion did not become common until the Great Awakening in the third and fourth decades of the next century. The early Puritans in New England practiced a more restrained form of religious piety. The minister of the First Church of Boston was a reserved scholar, not a charismatic leader. John Cotton wanted to bring his congregation to the experience of divine grace by instructing them in knowledge of the Scriptures. Prayer and discipline were valued above emotional confession.

A modern definition of schizophrenia is "a mental disorder characterized by delusions of both persecution and omnipotence." The Puritan fear of a jealous and wrathful God often appeared as "delusions of persecution." Edwards's picture of God holding sinners "over the pit of hell, much as one holds a spider, or some loathsome insect," is a graphic example of how the guilt of original sin could fire the Puritan imagination with dramatic visions of persecution.[4] And the complementary experience, the reception of divine grace, often was the equivalent of a "delusion of omnipotence." Again Edwards exclaimed, "How happy I should be, if I might enjoy that God, and be rapt up to God in Heaven, and be as it were swallowed up in Him."[5] Just as the doctrines of Calvinism included the paradox of God as jealous tyrant and merciful father, the religious experience of the Puritans brought together self-loathing and self-glorification, anxious guilt and undeserved grace, visions of persecution and the joyful delusion of supernatural favor. The language of modern psychology would seem impertinent, if not incomprehensible, to the early Puritans in America, but they were not at all unaware of the interconnected roots of love and hate deep in the human psyche.

THE PURITAN EPIC

The double nature of the Puritan God was dramatized by Michael Wigglesworth in an extraordinary epic poem, eighteen hundred lines, entitled *The Day of Doom, or a Poetical Description of the Great and Last Judgment*. Printed in 1662, ten years after the death of John Cotton, *The Day of Doom* became the most popular book in America, except for the Bible, for the next hundred years. The poem went through so many editions that every second family in New England could have possessed a copy. No other work of fiction has ever enjoyed such a popular reception in the New World.

Wigglesworth dramatized the sovereign God of the Puritans and His arbitrary decision to save "none but mine own Elect." The poem contains a dialogue held on the Day of Judgment between the spirits asking for admission to Heaven and God represented as a harsh Judge condemning souls to Hell. The poem illustrates Calvin's doctrines of original sin, predestined election, and limited atonement. The point is made repeatedly that good works and moral conduct in this world will not guarantee any reward in Heaven. The spirits hoping to gain entrance into Paradise by persuading God of their righteousness are reminded in turn of their condition as fallen men: "However fair, however square your way and work hath been/Before men's eyes, yet God espies iniquity therein."[6]

The poem does not reveal the exercise of much forgiveness at the

Last Judgment. It is hardly reassuring to learn that God is just yielding enough to assign unbaptized infants to "the easiest room in Hell." It is explained by God in the poem that all men, including any who die in infancy, share the mark of original sin—"You were born in state forlorn, with natures so depraved." The punishments called for by "God's fierce Ire" are vividly described by Wigglesworth. After binding of their hands and feet, the damned are cast into a lake "where Fire and Brimstone flameth" to suffer forever the torment of Hell. Only the predestined few are saved by God, and part of their reward is to contemplate the agony of the damned. A few centuries later James Russell Lowell facetiously described this Puritan epic as "the solace of every fireside, the flicker of the pine knots by which it was conned perhaps adding a livelier relish to its premonitions of eternal combustion."

The epic poet in the Massachusetts Bay Colony accomplished far more than just presenting the familiar doctrines of Calvin's theology; Wigglesworth also dramatized the psychological forces powerful in the Puritan imagination. *The Day of Doom,* no doubt, seems morbid and fanatic to modern readers, surely the work of an unhealthy imagination, but the poem's extraordinary popularity in the late seventeenth century should caution us against an easy rejection of the work as merely extreme or perverse. The poem was obviously accepted by a majority of its contemporary readers as a true picture of God's justice and a vital reminder of man's inherent sinfulness. The arguments presented on God's behalf for condemning infants to eternal punishment are not likely to persuade modern readers, but the epic poet did more than present the abstract doctrines, he also dramatized the psychological attitudes which once conditioned the acceptance of such doctrines. The secret guilt, the anxiety, the prejudice, the self-righteousness, and the yearning for death inherent in the Puritan doctrine of original sin are all revealed in *The Day of Doom.*

The apocalyptic vision from the Revelation of St. John was developed by Wigglesworth into a very dramatic account of death and punishment. *The Day of Doom* is filled with enough violence and terror to satisfy the curiosity of the most vengeful and morbid Puritan conscience. The focus upon death was determined in part by the Puritan concern with the decisive moment in the history of the soul, the moment of Judgment when God will separate the damned and the regenerate. Wigglesworth drew upon the fascination with death that is latent in Christianity. In the glorification of martyrdom, in the worship of a sacrificial victim dying on a cross, or merely in the contemplation of Heaven and Hell, the Christian imagination may dwell upon the images of death. The poet of *The Day of Doom* borrowed his evidence from the Bible in order to build his vision of death into a frightening picture of God's anger and justice.

But why were the Puritans in New England so fascinated by visions of death and darkness? Had they not boldly crossed the Atlantic in order to begin a new life? Was it the very precarious nature of their new life at the edge of the wilderness that forced some of the early settlers to think often about the significance of death? It is true that more than half the original settlers at Plymouth died during the first winter. But that does not explain the growing concern with death which later dominated the imagination of a man like Michael Wigglesworth. Even granting the fact that he was almost constantly in precarious health, isn't there a more general reason for his preoccupation with mortality? One modern theory is offered by Norman O. Brown in *Life Against Death.*

Brown draws a connection between a strong death wish and a fear of sexual desire. The connection is apparent in many accounts of the Puritan experience in New England, and may be supported by evidence from *The Day of Doom.* Some women among the second generation of Puritans in America were actually branded with the letter *A* as a punishment for having committed adultery. In the third generation the mere suspicion of sexual crime could be cited as intercourse with the Devil in the forest, and the suspect could be hanged as a witch. What impulse was strong enough to cause a judge to sentence a woman to be hanged for imaginary crimes? The outbreak of hysteria that swayed the magistrates of Salem was in part a strong fear of sexual freedom, a form of jealousy that became more intense and violent in the tightly organized and self-righteous community. Two hundred years later Nathaniel Hawthorne would analyze such feelings by showing the Puritan reaction to the seductive beauty of Hester Prynne. In Hawthorne's novel the death wish of the Puritan minister is inseparable from his sexual fear and inhibition.

The Puritans, of course, were not about to retreat from the advances made by Martin Luther in his revolt against the values of monasticism. Celibacy was no longer a requirement for holiness. The migration to New England had not been an attempt to escape from the corrupt world to find purity behind the walls of a monastery; the immigrants did expect to perpetuate their community of saints. Even the frail author of *The Day of Doom* had three wives and eight children. The Puritans therefore reserved their censure of carnal appetite for any illicit arrangement: hence the powerful condemnation of adultery and the consternation of Governor Bradford when he had to report that "even sodomy and buggery (things fearful to name) have broke forth in this land oftener than once." Any possible abuse of carnal desire called into focus the Puritan fear of punishment. Any relationship apart from marriage appeared to be a direct threat to the survival of the community of saints. When Thomas Morton set up a maypole not far from Plymouth in 1627, and advocated mild sexual freedom for the adherents of his group, the Puritans had him first confined to the stocks for the "beastly practises of ye mad Bacchanalians" and then shipped back to England. A few hundred years later in "The May-pole of Merry Mount," Hawthorne would dramatize that conflict between the "gay sinners" and the "grisly saints."

The Puritans cut down the maypole set up by Morton's band of revelers, because, as reported in Morton's account of the incident, "they termed it an idol." The celebration of male potency dramatized by the maypole dancers was considered offensive to the jealous God of the Puritans. Likewise in *The Day of Doom* all sexual power is sacrificed to the worship of the sovereign Father. Any glorification of carnal appetite was condemned by Wigglesworth in the manner of Revelation: "If any man worship the beast and his image . . . the same shall drink of the wine of the wrath of God . . . and he shall be tormented with fire and brimstone." The surrender of Puritan desire to the censure of a jealous God was filled with the tension of sexual rivalry between father and son. The fear and jealousy implicit in the sexual conflict described in Freud's theory of the oedipal relationship were central to the Puritan vision of an omnipotent God punishing His only Son upon a cross or threatening to punish all men because of their original sin.

To escape the supernatural punishment, the Puritan spirit abjectly surrendered all human power to the sovereign Father. But in that surrender there was a kind of victory. Didn't the Puritan secretly enjoy trembling beneath the "iron rod" of a vengeful Lord? Jonathan Edwards admitted: "My heart as it were panted after this, to lie low before God, and in the dust; that I might be nothing, and that God might be ALL."[7] Michael Wigglesworth obviously admired the powerful display of "God's revengeful ire," and described the cruelty of divine wrath with great relish. And later in Hawthorne's novel the Puritan minister was never so happy as when he scourged his own flesh in a torment of self-accusation and masochistic penance. (D. H. Lawrence observed years ago that Dimmesdale's flagellation may be the Puritan equivalent of masturbation.) If the Puritan fear of God was partially rooted in sexual rivalry, then the excessive Puritan interest in physical torment—see the images in *The Day of Doom* of burning, tearing, and horrible destruction—can be understood as the twisted emergence of suppressed carnal instinct. Thus in his display of orthodox Calvinism the epic poet dramatically revealed many of the psychological forces that conditioned his experience of the conventional faith. His theology was standard Puritan doctrine, but his art is charged with the tensions of sexual jealousy, delight in torture, death-longing guilt, and abject surrender at the feet of the omnipotent Father.

The Day of Doom illustrates the complete dominance of the superego in the Puritan mind. The natural impulses of the id find perverse expression only in the humiliation of the flesh and the fascination with eternal punishment. The prerogatives of the ego are mocked by an arbitrary God unwilling to tolerate any display of human ambition. But the superego, the psychological voice of the father, reigns over all as a "Power imperial." After rejecting the father figures of the Old World, the kings and bishops and popes, the early Puritans in America, reading their Holy Scripture at the edge of a strange wilderness, focused all their reverence and fear upon the one symbolic father available in the New World, the Puritan God with his power and grace. It would take many generations in New England before the settlers could free themselves from the grip of that sovereign and divine authority. The immense popularity of *The Day of Doom* lasted well into the eighteenth century.

2

JEREMIAH IN NEW ENGLAND

Great expectations were voiced by Governor Winthrop at the beginning of his adventure to the New World. He prayed for the guidance to found a colony that would become "a model of Christian charity." He asked God to bless the Puritan colony with "praise and glory, that men shall say of succeeding plantations: 'The Lord make it like that of New England!'"[1] But only forty years later the mood of much Puritan writing in America was bitter and disillusioned. The covenant had been broken, and God was angry. The sermons of Puritan ministers in the third generation often turned into jeremiads—dire warnings about the sinful nature of man and the punishment to be expected from God. As the future of the Puritan mission in the New World appeared to be at stake, the sermons became even more apocalyptic. Predictions of the Last Judgment were common. Perry Miller has explained in *The New England Mind: The Seventeenth Century* how the jeremiad developed into a form of art and ritual. The exaggerated vision of the typical jeremiad should not be accepted as a realistic guide. New England surely had not fallen into the condition of "utter sinfulness" which the ministers were picturing. Nevertheless, the "second fall of man" was not all the invention of the frightened clergy. The hopeful promise of the original Puritans in America had substantially turned in the third generation to foreboding and recrimination. Things appeared so threatening by 1679 that a synod was convened to make "full inquiry . . . into the Causes and State of God's Controversy with us." The delegates to the synod agreed on the necessity of a desperate renewal of the covenant, "the Lord having written his displeasure in dismal Characters against us."[2]

Many events contributed to the depressed mood of the delegates to the Reforming Synod. Some of the causes were immediate. The restoration of the monarchy in England, for example, meant new governmental interference for the colonies and new regulations for commerce. Great losses of life and property had been suffered during the Indian raids of 1675-76 known as King Philip's War. Terrible fires destroyed parts of Boston in 1676 and again in 1679. Epidemics of disease on a scale unknown to the early Puritans were sweeping across New England. Therefore it was hardly surprising to have the delegates to the Reforming Synod declare in 1679 "that God hath a Controversy with his New England people."

The underlying causes of the disillusionment are less visible and yet more significant. War and fire and pestilence were interpreted as signs of God's wrath and punishment. But what had the Puritans done in New England to deserve such torment? Had Zion been turned into Babylon? Why did the Day of Judgment appear to be drawing close? Three forms of change were helping to destroy the Puritan vision of man's relationship with God: the increasing material wealth and opportunity in New England were enabling the settlers to be less dependent upon Providence; the separatist tendencies inherent in Puritanism were dividing congregations and splitting some of the tenets of the faith; and a decline in the experience of conversion was threatening the very survival of the community of saints.

MATERIALISM

The growth of material wealth was the first and the most lasting threat to the Puritan vision of building the City of God in the wilderness. The history of America has often been described as the substitution of mere worldly success for the original Puritan ideal of salvation. The story of dreams exchanged for dollars is conventional enough in American literature. But the dialogue between spiritual goals and worldly success achieved a special focus among the third generation of Puritans in America. Perhaps because the original hope for a model Puritan community in the New World had been so intense, the disillusionment was exceptionally bitter. Having failed to achieve their high expectations on the fresh soil of a new continent, who could the Puritans blame but themselves? The rhetoric of self-accusation and doom saying reached a level of intensity in the third generation since unequaled in American writing. The lamentations of Jeremiah in the Old Testament are mild in comparison. In his account of the Puritan experience in America, *Magnalia Christi Americana*, Cotton Mather wrote near the end of the seventeenth century that "religion

brought forth prosperity, and the daughter destroyed the mother."[3]
William Bradford's history *Of Plymouth Plantation* had earlier come to
the same negative conclusion: "And thus was this poor church left, like
an ancient mother grown old and forsaken of her children. . . . She that
had made many rich became herself poor."[4]

A visitor to the Massachusetts Bay Colony in 1671 described many
of the "civil and ecclesiastical masters" as not only "damnably rich"
but also "covetous and proud." Cotton Mather was likewise concerned
about "the enchantments of this world" causing the men and women
of New England "to forget their errand into the wilderness." During
the first generation in America all able members of the small population
had to help in the work of planting crops and building shelters. Mere
survival was interpreted as the miracle of God's protection. During the
second generation the success of Cromwell in England temporarily
lessened the tide of migration across the Atlantic, and thereby created
severe economic difficulties in the young colonies. Many Puritans even
returned to England. Necessary supplies became more uncertain than
ever. But as the colonies in America entered their third generation,
material conditions were improving, the population was then increasing
rapidly, and a relative prosperity could be enjoyed. The growing materialism, however, was steadily at work undermining the power of God in the
Puritan imagination.

The early settlers in Massachusetts had felt completely dependent
upon their special covenant with the Lord. But after three or four decades in New England it was obvious that many of the unregenerate
settlers were enjoying as much prosperity as the Puritan saints. Was
God responsible for all that happens to man? Was it possible for individuals with determination to improve their own destiny? New answers
to those questions began to diminish the sovereignty of God in the Puritan mind.

The jeremiads preached again and again to the third generation indicate the growing anxiety of the Puritan leaders in Massachusetts. The
ministers were forced to exaggerate the specter of doom in order to
awaken the people who were distracted by worldly concerns. The attempt to provoke fear and guilt was necessary because the original fear
of God had been waning in the face of new comfort and complacency.
The wilderness was gradually turning into farms and settlements. Disputes about more land were constant, but the disputes were political
and economic. Fear of the strange wilderness and the consequent dependence upon God were yielding to confidence and self-assertion.

As the men and women of New England began to think less of their
God, they started to think more of themselves. The doctrine of original

sin came to be regarded with a new skepticism. The idea of original sin was difficult to reconcile with the growing pride in human achievement. Perhaps Calvin had exaggerated the guilt of original sin. Perhaps he had been misled by the corruption of the Old World. Such excuses came naturally to the inhabitants of New England, who did not want to deny their own feeling of accomplishment. Of course there was always sufficient evidence of human sinfulness. Even on the fresh green breast of a new continent the Puritans had failed to keep from persecuting and hanging one another. Did that not prove the contention of Augustine and Calvin that man is a fallen creature and can only be saved by divine grace? The ministers of the third generation continued to remind their congregations of man's wretched sinfulness. But the rhetoric of the jeremiads seemed to intensify as part of a desperate and futile attempt to persuade the people to hold fast to an obsolete faith. The failure to establish a perfect communion of saints in the New World could be balanced by the obvious material progress. Why insist on the fallen nature of men and women who were clearly improving themselves? Why be concerned about original sin, when the unregenerate could also achieve the same prosperity? Such questions illustrate the confusion of salvation and success that was beginning to appear in the Puritan experience, a confusion that helped to undermine the doctrine of original sin, and a confusion of religious and secular concerns which future generations would continually enlarge.

The growing materialism of New England also encouraged a drift toward the acceptance of the Arminian philosophy, which questioned Calvin's doctrine of predestination and maintained instead that man could influence his own future. The Puritan leaders of New England decried the Arminian point of view as heresy because it detracted from the absolute sovereignty of God. But with the gradual economic development of the Puritan settlements the acceptance of the Arminian philosophy was inevitable. The early Puritans who shared in the economic growth of the Bay Colony were anxious to interpret their good fortune as a tangible sign of God's favor. As long as the work done by man was not seen as an attempt to influence God, the doctrine of predestination might remain unchallenged. Once the connection was made, however, between material wealth and divine favor, it became rather common to reverse the logic of cause and effect. Then the settlers in Massachusetts began to expect their own efforts to be automatically rewarded by a proud Father. The covenant of grace was thus replaced by a covenant of works, and the jealous, absolute God of Calvin was replaced by a divine Accountant paying out heavenly wages. As Max Weber explained long ago, the roots of capitalism and Puritanism are inseparable. The growth of economic rewards was strengthened by the gradual acceptance of the Arminian philosophy, and both helped to usurp the power of the Puritan God.

The developing commercial life of New England inevitably produced social distinctions, which in turn forced adjustments in religious affairs. Those who were enjoying commercial success also wanted a share of the power that could be granted only by the church. With political rights dependent upon church membership, and with less than one-fifth of the population admitted to membership, strong pressure soon developed to force the churches to open their doors. The standard for admission was supposed to be the transforming experience of divine grace. To accept the unregenerate into the congregation, the Puritan leaders argued, would mock the covenant and debase the communion of saints. But the requirement of conversion proved to be too exclusive and too impractical. Although the Bible claims that it may be "easier for a camel to go through the eye of a needle, than for a rich man to enter into the kingdom of God," even the Puritan churches in New England could not long exclude the growing number of unregenerate but prosperous and respectable settlers. The first generation in Massachusetts had enjoyed the privilege of all starting together in a divine enterprise; economic and social distinctions had been reduced by the common migration to a new continent; the saints were all equal under their covenant. By the third generation, however, the growing pressure of social and economic change forced important revisions in church polity.

From the earliest days of the Massachusetts Bay Colony, there had been a small group of merchants who occasionally found themselves at odds with the local ministers. While the economic theory of John Cotton was derived from the medieval concept of a "just price," some merchants in Boston were deriving economic profit from a fluctuating market. The merchants had to tread carefully between the restrictions on trade imposed by the government in England and the censure of unjust profit heard from the local Puritan ministers. The power of the merchant class did not emerge clearly until late in the century when some outside events helped to support their position. The charter of the Bay Colony was annulled in 1684. When the charter was renewed seven years later, its terms were significantly different: political rights were based upon property rather than on church membership. The merchants of Boston were ready to benefit from the limitations placed upon ecclesiastical power. At the same time mercantile relations with England greatly improved. The merchants then felt sufficiently confident to make a show of force. Long irritated by the narrow and exclusive standards of the oldest churches in the Boston area, a group of merchants in 1699 decided to open a new church to be fashioned along "broad and catho-lick" lines. The doors of the new Brattle Street Church were open wide to all who wished to profess the Christian faith. Even the Half-Way Covenant was disregarded. The merchants thus scored a victory against the exclusive will of the Puritan ministers, and a schism was thereby opened in American experience that would never again be closed. Only a few years later, as if to confirm their new power, the merchants had Increase Mather removed from the presidency of Harvard, and a man of their own choosing put in his place. With a layman installed as president of Harvard in 1707, the Massachusetts Bay Colony was indeed entering a new century.

Within three generations of the founding of the Bay Colony, the growing materialism had thus succeeded in diluting strict Puritan dogma and challenging exclusive church membership. The doctrines of original sin, predestined election, and limited atonement had all been reduced in importance. The covenant of grace was rapidly losing ground to a covenant of works. The sovereign authority of God was declining in the Puritan imagination. The success of the merchants in Boston forced the Puritan ministers to react defensively. The growing worry of the Puritan leaders was dramatized in the strong rhetoric of the jeremiads. The full tension of the predicament was revealed by the almost paranoid career of Cotton Mather. It was at the turn of the century that he gloomily observed how the Puritan churches in New England had "brought forth prosperity, and the daughter destroyed the mother."

SEPARATISM

A second form of attack on the authority of the Puritan God came from the practice of separatism. Martin Luther dramatized the basic principle of separatism with his decisive break from the Roman church. Until the early sixteenth century the church had been able to control potential reformers by either silencing them completely—men like John Huss were burned at the stake—or by accommodating them within the government of the church, allowing a man like Ignatius of Loyola to organize the Society of Jesus. But Luther was too popular to be silenced and too independent to be controlled. Once the unity of Christ's kingdom in Europe had been broken by the Reformation, it was impossi-ble to limit or even to predict the number of different Protestant sects that might emerge. Independent of any central authority, the reform movement could not resist further division and subdivision. In America the multiplication of sects and churches would continue until writers like Emerson and Thoreau in the nineteenth century were able to proclaim that every man should be his own priest and produce his own scripture. Martin Luther, of course, could never have imagined freedom carried to such an extent, but only one successful revolution was necessary to establish a principle for all of those to follow.

The Reformation reached England in the 1530s when Henry VIII defied the authority of Rome and proclaimed himself "Singular Protector, only Supreme Lord, and as far as the law of Christ allows, even Supreme Head of the English Church." Having gained immense power by seizing church land and money in England, Henry VIII was naturally reluctant to have the Reformation proceed any further. Separation from Rome had been greatly to Henry's advantage, but any further splintering of the church within England would only dilute his newly acquired power. If he was to maintain a strong state church under his own authority, Henry VIII knew that the plans of the more radical Protestant reformers would have to be cautiously opposed. The difficult task of steering a middle course for the English church between the threats of Rome and the growing demands of the Puritans eventually became the responsibility of Queen Elizabeth. For more than four decades Elizabeth carefully played one side off against the other, withstanding both excommunication from the pope and bitter complaints from the Puritans, while all the time holding and increasing the power of her middle position.

During Elizabeth's reign John Cotton was born in Derby and received much of his education at Cambridge. As a young boy in Derby he could have witnessed the hanging of Roman Catholics; and as a young man at Cambridge, he would have become familiar with the suppression of Puritan reformers like Thomas Cartwright and Peter Baro. John Cotton was forced to recognize quite early the power of a central, unified, state church, and the possible fate of radical dissenters. Although he gained a reputation as a Puritan spokesman in England, and then migrated to the Bay Colony in 1633, John Cotton did not forget the lesson of caution. He refused to view his move from England as a definite separation from the English church. Complete separation was considered illegal, if not heretical, and the specter of separatism frightened and disturbed the cautious mind of John Cotton. Before joining the Massachusetts Bay Colony he tried to reassure himself that he was not just following the example of the radical separatists who had settled a decade earlier at Plymouth.

The men and women who arrived at Plymouth in 1620 had deliberately broken away from the Church of England, and consequently had been "hunted and persecuted on every side." After seeking refuge for a while in the Netherlands, this small group of "schismatics" sailed aboard the *Mayflower* to plant their radical congregation in America. Although the settlers at Plymouth still professed token allegiance to king and country, their political and religious opinions continued to provoke suspicion and hostility. When the much larger Massachusetts Bay Colony was founded ten years later, the new settlers were careful to distinguish their position from the separatism practiced at Plymouth. But the distinction was easier to maintain in theory than in practice. Although still professing some loyalty to the Church of England, the settlers in the Bay Colony soon began to establish local churches at Salem and Boston very similar to the congregation at Plymouth. Historians have long debated whether the Puritans settling in the Bay Colony were hypocrites only professing allegiance to the Church of England while still within earshot of Canterbury, or if their minds were truly changed by the exigencies of frontier life in New England and the proximity of the Plymouth example. In any event, the practice of nonconformity soon outstripped the theory. The churches of Boston and Salem were separatist in fact if not in principle. Each was a local church offering communion only to its own members. Each church required members to show evidence of spiritual conversion to the extent of regeneration. A few years later John Cotton, who had long feared the idea of separatism, would coin the term "congregationalism" to describe in a favorable manner the practice of church organization in the Bay Colony.

The compromise of theory and practice established in Massachusetts was soon tested by the uncompromising Roger Williams. Called to minister to the Boston church in 1631, he refused because that congregation would not formally declare its separation from the Church of England. Instead it was maintained by Governor Winthrop that "we esteem it our honor to call the Church of England from whence we rise, our dear mother . . . and shall always rejoice in her good." Then in 1635 Roger Williams was elected minister of the church at Salem, and he requested that church to declare its separation from all others in England and Massachusetts. Within a few months he was ordered by the General Court of Massachusetts to separate himself from the colony. He fled to the wilderness of Rhode Island.

By founding the settlement of Providence, Roger Williams further encouraged the practice of separatism. The availability of land in Rhode Island invited other Puritans to follow his example. Eventually Rhode Island became a haven for various dissenters, and other settlements in New Jersey and Pennsylvania followed the same pattern.

The case of Anne Hutchinson illustrates another form of division suffered by the Puritans in New England even during the first generation. Before coming to America Anne Hutchinson had been a disciple of John Cotton's in England. She had listened with great enthusiasm to Cotton's sermons about the direct experience of God's redeeming grace. She began to cause trouble in the Bay Colony by ignoring the careful limits placed upon that doctrine. Whereas John Cotton advocated a need for inward signs of divine grace along with outward conformity to the law of church and Scripture, Anne Hutchinson placed all emphasis upon the inward experience of faith, and mocked legal conformity as a mere "covenant of works." Her attitude was condemned by many in the new colony as a dangerous example of Antinomianism. John Cotton was slow to realize that his own parishioner was interpreting his teaching in a dangerous manner. Having been familiar with Anne Hutchinson for many years before their immigration to the New World, John Cotton did not foresee the confrontation in Boston that her unguarded conversations would cause. Thus accusations of heresy multiplied against Anne Hutchinson, and before her teacher had a chance to counsel moderation or attempt some negotiation of the controversy, a full synod was convened in 1637, and then a General Court, to place the opinions of Anne Hutchinson on trial. She complicated her own difficult case by maintaining her unbending manner in the presence of the magistrates, and by proclaiming boldly that she had received special revelations from the Lord. That was too much for the magistrates. To claim "immediate revelation" was to ignore the law of Scripture and the established church. If anyone was allowed to claim direct access to God, then the authority of the Scripture and the need for clergy would be seriously challenged. The magistrates acted quickly to preserve the power of the law; the Antinomian heresy had to be suppressed; Anne Hutchinson was deprived of all civil liberties, including residence. At a church trial in Boston early the next year, the heretic was excommunicated. She followed the path of Roger Williams into exile in Rhode Island.

The suppression of heresy illustrated by the punishment of Anne Hutchinson was made possible by the close working together of civil and clerical authorities. The elders meeting in the synod of 1637 laid the groundwork for the court trial held by the magistrates a few months later. And the outcome of the civil proceedings foreshadowed the verdict of the church trial held the following year. Historians have often debated the justice of calling the Massachusetts Bay Colony a "theocracy." Edmund S. Morgan claims in *The Puritan Dilemma: The Story of John Winthrop* that "of all the governments in the Western world at the time, that of early Massachusetts gave the clergy least authority."[5] In his recent *A Religious History of the American People* Sydney Ahlstrom concludes:

"To call it a 'theocracy' is therefore absurd."[6] Nevertheless the case of Anne Hutchinson illustrates quite clearly the common purpose of civil magistrates and church elders in the early years of the Massachusetts Bay Colony. Separate trials were held by court and church to achieve a common goal—to enforce religious orthodoxy and suppress the Antinomian heresy. Whether or not this form of double inquisition should be called a "theocracy" is unimportant. For Anne Hutchinson either exile or excommunication would force her into the same wilderness. As long as opinions of the Puritan elders coincided with the will and authority of the civil magistrates, the Bay Colony was a theocracy in practice if not in theory.

The close agreement between civil and religious authority during the early years of the Puritan experience in Massachusetts was based upon the restriction of political franchise to members of the church. As long as church membership in turn was available only to the communion of visible saints, Puritan orthodoxy was thus maintained by a double method of selection and exclusion. Exile and excommunication were the most effective weapons, short of capital punishment, for dealing with possible heresy. So many of the religious extremists who were banished from the congregations of the Bay Colony began to follow the path of Roger Williams and Anne Hutchinson to Rhode Island, that the settlement of Providence became known to orthodox Puritans as the "sewer of New England."

The tactics of exclusion, however, could not deal indefinitely with each new threat of Antinomianism. During the first two generations in Massachusetts, the strategy was largely successful, because the civil and religious authorities still shared a common purpose. But thereafter such concerted action against religious heresy became more difficult. As the population continued to grow and different economic interests took root, the attention of the civil authority to secular matters began to diverge from the desire of the clergy to enforce strict religious conformity. Requirements for church membership were partially relaxed when the controversial Half-Way Covenant was adopted in 1662. Extending church membership automatically extended the political franchise. Soon magistrates were elected with more interest in the commercial than the spiritual development of the colony. Consequently some degree of religious tolerance began to emerge. Although the outspoken heretics, the Quakers for example, could still be sentenced to exile, the opportunity of Rhode Island could not itself be banished from Puritan consciousness. Stories about the relative freedom and religious toleration practiced in Rhode Island inevitably found their way back to Massachusetts.

The widening division between civil and religious power was confirmed by the Bay Colony's new charter in 1691. Political franchise was now based on property rather than on church membership. Even some degree of religious toleration was imposed by the new charter. The civil magistrates therefore felt less concern with combating any new appearance of Antinomianism. The last desperate inquisition staged by the dying theocracy of Massachusetts was the infamous witch hunt in 1692. A small number of "witches" were actually hanged or pressed to death by stones, but the magistrates soon came to repent their extreme judgment. Samuel Sewall, who was a special commissioner in the Salem witchcraft trials, publicly recanted his part in the affair. He stood up silently in Boston North Church while his acknowledgment was read aloud to the congregation. Samuel Sewall later became chief justice of the colony's superior court. The embarrassment caused by the witchcraft persecution thus served to divide further the civil and clerical authorities. Men like Sewall could not be tempted again to support the cause of religious persecution. The clergy would have to fight the Devil by themselves. The intensity of Puritan rhetoric began to increase at this time; jeremiads were thundered from every pulpit, because the real authority of the religious leaders was declining. Powerless to stop the increasing spread of Antinomianism, the Puritan ministers finally pretended they were fighting against the beast from the Book of Revelation—"having seven heads and ten horns, and upon his horns ten crowns, and upon his heads the name of blasphemy."

DECLINING PIETY

While the first immigrants to Massachusetts enjoyed the spiritual intoxication of founding a holy settlement in the New World, "a city upon a hill" to serve as a model for all Christians, the following generations were left to experience failure and disillusionment. Declining religious enthusiasm was partially a reflection of the causes already examined, growing material comforts and inherent separatist tendencies, but the decline also followed naturally from the high pitch of the initial expectations. The exaggerated hope shared by the first Puritans reaching out for a New Jerusalem inevitably led to disappointment and bitterness. Toward the end of the next generation, the religious mood of New England darkened. Increase Mather, a minister in the second generation, lived long enough to lose his faith in the divine mission of New England, and he began to preach instead about the inscrutable mystery of God's purpose. In Mather's eyes the covenant had been hopelessly broken.

The natural decline in religious enthusiasm appeared quite clearly in the second generation controversy over baptism and church membership. Each church in the Bay Colony had been organized by men and women professing obedience to the Holy Scriptures and claiming the transforming experience of God's grace. Only the visible saints were admitted to the sacrament of Holy Communion, and only their children were allowed to be baptized. Such an exclusive system could not perpetuate itself for very long. In the second generation many children of the original church members simply could not attest to a personal experience of divine grace, and therefore they had to remain in "external covenant"—baptized but not admitted to full communion. And their children in turn were then denied the rite of baptism. Pressures to open up this narrow system soon became quite strong. Not only the children of the original settlers, but also many of the new immigrants coming into the colony, demanded a loosening of the standards for church membership. At the full synod convened in 1662 to resolve this problem, the famous Half-Way Covenant was adopted. Children could now be baptized if their parents had received that sacrament, but full communion was still reserved for those prepared to confess the experience of regeneration. The membership of the church was thus partially diluted by men and women unable to experience or simply indifferent to the full piety described by Augustine and Calvin. The churches in New England soon had many respectable members, but only a minority still prepared to claim the transforming power of divine grace.

The Half-Way Covenant was widely accepted throughout New England, but in some places it met with bitter opposition. The more liberal churches were prepared to relax the standards for membership, but other churches refused to follow. A majority of the congregation at the First Church of Boston opposed the adoption of any halfway measures. Consequently the minority was forced to separate and to establish a new church. In that manner the "Old South Church" of Boston came into being. Thus a measure designed to lessen tension over the question of church membership in some places actually increased the controversy. And the new, more inclusive covenant ironically intensified the factionalism among a number of the churches.

The Half-Way Covenant was, at best, a temporary compromise designed to resist the complete disintegration of membership requirements. But the compromise inevitably worsened the problem that it was designed to correct. When the church doors were opened to the unregenerate, the proportion of visible saints in the congregation rapidly declined. When Cotton Mather as a young man began to assume much of the burden of the Puritan cause, he saw the enemies of the righteous multiply so quickly that he sometimes wondered if the remaining Puritan saints were not marked for destruction. His long career was a bitter fight against the tide of disintegration.

The Half-Way Covenant represented a partial surrender of the Puritan hope of building the City of God in the wilderness. Either the English Puritans had been selected by God to establish a holy commonwealth in the New World, or their mission was a vain prophecy and a self-delusion. When the original covenant was abandoned, the lamentations of Jeremiah were heard again in New England. The long and bitter arguments about church membership and baptism could not disguise the growing sense of failure. The elders of the church might come together in another synod to discuss the cause of God's apparent wrath, but that could not stop the spreading controversy, nor reverse the trend of disillusionment. The Puritan ministers might continue to preach dire warnings of approaching Judgment (in one jeremiad after another it was proclaimed that God would avenge the broken covenant), but that could not provide the needed experience of transforming piety, nor restore the original sense of divine mission shared by the founders of the colony. The sovereign light of the Puritan God was fading among the children of New England.

COTTON MATHER

How could the orthodox faith of the first generation be restored? The children of the early Puritans needed a Moses to talk with God about their broken covenant. Instead they had Cotton Mather. The extraordinary grandson of John Cotton, the pious and scholarly son of Increase Mather, this reactionary champion of religious orthodoxy inherited the banner of the Puritan cause in Boston at a time when attack was coming from all sides: growing secular concerns were distracting the faithful, separatist tendencies were splitting the churches, and the confession of grace was declining. The career of Cotton Mather was a stubborn and futile battle against all of the forces undermining the sovereignty of the Puritan God.

At the age of twelve, already knowing Latin, Greek, and some Hebrew, Cotton Mather entered Harvard College. His curiosity for knowledge of all kinds remained a commanding force throughout his life. His private library became the largest in New England. But the years spent by the young scholar at Harvard were not happy ones. He could not find any match for his own deep piety or seriousness among his fellow students. His unhappiness at Harvard foreshadowed the pain and frustration that Cotton Mather would suffer to the end of his life. Although he later performed unprecedented feats of scholarship in the New World, writing and publishing more than four hundred and thirty books and pamphlets, he was frequently mocked and maligned by his contemporaries. When he was awarded the degree of Doctor of Divinity by a European university, an honor attained by very few in New England, his detractors in Boston published a scurrilous poem to defame him. When he was accepted as a fellow of the Royal Society, another rare distinction for a citizen of Massachusetts, his enemies found some technicality in the rules of the society to cast doubt upon his being a legitimate member. After he devoted thousands of hours to compiling a monumental scholarly work, his *Biblia Americana,* no publisher at home or abroad would print such an enormous book. It still remains in manuscript. No wonder Cotton Mather wrote in his diary: "The Life of men is full of Labour; and it is generally a Labour in Vain."[7] Fully committed to defending the faith of his fathers, Cotton Mather could only dimly perceive how the rules of the game had been changed against him. He should have lived two generations earlier.

At the age of sixteen Cotton Mather made the required profession of faith to become a member of his father's church. The next year he preached his first sermon, and the following year he began to serve as pastor of the congregation. His life from that time forward was filled with the duties and concerns of supporting his father's ministry at the Church of North Boston. Because his father was often busy as president of Harvard College, or away in England trying to negotiate a new charter for the colony, the full responsibility of the church was left to its young pastor. Sometimes called upon to preach five or six sermons a week, counsel the children, tend the poor, meet with the elders, pray for the sinners in his congregation, and defend the Word of God against all enemies, Cotton Mather performed his many obligations with an extreme diligence characteristic of his determination to be worthy of his Puritan heritage. But he was met in return with "cruel Hatred . . . personal Revenges . . . and villainous Abuses." Toward the end of his career he lamented that he was "by far the most afflicted minister in all New England." After decades of trying to advance the Puritan cause in Boston, Cotton Mather complained that "the Town is become almost a Hell upon Earth, a City full of Lies, and Murders, and Blasphemies. . . . Satan seems to take a strange Possession of it."[8]

Mather's private life was also a record of disappointment and frustration. Caught between the ideal of chastity and a strong sexual desire, he often condemned himself as a "poor sinful creature." He prayed earnestly that "I will endeavour to be always exemplary for my

Chastitie," but he often had to confess "I am strongly haunted by the èvil Spirit, with Temptations, that horribly vex my very Soul within me." Anxious prayer, strict fasting, and guilt-ridden desire were the prologue to his first marriage vows. But he lived to preach funeral sermons for two of his wives, and then was convinced that the sexual demands of his third wife were evidence of insanity.

Cotton Mather also outlived all but two of his fifteen children. At the birth of his first son, named "Increase" after Cotton's father, he wrote in his diary: "I received a wonderful Advice from Heaven, that this my Son, shall be a Servant of my Lord Jesus Christ throughout eternal Ages."[9] But all hope for this favorite son turned to bitter disappointment. Eventually Cotton Mather had to admit that his "wicked Son Increase" had turned out to be "ungodly, distracted, hard-hearted," and completely lost in "foolish and vicious Courses, which must bring him to Misery." The behavior of this wayward son caused his father to suffer "unspeakable Trouble and Anguish and Confusion." Public scandal occurred when "an Harlot big with a Bastard, accuses my poor son Cresy, and layes her Belly to him."[10] Finally the intended "Servant of my Lord Jesus Christ" disappeared forever at sea.

True to his Puritan faith, Cotton Mather understood his many afflictions as proof of the doctrine of original sin. He continually searched his own soul for transgressions that might be increasing the anger of God. He attempted to strengthen his religious exercises: adding more prayers to his daily schedule; observing more fast days until his health was threatened; giving more charity to the poor until his own insufficient resources were almost depleted; visiting the houses of the dying and the jail cells of the condemned in order to witness their final suffering; always demanding more of himself, praying, writing, ministering— determined to prove himself worthy in the eyes of God. Cotton Mather was resolved never to lose a single occasion for saying a memorable or improving word to his wife, children, congregation, and posterity. No minister in New England was more conscientious; no Puritan writer was more prolific. But still his private and professional troubles continued to multiply. Smallpox, witches, Indian massacres, sickness, heresy, grief, all these he could cope with, unshaken in the basic tenets of his faith. He never expected life to be other than difficult. But the rebellion of his own children and the splitting apart of his own congregation were events that his Puritan mind was not prepared to meet. Because his devotion to his own father was so total, Cotton Mather could not begin to understand the ingratitude and disobedience of his son. Because his commitment to serve the Puritan God was so complete, Cotton Mather could not understand the indifference and occasional hostility of his congregation. The commandments of the superego were so powerful to Cotton Mather, whether the voice of conscience came from Increase Mather or God the Father, that he could not comprehend the willful disobedience of such authority. The riotous behavior of his son and the factious dissent of his congregation therefore attacked the very principle of Cotton Mather's devotion to his Puritan God. A revolution advancing the psychological forces of the id and the ego against the authority of the superego was gaining territory on all sides of Cotton Mather, and all he could do was lament the growing power of the Devil. Facing the world, he remained the rigid advocate of the orthodox faith, allowing his frustration to show only in occasional outbursts of temper and petulance. But facing himself in the pages of his diary, he found the armor of the Puritan occasionally cracked, and the dark light of doubt became visible. "I have been lately Tempted with a new Assault from Hell, violently made upon me. I am assaulted with Sollicitations to look upon the whole Christian Religion, as—(I dare not mention what!)"[11] Cotton Mather was even afraid of polluting his mind and diary with the mere thought of skepticism, but eventually his honesty overcame his fear, and he confessed "Temptations to Impurities; and sometimes to Blasphemy, and Atheism, and the Abandonment of all Religion, as a mere Delusion; and sometimes, to self-Destruction itself."[12] With such doubts hidden in his soul, Cotton Mather continued to support the faith of his fathers. The diary of Cotton Mather is an extraordinary document in the intellectual history of New England. Unlike so many private journals of the age, it is more than just a dull record of daily events. The honest power of Mather's introspection revealed the trial of his Puritan spirit caught in the world of flesh and time.

Cotton Mather's role during the epidemic of witch hunting in Salem was a dramatic example of his Puritan conscience on trial. When some young girls in Boston showed signs of bewitchment, Cotton Mather investigated the matter, and even invited one of the girls to stay for a while in his own house. The behavior of the girl was so extreme—the minister was attacked with blows and kicks—that he could only ascribe such conduct to the influence of the Devil. When the girl and her sisters accused a helpless old woman of having bewitched them, the woman was put on trial, condemned, and hanged. Within a few years at least two hundred men and women in Salem and Boston were likewise accused of witchcraft and devilish practices. Twenty of them were executed; eight "firebrands of hell" were killed at one time. What position did Cotton Mather take toward these proceedings? He does not deserve as much blame as some of his detractors have insisted; nor were his actions as commendable as his apologists have maintained. Although he had firsthand contact with the "bewitched" girls from the beginning of the panic, he never appears to have doubted the truth of their reports. Certainly he never doubted the existence of witches nor the subtlety of the Devil. Such doubt would have been totally foreign to his Puritan education. Nor could he ignore the punishment prescribed by Scripture: "Thou shalt not suffer a witch to live." Thus Cotton Mather could see no other choice but to commend the special judges for "the speedy and vigorous Prosecution of such as have rendered themselves obnoxious, according to the Direction given in the Laws of God, and the wholesome Statutes of the English Nation, for the Detection of Witchcrafts."[13] Blind doctrine therefore prevailed. Cotton Mather even praised the judges for "a most charming Instance of Prudence and Patience." He offered to take as many as six of the bewitched girls into his own house to help cure them with fasting and prayers. What he could not do was to consider the possible innocence of the accused men and women. But almost twenty years later he was still puzzled by the significance of the whole tragic episode, and "entreated of the Lord, that I might understand the Meaning of the Descent from the Invisible World."

Although Cotton Mather had acted during the witchcraft hysteria in a manner totally in keeping with his Puritan education and duty, he later became the target of considerable criticism. His enemies seized upon the occasion to use him as a clerical scapegoat for the whole affair. A book was circulated by Mather's opponents that exposed the injustice of the witchcraft trials, and cast much of the blame upon the Puritan minister. The instigators of this attack were the same men who were dividing the congregations of Boston by opening the new Brattle Street Church. Cotton Mather railed against the founders of the rival church as "ignorant, arrogant, obstinate, and full of Malice and Slander." But the wealth and power of Boston soon went to church services in Brattle Street, and Cotton Mather was unable to clear his own reputation from the slanders of the enemy broadsides. His real opponents were not devils from "the Invisible World," but prominent men in Boston like John Leverett and Thomas Brattle, who had, ironically, been his fellow students at Harvard. These men represented the new tendencies in Boston that Cotton Mather fought vainly against: the growing power of the mercantile interests and their modifications of the orthodox Puritan faith.

At the age of twenty Cotton Mather had felt certain that he stood in the vanguard of God's work in the New World. He had been educated and ordained to carry forth the holy mission of his fathers. Ten years later had come the "diabolical Vexations" in Salem, and Cotton Mather was forced to wonder how "the Inextricable Storm from the

Invisible World assaulted the Country." After another ten years had passed, the balance of power and influence in Boston had clearly shifted against Cotton Mather and his Puritan cause. Still he continued to resist the declining sovereignty of the Puritan God. And with increasing boldness his enemies used their secular power to ridicule and frustrate his efforts. He counterattacked by forming the Society for the Propagation of the Christian Religion and another Society for the Suppression of Disorders, but such efforts could not hold back the tide of invective and abuse. Cotton Mather soon complained that Boston was filled with "riotous Young Men" who would come under his window late at night and "sing profane and filthy Songs." When the third regular newspaper of Boston, the *New England Courant,* with a group of writers likened by one contemporary to London's "Hell Fire Club," continued defaming the Puritan clergy, Cotton Mather protested in vain against "the wicked Printer, and his Accomplices, who every week publish a vile Paper to lessen and blacken the Ministers of the Town, and render their Ministry ineffectual."[14] Near the end of his life a "fired Granado" was thrown into his house, but an "Angel of God" saved him from death. The fuse of the hand grenade broke off, and thus Cotton Mather was even denied the satisfaction of martyrdom.

Of his 437 publications only Mather's *Essays To Do Good* and his *Magnalia Christi Americana* have enjoyed some lasting influence. His most popular book, *Essays To Do Good,* was frequently reprinted during the eighteenth century, and Benjamin Franklin admitted that it "gave me such a turn of thinking, as to have influence on my conduct through life." *Essays To Do Good* is a handbook of morals and manners, a practical American how-to-do-it book, foreshadowing Franklin's *Poor Richard's Almanack.*

Cotton Mather's greatest work was the seven-volume *Magnalia Christi Americana,* or *The Ecclesiastical History of New-England.* In the midst of disintegrating hope for the Puritan cause in Massachusetts, Cotton Mather decided to write a full account of the holy mission of the Puritans in America from 1620 to 1698. The seven volumes contain history, biography, theology—an enormous supply of information about seventeenth-century New England. The work, of course, is a Puritan apology. It was Cotton Mather's intention to pay tribute to the faith of his fathers, and to demonstrate the will of God in the founding of Massachusetts.

Mather's heroes were the great men of the first generation, who crossed the Atlantic and dedicated their settlements in the wilderness to the glory of God. Frequently a note of nostalgia is sounded in the narrative, nostalgia for the heroic days when his grandfathers, John Cotton and Richard Mather, preached in Massachusetts. At the age of six Cotton Mather had stood by the deathbed of his paternal grandfather. The impression of honor and authority never faded from his imagination. The heroic stature of the early Puritan leaders was described by Cotton Mather in epic dimensions: a bold voyage to a new continent, building settlements in the wilderness, fighting the devilish Indians, coping with the harshness, privation, and danger of frontier life, discovering heretics among the faithful, and preserving the communion of visible saints. In the pages of the *Magnalia* the details of Puritan life are transformed into heroic legend, and the history of New England begins to resemble a biblical myth. But the dreams of a golden age were a triumph of hope over reality. Cotton Mather was happier imagining an heroic past, than he was in dealing with the confused and frustrating present. Mocked and abused by the philistines of Boston, Cotton Mather often felt like Milton's tragic hero, "Eyeless in Gaza at the mill with slaves." And like the greatest of all Puritan writers, his imagination turned to the vision of Paradise on earth —innocent, heroic, and lost.

Cotton Mather died in 1728, convinced that Winthrop's "city upon a hill" had become "a City full of Lies, and Murders, and Blasphemies." The paradise of his grandfathers had become "a Hell upon Earth." If Cotton Mather was born too late, he also died too early. The year of his death ironically brought New England to the verge of the Great Awakening. Toward the end of his life Cotton Mather was more convinced than ever that the Second Coming was approaching. Amid fire and angels Christ would soon descend from Heaven to proclaim the advent of the millennium. Instead young Jonathan Edwards was riding his gray horse on the trail to Northampton.

3

THE GREAT AWAKENING

The apparent decline of the Puritan faith in America was temporarily reversed in the 1740s by an unexpected increase in religious conversions. During the Great Awakening the Puritan churches from Georgia to Maine received new members at an unprecedented rate. If the thousands of jeremiads preached in New England during the long career of Cotton Mather had failed to halt the decline of piety, why did the spirit of revivalism prove so successful just a few years after his death? The subject of the Great Awakening—what happened and why—is still one of the most controversial in the history of religion in America.

The surge of religious enthusiasm that surprised the colonies in the 1740s had been foreshadowed by smaller revivals among the churches of western Massachusetts and Connecticut. For nearly sixty years the ministry of Solomon Stoddard in Northampton influenced the course of the Puritan faith in western New England. Stoddard experimented with the membership requirements of his church in order to attract more people to the experience of spiritual conversion. He was one of the first ministers in New England to abandon the Half-Way Covenant, and invite the whole congregation to the sacrament of Holy Communion. In Northampton a public confession of grace was no longer required for church membership. All the people in the congregation who would come forward to receive the Lord's Supper were accepted without further question as converted members of the church. The simultaneous conversion of a whole group of people, a practice heretofore almost unknown in New England, soon became the dynamic principle of revivalism. The church in Northampton continued to add new members in a series of group conversions that Stoddard called "seasons of harvest."

When Stoddard died in 1729, the influential pulpit of Northampton passed to his grandson Jonathan Edwards. At first the new minister felt his congregation to be "very insensible of the things of religion," but in a few years Edwards began to note a dramatic change. He witnessed a surprising increase in the size of his audience and a growing spiritual concern among many who listened to his sermons on divine grace. "This town," Edwards wrote to a fellow minister in 1734, "never was so full of Love, nor so full of Joy. . . . I never saw the Christian spirit in Love to Enemies so exemplified in all my Life as I have seen it within this half-year."[1] Edwards had no doubt but what the unexpected revival was "a glorious work of God." In less than a year more than three hundred new church members were brought to a conviction of regeneration by the dynamic preaching in Northampton. The celebration was temporarily dampened when Edwards's uncle-by-marriage despaired of ever being saved and deliriously cut his own throat. (Edwards attributed the suicide to the rage of Satan.) A few years later Edwards wrote a long account of the revival in Northampton: *A Faithful Narrative of the Surprising Work of God in the Conversion of Many Hundred Souls in Northampton and the Neighboring Towns and Villages.* This account was widely read on both sides of the Atlantic, and it helped to inspire the greater wave of revivalism that was soon to follow. John Wesley read Edwards's book while walking from London to Oxford, and reportedly exclaimed: "Surely this is the Lord's doing, and it is marvelous in our eyes."[2]

When the Great Awakening began in 1740, there were few critical voices raised in disagreement. The spirit of revivalism was reported from Georgia to Maine, from the seacoast to the frontier, among educated and illiterate, young and old, black and white, rich and poor. Jonathan Edwards called it "a time of glorious outpouring of the Spirit of God to revive religion." Recent attempts by historians to explain the Great Awakening in terms of one social class, one political force, one economic interest, or one geographical area are contradicted by the ample historical evidence that the awakening did not follow conventional boundaries, social, political, or geographical. Similar revivals appeared at approximately the same time in France, Holland, Germany, Switzerland, and most dramatically in England.

All these revivals shared a quickening of interest in the fundamental question of Calvinism—what must I do to be saved? Attendance at church lectures and services rapidly increased. Itinerant preaching and even lay exhortations became popular and widespread. Many of the people who confessed an awakening to divine grace were inspired by the words of Christ: "Except a man be born again, he cannot see the kingdom of God." The example of Paul on the road to Damascus was the accepted model of sudden and unexpected conversion, but the experience generated by the Great Awakening in New England often depended more on the excitement of group participation. Listening to evangelical sermons, the congregation might fall to moaning, shrieking, fainting, and crying. The two central emotions of Calvinism—fear of damnation and fervent hope for divine grace—were both pushed to dynamic extremes. Revivalist preachers would torment a congregation with visions of eternal punishment until the extreme tension would issue forth in a flood of confession and the relief of spiritual conversion. Even an observer as disinterested and skeptical as Benjamin Franklin admitted: "It was wonderful to see the Change soon made in the Manners of our Inhabitants; from being thoughtless or indifferent about Religion, it seem'd as if all the World were growing Religious."[3] The explanation of Jonathan Edwards was echoed by a more zealous observer: "The Dispensation of Grace we are now under is certainly such as neither we nor our Fathers have seen. . . . I believe there has not been the like since the extraordinary pouring out of the Spirit immediately after our Lord's Ascension. The Apostolical Times seem to have return'd upon us."[4]

Itinerant preachers were a common feature of the awakening; the most famous was the Reverend George Whitefield. On his tour of the colonies in 1740, he traveled from South Carolina to Maine, preaching more than 130 sermons in seventy-three days. The consequences were extraordinary. In Boston more than 25,000 people assembled on the Commons to hear his final sermon. His emotional and extemporaneous style of preaching held great appeal for audiences bored with the customary recitation of sermons from pedantic notes and closely written manuscripts. Whitefield's first tour through New England was a triumph of crowd manipulation. News of his coming would be advertised well in advance; expectations would be built up to a high degree of excitement; large crowds would gather in church or field; and then the powerful voice of the revivalist preacher would hypnotically unite his audience into one band of sinners, trembling, crying, and finally exulting in the release of mass emotion. One Connecticut farmer, who dropped his tools in the field and ran twelve miles just to hear a sermon by Whitefield, described his response:

> When I see Mr. Whitfield come upon the Scaffold, he looked almost angelical—a young, slim, slender youth before some thousands of people, and with a bold, undaunted countenance. And my hearing how God was with him everywhere as he came along, it

solomnized my mind, and put me in a trembling fear before he began to preach, for he looked as if he was cloathed with authority from the great God. And a sweet, solomn Solemnity sat upon his brow, and my hearing him preach gave me a heart wound, by God's blessing.[5]

In the first stages of the awakening, there were few who could resist the emotional contagion. During the sermon Whitefield preached in Northampton, Jonathan Edwards "wept the whole Time." The established clergy of Boston were three-to-one in favor of the revival. Ironically the only remaining son of Cotton Mather stood in mute opposition, and in 1741 he was asked to surrender the pulpit of his church. Whitefield blamed conventional ministers like Samuel Mather for the lethargy and deadness of spirit in New England: "I am verily persuaded, the Generality of Preachers talk of an unknown, unfelt Christ. And the Reason why Congregations have been so dead, is because dead Men preach to them."[6] Whitefield boldly sounded the trumpet for regeneration, and as Edwards once remarked: "The noise amongst the dry bones waxed louder and louder."

The example of George Whitefield was soon imitated by other itinerant preachers. But those who followed in the wake of the great revivalist could neither match his remarkable success nor escape the controversy his preaching had aroused. The "divine fire lately kindled" by Whitefield was fueled anew by the preaching tour of Gilbert Tennent in the early months of 1741. One minister in Boston reported that after Tennent's visit more than five hundred people came to him seeking religious counsel, and the minister of the Brattle Street Church admitted that in one week's time more people had come to him for advice about their salvation than in the preceding two decades. But still the crowds attracted by Gilbert Tennent could not match the excited mobs who had turned out for George Whitefield, and the voices of opposition began to grow stronger.

The notoriety of itinerant preaching reached a new height with the fanatical performances of James Davenport, who toured New England in the summer of 1741. In the impassioned harangues of Davenport the excesses of the awakening were fully exposed. Brought to trial in Connecticut for disturbing the peace, Davenport was found "disturbed in the rational Faculties of his Mind," and was transported under guard out of the colony. Undaunted by such treatment, Davenport next took his evangelical campaign to Massachusetts. There he aroused opposition on all sides. A contemporary witness described Davenport's preaching in the *Boston Evening Post*:

He has no knack at raising the Passions, but by a violent straining of his Lungs, and the most extravagant wreathings of his Body, which at the same Time that it creates Laughter and Indignation in the most, occasions great meltings, screamings, crying, swooning, and Fits in some others. . . . Were you to see him in his most violent agitations, you would be apt to think that he was a Madman just broke from his Chains.[7]

Davenport tried desperately to fight back by branding all his critics as "unconverted." Always his own worst enemy, Davenport by his attacks on local ministers simply turned more people against him. Even Gilbert Tennent, the man Davenport was trying to imitate, found him "enthusiastical, proud, and schismatical." Clearly the antics of Davenport were a disservice to the cause of the awakening. A court in Massachusetts also found him mentally unbalanced. The symbolic climax of his career was reached a year later in New London when Davenport persuaded a crowd to hold a public book burning. Moving around the flames, the minister then told his wild audience that "in order to be saved they ought to burn all their idols." They built a great heap of silk gowns, cloaks, fans, gloves, etc. According to a witness: "Davenport's own idol with which he topped the pile was a pair of old, wore out, plush breaches." But when the crowd had a chance to observe the preacher "strutt about bare-arsed," their enthusiasm waned, and it was decided that "making such a sacrifice was not necessary for their salvation."[8]

The foolish conduct of Davenport did much to call forth the opponents of the awakening. How had it come to pass, the critics wanted to know, that so many people "were seriously, soberly, and solemnly out of their wits"? Charles Chauncy, the minister of the First Church of Boston, suggested the "cause of this enthusiasm is a bad temperament of the blood and spirits; 'tis properly a disease, a sort of madness."[9] Chauncy was the most persistent critic of revivalist conduct. He was appalled by the "freakish or furious" behavior, the shrieking, the trembling, the convulsions, all in the name of divine grace. Most of all, Chauncy was annoyed by the claim of the new converts to have "familiar converse" with God and a "peculiar intimacy with heaven." Although Chauncy was able to describe the behavior as "deluded imagination" and "madness," he could not explain its origin.

Recent historians have also tried in vain to identify a particular cause of the Greak Awakening. Richard Mosier calls it "a revolt of the back-country producers from the stringent controls of the mercantile aristocracy which ruled from afar."[10] But such an explanation does not account for the awakening in Boston where many of the established ministers offered their support. Eugene White, on the other hand, describes the revival as a "deep-rooted social movement . . . confined to the cities and the settled areas of the East."[11] But it did extend from the cities to the western and southern frontiers, and periodic revivals became a popular feature in frontier settlements. Clinton Rossiter attempts to solve the problem by introducing class distinctions: "It appealed primarily to the poor and despised; it revolted the well-born, well-educated, and well-to-do."[12] But the infamous James Davenport was well born and well educated; he was a graduate of Yale and the great-grandson of New Haven's founder; nevertheless, the excitement of the revival appealed to him as strongly, if not more so, as to anyone else. Perry Miller's explanation of the Great Awakening also relies upon an assumed class distinction. Even when he views the events as international in scope, he believes "the upper or the educated classes . . . turned to eighteenth-century rationalism," while the aspirations of "the lower classes . . . finally found vent in the revivals."[13] This formula is contradicted by Miller's own account of Jonathan Edwards, which praises Edwards for his wide-ranging comprehension of Locke, Newton, and the rationalism of the eighteenth century, and also gives him credit for writing the most profound defense of the Great Awakening.

Miller's picture of the awakening as "an uprising of the common people" has encouraged other historians to view it as a rehearsal of the political revolution thirty-five years later. Richard Mosier does not hesitate to describe the Great Awakening as "the first step in a movement which culminates in the American Revolution," and Alan Heimert, a student of Perry Miller's, in his recent and controversial book *Religion and the American Mind: From the Great Awakening to the Revolution,* strongly argues that the revivalists, and not their rational opponents, set the spirit of revolution in motion. Certainly the actions of the revivalists had some unforeseen political consequences, but Jonathan Edwards was looking forward to the Kingdom of God, and would have had no interest whatsoever in the founding of the American Republic.

The causes of the Great Awakening were not primarily economic or political; they were rooted deep in the Puritan imagination, and were called forth by recent changes in Puritan worship. What Edwards viewed as a "glorious outpouring of the spirit of God" was anticipated by generations of Christians in New England. When the Half-Way Covenant was abandoned by Solomon Stoddard, and the sacrament of Communion was offered to all regardless of prior conversion, the result was a great increase in church membership. When Jonathan Edwards assumed the pulpit of his grandfather's church in Northampton, he continued to use the sacrament of Communion to encourage conversion. It is not a coincidence that the great revivals began in Northampton. When White-field and Tennent preached to crowds throughout New England, they also encouraged all to accept Christ by coming to the Lord's Table. Again many conversions resulted. The success of the Great Awakening thus depended upon the rejection of the Half-Way Covenant, and the new availability of church membership. Cotton Mather and his father had been alarmed when Solomon Stoddard first introduced such open practices in western New England. Cotton Mather's son was dismayed when the revivalist methods reached Boston. From one generation to the next the Mather family refused to abandon the congregational prin-ciple of limiting church membership to the visible saints. Each candidate for membership was required to stand individually before the congrega-tion and profess his experience of divine grace. But when revivalist preachers began to invite the unregenerate to come forward together, many who were hesitant to make an individual confession of grace found comfort in group participation.

The practice of multiple conversion also intensified the emotional drama of the conversion experience. Instead of the sober and respectable confession of a single person seeking admission to the communion of saints, the churches now witnessed the unregenerate crowd shrieking and moaning and writhing their way to drink at the Lord's Table. The ex-perience of conversion thus assumed all the dynamic aspects of crowd hysteria, and forceful preachers like Whitefield and Tennent could bring more sinners to Christ in a short time than conventional ministers had been able to do with years of patient doctrinal exposition. Puritan leaders, of course, had always recognized the importance of emotion in the conversion experience. John Cotton had described regeneration as a change of heart and not just a rational affirmation. But the drama of group conversion granted a much larger role to the dynamic force of emotion. No one understood the principle of mass suggestion more thoroughly than Jonathan Edwards. He maintained that "true religion, in great part, consists in holy affections," and the power of his preach-ing was increased by his direct challenge to the feelings and emotions, the "affections" of his congregation.

Revivalist preachers intensified the emotional drama of conversion by drawing upon the power of fear. For generations Puritan ministers had attempted to frighten their listeners into a conviction of original sin and thereby inspire a desperate hope for salvation. Increase Mather had warned his congregation: "Thy soul is hanging over the mouth of hell by the rotten thread of a frail life: if that breaks, the devouring Gulf will swallow thee up forever."[14] Even the self-avowed rationalist Charles Chauncy invoked the same rhetoric of fear: "There is nothing betwixt you and the place of blackness of darkness, but a poor frail, uncertain life. You hang, as it were, over the bottomless pit, by the slender thread of life, and the moment that snaps asunder, you sink down into perdition."[15] Are such fearful warnings very different from Jonathan Edwards's famous vision?

> The God that holds you over the pit of hell, much as one holds a spider, or some loathsome insect over the fire, abhors you, and is dreadfully provoked: his wrath towards you burns like fire. . . . You hang by a slender thread, with the flames of divine wrath flashing about it, and ready every moment to singe it, and burn it asunder.[16]

Why is it that no one can remember the words of Increase Mather or Charles Chauncy, and no one can forget the similar words of Jonathan Edwards? It may be true that Edwards's sermon is more artfully constructed and more insistent with its imagery; the spider is certainly a powerful addition; but merely comparing the style of the sermons will not reveal their essential difference. Increase Mather preached to the same congregation for fifty-nine years. Some members of his church in Boston may have listened to more than ten thousand Mather sermons. Solid instruction, no doubt, but not many surprises. How could he call for an awakening? How could he make the rhetoric of fear sound convincing? But Jonathan Edwards traveled to Enfield by special invitation to deliver his famous sermon "Sinners in the Hands of an Angry God." It was not an ordinary Sunday for the congregation. They were eager to see and hear the great preacher from Northampton. And Jonathan Edwards came with the avowed purpose of a revivalist. "The use of this awful subject," he frankly stated, "may be for awakening unconverted persons in this congregation." The audience was ready for him. They shrieked and moaned with fear; some fainted; some cried for mercy; few could resist the drama of conversion.

If revivalist preachers were more successful at arousing the fear and terror of their special audiences, they were also better able to provide an escape from anxiety in the experience of regeneration. The leaders of the revival had the advantage of appealing to the uncommon expectations built up during the Great Awakening. The unregenerate often came to a revivalist sermon with the intention of taking some part in the excitement of conversion. Or they might become so influenced by the enthusiasm of the crowd that personal hesitation was sacrificed to the psychology of the group. By abandoning the Half-Way Covenant, and by allowing multiple confessions of grace, the revivalist preachers made it as easy as possible for the crowd to come forward to acknowledge Christ. Jonathan Edwards's listeners at Enfield would have been waiting expectantly for his call at the end of the sermon: "Therefore, let every one that is out of Christ, now awake and fly from the wrath to come." Every good revivalist sermon must contain a stage cue for audience action.

If the power of a sermon depends in part on the reputation of the minister and the special expectations of his audience, then the importance of itinerant preaching for the Great Awakening can be fully appreciated. The farmer who ran twelve miles to hear George Whitefield preach found the itinerant minister "cloathed with authority from the great God." The same farmer probably could have gone to his local church and listened to more solid doctrine. But intense expectation and dynamic emotional release are the ingredients of a successful revival. The Great Awakening was an extraordinary stirring up of the Puritan faith, and the exchange of ministers, the itinerant preachers, the lay exhorters, all helped to increase the disturbance. It is not surprising that the aftermath of the Great Awakening found the traditional parish system in widespread disarray.

Debate among historians about the causes of the Great Awakening has been surpassed only by critical disagreement about the consequences. Much confusion has resulted from a failure to separate the short-term effects of the awakening from its long-range implications. At the beginning of the revival even Charles Chauncy spoke highly of its promise; later he became its most persistent critic. When the excitement of revivalism first began to spread across New England, even the older clergy were pleasantly surprised by the new influx of church members. In one small area of Connecticut eleven ministers together proclaimed the awakening "a great and glorious work of divine grace, and a great reformation of religion." The general chorus of praise seemed at first to preclude any chance for protest. To criticize what many believed to be the overture to the millennium and the proof of God's mercy required considerable detachment and courage. Any expression of doubt about the value of the revival might expose the skeptic to charges of being ungrateful, hardhearted, and hopelessly unregenerate. Thus at the beginning of the Great Awakening the tide of religious enthusiasm was dominant, and potential opponents by and large remained silent.

But they were not silent for long. Ministers who were secretly alarmed by the tactics and success of George Whitefield unleashed their resentment against his unfortunate imitators, especially the pathetic Davenport. And once the critics recognized their own strength, divisions were created that could not be reconciled. The harmony reported during the first year of the awakening was soon replaced by schism, invective, and bitterness. Battle lines were drawn for and against the methods and meaning of revivalism. Congregations began to split apart because of their inability to agree about either the validity or the significance of the awakening. The Congregationalists divided into factions known as "new light" and "old light." The same division among the Presbyterian churches was styled "new side" and "old side." The splintering caused much rancor, and led to extreme statements from both positions. The polarization created a number of important changes in Puritan theory and practice.

The division of congregations into pro- and anti-revivalist factions was encouraged by the itinerant preachers, especially by Whitefield. He not only dramatized an exciting form of preaching to many who had experienced only the dry reading of sermons by their local ministers, Whitefield also condemned the local clergy as "dead men" and dismissed their traditional preaching as "a sad Symptom of Decay of vital Religion." Congregations were thus invited to compare ministers, and more than ever before in New England the clergy found themselves vying with one another in a kind of popularity contest. Tennent's sermon "On the Danger of an Unconverted Ministry" openly encouraged his listeners to travel "a few Miles farther than ordinary" if they felt dissatisfied with their local church. Such advice was anathema to the established clergy of New England. Small wonder that Tennent's sermon was blamed for "all that Discord, Intrusion, Confusion, Separation, Hatred, Variance, Emulations, Wrath, Strife, Seditions, Heresies, etc. that have been springing up in so many of the Towns and Churches thro' the Province."[17] For many local ministers it soon became an intolerable situation. Few could hope to match the excitement generated by the appearance of a great itinerant like Whitefield. The men and women who traveled miles to hear the open-air sermons of Whitefield and Tennent would return the following Sunday to their parish church, stirred with expectations that could not be fulfilled, and ready with criticism that could not be silenced.

Even more disruptive to the traditional ministry were the many lay exhorters, men neither educated nor ordained to preach, who were moved by the revivalist spirit to take upon themselves the task of spreading the Gospel. Their preaching was often a mixture of incoherent frenzy and ignorant sentimentality. The antics of the lay exhorters were often worse than the extreme conduct of the itinerants. The established clergy observed with horror while "Numbers of illiterate Exhorters swarm about as Locusts from the Bottomless Pit." In 1742 the General Assembly of Connecticut passed a law "regulating abuses and correcting disorders in ecclesiastical affairs." The law was designed to prevent itinerant preaching, and James Davenport was soon ejected from the colony when he ignored the provisions of the new statute. The law was also designed to suppress the practice of lay exhorting, and jail sentences were provided for laymen who might still dare to "publicly teach and exhort the people." But no law could heal the bitterness that had already divided congregations; the feelings on both sides were too strong.

Much of the bickering and controversy that surfaced in the aftermath of the Great Awakening was nourished by the aggressive criticism which the pro-revivalists aimed at their opponents. Following the example of the itinerant preachers who branded many established ministers as "unconverted," the members of the crowd who believed themselves to be newly awakened began to judge the religious behavior of their neighbors with more severity. As this spirit of censoriousness spread, suspicion and angry debate broke apart congregations and inflamed separatist tendencies.

Many preachers found themselves caught in the middle of the pro- and anti-revivalist factions. Attempts at compromise were rarely successful. Conciliatory gestures toward the pro-revivalist group would bring accusations from the old lights of radical enthusiasm and dangerous heresy. Any expression of sympathy for the opponents of the awakening would bring charges from the new lights of being unregenerate and hardhearted, while attempts to remain above the controversy, indifferent to the passion generated on either side, would only provoke the dissatisfaction and wrath of both groups. Ministers soon found themselves losing a large part, if not all, of their congregations. New churches were formed at an unprecedented rate. Some democratic choice had always been implicit in the method of calling for a new Puritan minister, but now the choice was exercised more widely. It had also been possible, although very unlikely, for a minister to be removed from his church, but now the likelihood of removal was greatly increased. Less than ten years after the wave of revivalism had receded, Jonathan Edwards was forced to surrender what had been the strongest pulpit of the Great Awakening.

The disorder which troubled many preachers in the wake of the great revival was echoed in the theoretical debate about the very meaning of religious faith. Differences of opinion about the validity and significance of the awakening forced the partisans on either side to rethink the basic assumptions of Puritanism. Jonathan Edwards wrote the majority of his theological work either to explain or to defend the revival. Much of his writing was a direct reply to his critics. The controversy stirred up by the awakening thus added a new chapter to Puritan theology in America, and Jonathan Edwards, before and after his dismissal from Northampton, was its principal author.

The debate over the meaning and value of the Great Awakening focused on the nature of the conversion experience. The powerful emotion reported by many new converts was scorned by the opponents of revivalism as mere "enthusiasm"—a disease of passion that fools men with delusions of grace. But the defenders of revivalism believed that such emotional power was the genuine blessing of God. The basic question thus became how to distinguish false enthusiasm from true inspiration. Men on both sides of the controversy believed that some human feelings were divinely granted and that some were not, but they could not agree on how to tell them apart. Critics of the awakening like Charles Chauncy argued that it was possible to distinguish enthusiasm from inspiration by noting the violent symptoms of the former. Chauncy listed the forms of behavior in *Enthusiasm Described and Caution'd Against* (1742) that characterize a false conversion: a wild countenance, a loose tongue, convulsions, shrieking, writhing, etc. His list is a catalog of the extreme behavior observed during the awakening. But Jonathan Edwards never expected the sudden experience of divine grace to be anything but powerful and violent. He was not greatly disturbed by the emotional behavior of the new converts. The violence of their experience was to Edwards a possible sign of their genuine conversion. Chauncy felt that toleration of such extreme behavior would only debase the image of man; Edwards felt that criticism of such conduct would negate the free gift of God. There could be no agreement for two Christians seeking grace, as long as one defined conversion as a rational assent to scriptural authority, and the other believed conversion to be a powerful and emotional transformation.

Both Chauncy and Edwards had to fight their battles on two fronts. While Chauncy strongly warned against the dangers of enthusiasm, he had to caution his own followers not to proceed uncritically, lest in their zeal they might also reject genuine inspiration. It was necessary to protect "real religion" while the "imaginary" was being rooted out. Edwards faced a similar dilemma. While promoting revivalism, he had to warn against an uncritical acceptance of Christ, lest the proponents of the awakening deceive themselves and disgrace their own cause. Edwards sometimes found his friends more embarrassing than his enemies. The predicament of each was heightened by the fact that both Chauncy and Edwards recognized that the outward signs of divine grace "may be counterfeited." Thus Chauncy had to decide whether enthusiasm was "a sort of madness" or just bold hypocrisy, and Edwards had to distinguish genuine conversion from mere delusion whether innocent or deceitful.

It is hardly surprising that historians have had great difficulty attempting to define the positions for and against the awakening. Jonathan Edwards has been viewed as the articulate champion of revivalism, pointing ahead to more than a century of missionary activity in America, and he has been seen as the last defender of strict Calvinism, harking back to the almost forgotten days before the Half-Way Covenant. Charles Chauncy has been praised as a clearsighted liberal, seeing ahead to Unitarianism if not all the way to scientific rationalism, and he has been dismissed as a stubborn reactionary, unable to respond to the spiritual power of the Great Awakening. Such contradictory views, however, are quite appropriate, because both men were headed in two directions at once. Edwards did borrow the new philosophy of John Locke to analyze and support the forward thrust of revivalism, but he also contradicted the awakening by reverting to strict rules for church membership, rules that even predated the Half-Way Covenant and the reforms of Solomon Stoddard. Chauncy did assume a modern pose of rationalism in order to censure the extreme behavior of the awakening, but his fear and distrust of the rapid changes caused by revivalism were deeply conservative and reactionary.

The debate between Chauncy and Edwards can be seen as a renewal of the Arminian versus Antinomian controversy. Chauncy believed that "real religion" could be demonstrated by the "sober, calm, reasonable" conduct of men. He emphasized human dignity and the power of man's will to give rational assent to scriptural authority. To the extent that Chauncy believed that man was able to influence his own salvation, his position was Arminian. He told his congregation that if they would "live soberly and righteously" they could anticipate the promise of redemption. Edwards, on the other hand, helped to start the revival in Northampton by preaching a series of sermons on justification by faith. His favorite quotation from the Bible was Saint Paul to the Ephesians: "For by grace are ye saved through faith; and that not of yourselves: it is the gift of God." He emphasized the sovereign power of God to save and damn regardless of human will. Edwards pictured all men as sinners, unable to redeem themselves, and therefore dependent upon the mercy of God. To the extent that Edwards believed in the availability of grace independent of moral conduct and scriptural authority, his position was Antinomian. He told his congregation that God was not bound to reward the good conduct of any man, but even the most wretched sinner might suddenly be transformed by God's merciful and irresistible grace.

Although the thrust of Chauncy's position was Arminian in character, his Puritan training was sufficiently orthodox to keep him from fully embracing an Arminian conclusion. Thus he stopped short of believing that it was completely within man's power to accomplish his own salvation, and occasionally Chauncy might remind his congregation that an all-powerful God holds sinners "over the bottomless pit, by the slender thread of life." Likewise a full acceptance of the Antinomian position was avoided by Jonathan Edwards. He warned against spiritual pride in *Some Thoughts Concerning the Present Revival of Religion in New England* (1743), and cautioned his readers to be critical of immediate revelation contrary to Scripture. Chauncy was conservative enough to resist the long-range development of his position through Unitarianism into rational humanism, and Edwards was too much of a Calvinist to be able to support the careless revivalism that was a principal legacy of the Great Awakening. Although much of Chauncy's thought appears to be rational, it is a mistake to place him among eighteenth-century rationalists. His definition of reason was closer to the "rational acceptance of Scripture" that Puritans had always acknowledged. The foundation of his world was still supernatural. Chauncy was more of a Puritan than a man of the Enlightenment. And although Jonathan Edwards raised the strongest voice in defense of the Great Awakening, it is a mistake to place him in the current of revivalism that ran on into the nineteenth century. His understanding of religious conversion was closer to Augustine and Calvin. He still emphasized the doctrines of original sin and predestination. Chauncy and Edwards were both rooted firmly enough in orthodox Puritan tradition to be able to resist their own tendencies in the directions of secular humanism and broad evangelicalism. The future did not belong to either man.

The anti-awakening forces eventually split into two groups which matched the division apparent within Chauncy's own character. One faction became very conservative, resisting all change, attempting to preserve the Puritan faith as it had been in the days of the Mathers. To this group the challenge of revivalism and the arguments for secular humanism were equally unwelcome. Antinomianism and Arminianism were both considered dangerous heresies that would destroy the true faith. This group, which included men like Samuel Mather and Samuel Niles, was fairly silent in its resistance to change, partly because these men had nothing new to say, and partly because they felt that bitterness and controversy were poisoning the religion of their fathers.

Another faction developed at the same time from the rational tendencies of Chauncy's philosophy. Ministers like Ebenezer Gay and Jonathan Mayhew conducted a liberal attack on the hard doctrines of Calvinism. The concept of original sin was criticized and rejected. Predestination was declared unjust and untrue. The doctrine of irresistible grace was interpreted as a bar to human initiative and achievement. The liberals were trying to reshape Puritan theology in accord with the emerging tendencies of the Enlightenment. The sovereignty of God was sacrificed for the dignity of man. The liberal attack on Calvinism led to a mild form of deism and eventually to secular humanism.

The pro-awakening forces also split into two groups which matched the division within Edwards's character. One party followed Edwards back into a form of strict Calvinism. Ministers like Joseph Bellamy and Samuel Hopkins continued to repudiate the Half-Way Covenant, and to insist on the absolute sovereignty of God, the sinfulness of man, predestination, and irresistible grace. The extensive religious writings of Jonathan Edwards provided a "New England theology" for his disciples to follow. Shortly after Edwards's death Hopkins wrote a biography of him in order to illustrate his religious exercises so "that others may hereby be directed and excited to go and do likewise."[18] But a man as remarkable in intellect and as uncompromising in conscience predictably had few genuine followers. The theological achievement of Jonathan Edwards remains unsurpassed in American philosophy; however, it has been a high summit commanding respect, and not a common position for many to reach.

A major portion of the pro-awakening forces moved away from strict Calvinism in the direction of pietism and evangelicalism. Among this large and influential group the tactics of revivalism were taken for granted. Standards of church membership, considered essential by Edwards, were abandoned. The scholastic roots of Calvinism were almost forgotten, and a broad appeal to emotion and sentiment passed for genuine religion. This form of revivalism spread rapidly and strongly through the South and the West. Few denominations were spared the pressure for evangelical activity. The same impetus had much to do with the phenomenal spread of Methodism in the next century. And sporadic revivals have remained at least a sideshow of American life to the present day. But the careless spirit of revivalism has tended to ignore or to discredit the intellectual content of the Puritan faith. The finest historian of the Great Awakening, Edwin Gaustad, is far too optimistic when he concludes that "New England's piety survived . . . in part . . . because the Edwardsean theology was a powerful, capacious channel through which it could steadily flow."[19] What did flow south and west was not "Edwardsean theology" but a debased form of revivalism with little Puritan respectability and less intellectual discipline. The special genius of Edwards was always to combine the intellect and the emotions, but the evangelical movement in America has generally sacrificed the former to the latter. The proponents of the Great Awakening thus branched into movements that sharply diverged. While the few genuine followers of Edwards were trying to save the Puritan faith by preserving a form of strict Calvinism, a larger party of evangelical preachers was forgetting theological distinctions and debasing its religion. Eventually the gap between intelligence and religious conviction became the hopeless division that Sidney Mead complains about in *Church History:* "Since around 1800 Americans have in effect been given the hard choice between being intelligent according to the standards prevailing in their intellectual centers, and being religious according to the standards prevailing in their denominations."[20]

JONATHAN EDWARDS

Jonathan Edwards was at the center of Puritan revivalism in America from the surprising conversions in Northampton in 1735 through the bitter aftermath of the awakening in the next decade. He was not only one of the best-known ministers and the principal theologian of the Great Awakening, but also the most articulate champion of the Puritan faith in its long battle with the forces of the Enlightenment. The popular nineteenth-century historian George Bancroft declared without reservation: "He that would know the workings of the New England mind in the middle of the last century, and the throbbings of its heart, must give his days and nights to the study of Jonathan Edwards."[21] Critical study of Edwards has accelerated dramatically in the past decade, and a definitive edition of his writings is nearing completion at Yale University. But the considerable attention focused on his career has not produced any critical agreement. Perry Miller believed Edwards to be profoundly "modern," while Peter Gay calls him "the last medieval American."[22] Vernon Parrington described Edwards as "an anachronism," while Alan Heimert sees his influence reaching ahead to the American Revolution.[23] Although their interpretations differ, all historians appear to share a common fascination with the extraordinary intellectual drama of Edwards's career—the tragic spectacle of a man laboring to make clear the very foundations of his faith, when the world at the same time was relentlessly turning against him. Add to his rise and fall on the world's stage the constant irony that dogged the career of Edwards, and the sum is a full tragic drama.

The life of Jonathan Edwards began with great expectations. He was born in 1703, the son, grandson, and great-grandson of Puritan ministers. As the only boy among eleven children he felt a pressure to follow in the footsteps of his father that was no doubt extraordinary. He was educated by his father until he entered Yale College at the age of thirteen. After graduation in 1720 and a brief period of ministerial work in New York, he returned to Yale to assume the duties of a senior tutor. There he remained until 1726 when he was invited to join the ministry of his grandfather's church in Northampton. Edwards's life followed the example set by John Cotton more than a century before: first the achievement of academic distinction as a scholar and teacher, and then a turbulent career as a minister. It is not surprising that both men ran into difficulties with their congregations. Neither John Cotton nor Jonathan Edwards ever fully succeeded in bending the temperament of a scholar to the popular routine of a minister.

The most important event in Edwards's life was his religious conversion at the age of seventeen. Twenty years later he described the extraordinary happening in his *Personal Narrative*. As the son of a Puritan minister he had been conditioned to anticipate conversion as the decisive experience of his life. His earliest surviving letter, which was written in his twelfth year, tells of the new converts to his father's church and rejoices at such a "very remarkable stirring and pouring out of the Spirit of God." But for a young boy already accustomed to experiences of intense piety, what new moment of transforming grace could be expected? He already knew the delight of private communication with God—"I used to pray five times a day in secret." He already acknowledged the Puritan calling—"I made seeking my salvation the main business of my life." His childhood could not have been more religious. But he also knew from the teaching of his Puritan father that salvation could come only by divine choice and divine action. When Jonathan Edwards was seventeen, the long anticipated moment arrived; he suddenly became convinced that God was filling his soul with grace:

> The first that I remember that ever I found any thing of that sort of inward, sweet delight in God and divine things, that I have lived much in since, was on reading those words, I Tim. i. 17. *Now unto the King eternal, immortal, invisible, the only wise God, be honor and glory for ever and ever, Amen.* As I read the words, there came into my soul, and was as it were diffused through it, a sense of the glory of the Divine Being; a new sense, quite different from any thing I ever experienced before. Never any words of scripture seemed to me as these words did. I thought with myself, how excellent a Being that was, and how happy I should be, if I might enjoy that God, and be rapt up to God in Heaven, and be as it were swallowed up in him.[24]

The experience did not come to Edwards while he was listening to any preacher, although he later tried to awaken people to God by the force of his own preaching. Nor did the experience come to him while he was communing with nature, although he later reconfirmed his impressions of God by feeling again the exultant happiness in the woods and fields of Connecticut and Massachusetts. The moment of conversion came while Edwards was reading the Bible—the one activity that he always considered to be the most significant in his life. Reading was Edwards's favorite occupation; he regularly spent twelve or thirteen hours a day in his study. His reading was broad and varied: Locke and Newton, Augustine and Calvin, Fielding and Richardson, and a generous portion of Cotton Mather. But every day Edwards read the Bible and took notes. His intellectual career makes sense only if it is remembered that in all of his philosophical speculation he never departed from a belief in Scripture as the basis for all authority. Although Edwards possessed rational powers as great as any man of the Enlightenment, he never questioned or doubted the truth of revealed religion. He fully accepted the doctrine of Augustine that "greater is the authority of the Scriptures than all the powers of the human mind." Edwards's experience of grace had come to him while reading the Gospel, and that center of his inspiration was never disturbed.

Edwards's experience of conversion was an annihilation of self, "swallowed up . . . for ever," and a spiritual rebirth in "the glory of the Divine Being." Although versions of this transformation are common in many religions, and similar experiences have been reported by people using certain drugs, the power Edwards felt was especially characteristic of the Puritan faith as described by John Calvin. One part of the experience involved a complete surrender of the will, a total submission of the self to a supernatural authority—infinite and sovereign. Edwards went to masochistic extremes to humble his ego and pride: "My heart as it were panted after this, to lie low before God, as in the dust; that I might be nothing, and that God might be ALL."[25] But no ordinary humility would content Edwards—"I cannot bear the thoughts of being no more humble than other Christians."

When Edwards believed his spirit to be emptied of pride and egotism, he then felt ready for the sudden influx of divine grace. "The sense I had of divine things, would of a sudden kindle up, as it were, a sweet burning in my heart; an ardor of soul, that I know not how to express." Edwards's attempt to define his experience in his *Personal Narrative* led him to formulate the paradox at the heart of the Puritan vision. He imagined God to be a combination of love and power:

. . . there came into my mind a sweet sense of the glorious majesty
and grace of God, that I know not how to express. I seemed to
see them both in a sweet conjunction: majesty and meekness joined
together; it was a sweet and gentle, and holy majesty; and also a
majestic meekness; an awful sweetness; a high, and great, and holy
gentleness.[26]

Edwards never lost sight of this paradoxical combination. His philosophy
and theology are rooted in the fundamental Puritan experience of fear
and consolation, awe and grace, "majesty" and "sweetness."

Although Edwards's feelings of grace came most frequently while he
was reading the Bible—"I felt a harmony between something in my heart
and those sweet and powerful words . . . every sentence seemed to be
full of wonders"—he also began to find the glory of divine things reflected in nature:

God's excellency, his wisdom, his purity and love, seemed to
appear in every thing; in the sun, moon and stars; in the clouds,
and blue sky; in the grass, flowers, trees; in the water, and all
nature; which used greatly to fix my mind. I often used to sit and
view the moon, for a long time; and so in the day, spent much
time in viewing the clouds and sky, to behold the sweet glory of
God in these things.[27]

Some critics have used evidence of this sort to credit Edwards with a
romantic sensibility and label him as an early Transcendentalist. It may
be true that Edwards shared the visionary ability of a young Wordsworth to see the world "apparelled in celestial light." Watching the sun,
moon, and stars, he was fascinated like Shelley with the hypnotic power
of light. Watching the grass, flowers, and trees, he may have experienced
the mystical delight in nature reported later by Thoreau and Whitman.
He did commonly ride out into the woods to find peace and privacy
for "divine contemplation." But visionary experience by itself does not
distinguish any particular religion or culture. The same feelings may be
explained in many different contexts. Wordsworth interpreted his
visionary experience in pantheistic terms; Shelley borrowed the vocabulary of the Neo-Platonists; and Whitman remained an unreconstructed
pagan. For Jonathan Edwards, however, any mystical delight in nature
could be understood only as an expression of divine grace. The visionary experience was a taste of God's majesty and sweetness. To Edwards
it was a vital confirmation of Puritan faith.

If it is misleading to talk about Edwards as an early romantic or Transcendentalist, it is equally wrong to deny entirely the visionary nature of his religious experience. The most influential book on Edwards has been Perry Miller's intellectual biography published in 1949. Miller claims that it is "utterly incorrect" to call Edwards a mystic, "at least, in any sense that would imply the merging of the finite individual with a distinctionless divine."[28] But Edwards's *Personal Narrative* again and again reports the mystical experience of lying in the dust, "emptied and annihilated," weeping aloud, while the "infinite fountain of divine glory and sweetness" invades all his senses. Miller's desire to explain the "rational system" of Edwards's theology caused him to slight the frequent evidence of mystical power.

Edwards often described the reception of grace with a vocabulary common to visionary writing. A heightened sensitivity to images of light is apparent in much of his work. God is often compared to a fountain of heavenly light—"the sun in its glory, sweetly and pleasantly diffusing light and life." And the soul of a Puritan is compared to "a little white flower . . . opening its bosom to receive the pleasant beams of the sun's glory." Such images are common enough, but Edwards's regular insistence upon them shows to what extent his vision of God was a transforming, hypnotic experience of light.

Edwards also felt his other senses invaded by divine glory. Metaphors of taste and hearing appear frequently in his accounts of religious experience. When Edwards walked as a young boy through his father's pasture, he heard the sounds of God singing round about him. He often responded himself with spontaneous prayers and hymns. Even more frequent than references to light and sound are the many references to taste. Edwards often explained that divine grace was received as a spiritual sweetness. He equated the "sight of the divine excellency of the things of God" with the "taste of the soul-satisfying, and life-giving good." He described the Bible as "refreshing ravishing food." Edwards used the metaphors of taste and hearing and vision to describe as accurately as possible the way he experienced divine grace as a ravishing of all the senses.

A Treatise Concerning Religious Affections (1746) is Edwards's most detailed and analytic account of religious experience. The urgent question in the aftermath of the Great Awakening was how to distinguish genuine religious conversion from mere false enthusiasm. In *Religious Affections* Edwards described what he considered to be the twelve reliable signs of divine grace. "True religion," he maintained, "in great part, consists in holy affections." Although Edwards inherited the old faculty psychology, which divided human powers into such arbitrary categories as understanding, affection, and will, he was eager to preserve the integrity of the self against division. Thus he argued that affections are "vigorous and sensible exercises of inclination," and inclination represents the working together of understanding and will. Religious conversion then is a transformation of body and soul, a rebirth of feeling as well as of spiritual understanding. The true convert must be inspired to the point where "the motion of the blood and animal spirits begins to be sensibly altered." When the recent editor of Edwards's *Religious Affections* wonders if we should "take the physiological trappings seriously," he surely misses the point.[29] Edwards must be taken at his word. The man who believed that he could see and hear and taste the glory and sweetness of divine things would not hesitate to acknowledge the physical dimensions of grace. That is one reason why Edwards remained a principal defender of the Great Awakening. Of course he knew that physical response alone was no guarantee of real conversion, but he was never willing to underestimate the violent power of God's blessing. Many of his sympathetic editors and critics of recent years, not to mention his opponents at the time of the awakening, have failed to reckon with the integral nature of Edwards's religious experience.

If Edwards's faith in the transforming power of divine grace placed him in the vanguard of the awakening, the same faith led him to his tragic separation from his congregation. Since the time of Solomon Stoddard the church in Northampton had admitted new members without an individual account of their regeneration. When Edwards first assumed the pulpit of his grandfather's church, he continued the easy and popular custom. But as he worked on his *Treatise Concerning Religious Affections,* Edwards became more convinced than ever that church membership must be granted only to visible saints. The leading families of Northampton, however, were not willing to turn the clock back to the heroic and pious days of the early Puritans in Massachusetts. If the doors of the church could not remain open, then perhaps it was time to ask their reactionary minister to leave. After twenty-two years in Northampton Jonathan Edwards was forced to surrender his pulpit and even forbidden to preach within the town limits. The events which precipitated Edwards's dismissal were more complex than can be described here, but the principal cause was his uncompromising belief that only the genuine experience of regeneration could qualify a person for membership in the church. He wanted to repeal the Half-Way Covenant, and turn back the tide of compromise and moderation that had diluted the Puritan faith for more than seventy years. But with his vision of a pure communion of saints Jonathan Edwards stood practically alone. Cut adrift from

Northampton, he took refuge in the small frontier town of Stockbridge, where his flock consisted of a few white families and some indifferent Indians.

The six years spent at Stockbridge turned out to be the most productive time in Edwards's intellectual career. His treatise on *Freedom of Will* was published in 1754, and *The Great Christian Doctrine of Original Sin Defended* appeared in 1758. Two further essays of this period, "The Nature of True Virtue" and "Concerning the End for Which God Created the World," were published seven years after his death. Edwards's reputation as a theologian rests primarily on these four works together with the earlier *Religious Affections.* In all these volumes Edwards was attempting to explain and defend the fundamental principles of Calvinism.

Edwards's defense of the Puritan faith moved forward on a double front. He wanted to demonstrate both psychologically and philosophically the truth of his religious experience. For Edwards the awakening had served as a great laboratory of religious behavior. For years he had been at the center of the revivalism controversy. But his understanding of divine grace remained firmly in the tradition of Augustine and Calvin. Whatever he learned about human psychology from his youthful reading of Locke, or from his observation of religious behavior during the awakening, Edwards faithfully applied to his defense of Calvin's theology. In the middle of the eighteenth century, Edwards was still attempting to explain the psychological truth of such doctrines as predestination and original sin. In the world of Voltaire and Benjamin Franklin, he had become an anachronism.

The reactionary nature of Edwards's thought has often been attributed to his provincial isolation in western Massachusetts. But he continued to receive a wide range of books from abroad, and he even studied from the actual copy of the *Principia* which Newton himself had sent to the young college in New Haven. Edwards's analysis of religious behavior was reactionary, but it was neither provincial nor accidental. He defended the basic doctrines of Calvin because he believed their vital truth had been demonstrated in his own experience. Had he not witnessed as a child of twelve the "very Remarkable stirring and pouring out of the Spirit of God" among his father's congregation? Hadn't he received as a boy of seventeen "a sense of the glorious majesty and grace of God?" Hadn't he seen as a young minister how the "surprising conversions" of the awakening could demonstrate the power of God in New England? What other theology was able to explain why wretched sinners might suddenly receive God's irresistible grace? At the psychological center of Calvinism was the transformation of fear into inspiration, the same dynamic exchange that Edwards recognized at the center of religious conversion. No other American writer has focused on the psychological moment of conversion with as much concentration as Edwards. It was the recurrent theme of the hell-fire sermons for which he is most remembered in the popular imagination. And it remained the focus of his psychology of religious experience worked out in his analytical writing of the last dozen years.

The doctrines of original sin and predestination, which seemed hopelessly reactionary to many of Edwards's contemporaries, were essential parts of his Calvinism. Without the conviction of original sin, Edwards argued, the potential Christian will not feel humble enough before God; he will not experience the abject fear that is the necessary prelude to conversion. And without the belief in predestination the sinner will not be ready to acknowledge the absolute sovereignty of God. Turning away from either doctrine, Edwards believed, would threaten or destroy the psychological force of conversion.

Edwards had been familiar with the new psychology of John Locke since his student days at Yale. He recognized quite early the advantage of Locke's theory of sense impressions in helping to integrate the experience of thought and feeling. Edwards's later analysis of religious behavior during the Great Awakening followed to some extent the integration suggested by Locke. Edwards did not see any contradiction between the new psychology and the Puritan faith.

The philosophy of the eighteenth century rationalists, however, would seem less compatible with the assumptions of Puritan doctrine. Edwards did read the major authors of the Enlightenment. He knew the work of David Hume with its logical rejection of miracles, and the writing of Voltaire with its skeptical ridicule of Christianity. How was Edwards able to reconcile the premises of rationalism with the preposterous miracles and dogmas of his own revealed religion? He never saw the question in that light, because to Edwards the truths of the Puritan faith were rational. Absolute dependence upon a sovereign God appeared to Edwards to be the common sense of experience. He did not see any necessary contradiction between religion and natural philosophy.

The leading Puritans in America for more than a hundred years had considered their religion to be compatible with reason and science. Cotton Mather had been interested in natural philosophy, and he proudly accepted membership in the Royal Society. He had been one of the first Puritan ministers in New England to look at drops of water through a microscope, and one of the first to view the stars with a telescope. His astonishment at what he saw merely increased his faith

in the wonders of creation. The more he learned about the infinite scope
of the heavens, the more he respected the power of the Creator. Mather
accepted the laws of force described by Newton as a confirmation of
the divine order ruling the universe. John Locke had published *The
Reasonableness of Christianity* in 1695, and Cotton Mather issued
Reasonable Religion in 1700. Jonathan Edwards was therefore prepared to accept the harmony of natural science and the Puritan religion.
He agreed with Cotton Mather that "Scripture is reason in its highest
elevation."

But Edwards was living in the middle of the eighteenth century. What
kept him from realizing that much of the Bible is irrational nonsense?
Spinoza had long since pointed out that the Bible "is in parts imperfect,
corrupt, erroneous, and inconsistent with itself." How could Edwards
have accepted the various miracles in the name of reason as well as faith?
Part of the answer undoubtedly rests in the vague and multiple definitions of the word "reason." If the word is defined as thinking logically
and systematically about available evidence, then Edwards could argue
that the Bible contains much of the basic data from which rational conclusions must be drawn. Edwards wanted to be just as empirical as any
natural scientist, and granted the admissibility of his scriptural evidence,
he probably succeeded. And if the word "reason" is defined as the power
of coherent intelligence, then Edwards could point to the ordered universe as proof of a rational Deity. As far as Edwards could see, the
discoveries of natural science tended to confirm the truth of revealed
religion. Hadn't Newton been able to demonstrate a coherent power
holding the solar system together? Edwards's study of the *Principia* only
served to reconfirm his belief in the reasonableness of the Puritan vision.
Throughout his career as a theologian Edwards attempted to put together a "rational system" of religious and philosophical thought. At
the age of seventeen he made a series of notes on natural science that
he hoped to expand into a great philosophical treatise to be published
in London. His observations of the "New World of Philosophy" ranged
from human anatomy and the structure of light waves to the nature of
stars and atoms. But when he started to write the history of the world
from Creation to the Last Judgment, his model was the standard design
of Puritan history based upon the records and prophecies of the Bible.
Natural philosophy was subordinated to revelation. At the time of his
death Edwards still had plans to describe the "grand design of God"
in the "form of a history," and his notes indicate that he still considered Scripture to be the highest form of reason.

Edwards did object to one definition of reason. He condemned the
"false and superficial reason" of men like Charles Chauncy who criticized

the "irrational" behavior of the Great Awakening. Edwards believed that any use of reason without the support of inspiration was life-denying. Rational judgment could not be trusted unless the mind was alive with feeling as well as thought. He argued in *Religious Affections* that to make any arbitrary division between intellect and emotion would be incorrect for either psychology or theology. He therefore concluded that men like David Hume, who appeared to rely solely upon rational argument, were insensitive to religious truth. Edwards could not share the vision of a skeptic nor see that Hume might represent the portent of things to come.

Skepticism and intelligence are so often equated in the twentieth century, it has been difficult for recent historians to see how a man with Edwards's intelligence could be entirely free of skepticism. Even the first Puritans in America, whom Edwards greatly honored, were capable of entertaining some doubts of accepted dogma. Anne Bradstreet, for example, who sailed to America with John Winthrop, wrote near the end of her life: "Many times hath Satan troubled me concerning the verity of the Scriptures, many times by atheism how I could know whether there was a God; I never saw any miracles to confirm me, and those which I read of, how did I know but they were feigned?"[30] Although she was a very pious woman, she struggled with the questions of doubt that would later be developed in the Enlightenment. But Jonathan Edwards never felt the struggle. He did not see any reason to doubt "the verity of the Scriptures." Even Cotton Mather had confessed in the pages of his diary "Temptations to Impurities; and sometimes to Blasphemy, and Atheism, and the Abandonment of all Religion." Edwards, however, apparently never felt that temptation. He sometimes complained of low spirits or sinful thoughts, but he could not summon his extraordinary mind to question or challenge the authority of his God. There was no hint of Prometheus in his character. Starting out as the only son in a large Puritan family, he became one of the last obedient sons of the Puritan God.

Was his career of obedience, however brilliant and resourceful, not already an anachronism in a century famous for its revolutions? Some recent historians have attempted to avoid such a negative conclusion. Perry Miller has described Edwards as "intellectually the most modern man of his age," and indeed "much ahead of his time."[31] Miller's conclusion is based on Edwards's alleged synthesis of ideas borrowed from Locke and Newton. Miller's biography is a daring "life of the mind" which follows the intellectual development of Edwards from his youthful writing through the great philosophical treatises of the Stockbridge years. But Miller was trapped by his own habit of forming intellectual patterns. Three important errors mar his biography. He imposed a coherent design upon much of Edwards's thought, which Edwards himself may have desired but never actually attained. He also misjudged the extent to which Edwards understood the discoveries and implications of Locke and Newton. And it was misleading of Miller to subordinate Edwards's very emotional piety to his efforts toward building a "rational system." Edwards's priorities were just the reverse. His rational efforts were all devoted to the greater glory of his Puritan God. "For to find out the reasons of things in Natural Philosophy," Edwards believed, "is only to find out the proportion of God's acting." Miller did, of course, admit that Edwards was not "an experimental scientist, nor was he a trained mathematician." Nevertheless, in Miller's biography, Edwards is presented in "the great line of the future," anticipating the natural scientists of the twentieth century. It was a bold strategy for Perry Miller to try to rescue Edwards from the depths of Calvinism by stressing his attempted synthesis of Locke and Newton. But Miller's biography of Edwards remains brilliant and futile. No one in Edwards's own time praised him for his "insight into science and psychology," and no one today is likely to care. Just as the religious speculations of Isaac Newton have always been an embarrassment to the historians of science, Edwards's scientific intuitions cannot be more than a curious oddity to religious historians. Miller's attempt to raise the ghost of Jonathan Edwards among the spirits of Locke, Newton, Planck, and Einstein was a triumph of wishful thinking over practical sense.

Another attempt has been made to rescue Edwards from obsolescence by those who still see some relevance in his theological conclusions. A good example of this defense is found in the recent Yale edition of Edwards's *Religious Affections*. In his lengthy commentary the editor, John E. Smith, argues for the "enduring contribution" of Edwards's theology. "There are three basic contributions made by the *Affections*, and each has a direct application to present religious thought and practice."[32] Smith praises Edwards for recovering "the distinctively religious dimension of life," and claims that such a recovery can be of help to a twentieth-century audience. Smith, however, tends to ignore the fact that Edwards's religion was inseparable from the strict doctrines of Calvinism, some of which were rejected as untenable by Edwards's own congregation more than two hundred years ago.

Smith also tries to revive Edwards's vague definition of reason as a component of spiritual perception. He would like to give contemporary religion some of the rational authority now usually reserved for natural science. But if Jonathan Edwards was unable to fit the many contradictions of his Puritan faith into a "rational system," how does Smith expect to accomplish a similar task today? When he recommends a union of faith and reason, he merely undermines the definition of reason and fails to understand why the scientific method during the past two hundred years has replaced the dogma of revealed religion as a guide to the natural world. It was Edwards's own inability to separate rational inquiry from prior assumptions about supernatural causes that prevented him from seeing "the great line of the future." Edwards read at least a part of David Hume's *Treatise of Human Nature,* "glad of an opportunity to read such corrupt books," and dismissed it as the work of the Devil.

And finally Smith argues for the "contemporary relevance" of Edwards's criteria for distinguishing genuine inspiration from counterfeit enthusiasm. Edwards is praised for explaining how a true conversion requires a change of heart. But again Smith tends to ignore the extent to which Edwards's vision of grace was rooted in the psychology of Calvinism. In order to make Edwards's sense of conversion agreeable to a modern audience, it is diluted by Smith almost beyond recognition.

Another recent apologist for Edwards goes even further in claiming twentieth-century relevance. James Carse maintains in *Jonathan Edwards and the Visibility of God* that Edwards must be recognized for his "radical this-worldliness." His sermons of terror are interpreted as artful warnings meant to awaken his congregation to an understanding of human evil, just as Picasso's "Guernica" should awaken a contemporary audience to the horrors of war. In drawing this analogy Mr. Carse ignores the dogmatic context of Edwards's philosophy. His sermons of terror were all designed to fill his audience with the desperate need for assistance from a supernatural world. Edwards was much less interested in man's inhumanity than he was in man's disobedience of God. The attempt by Mr. Carse to apply the warnings of Edwards to the present "century of the atomic bomb and the urban slum" is rather misconceived and naive.[33] Edwards himself would be embarrassed by the effort to rescue him from "foolish other-worldliness."

The value of Edwards today does not rest in his early intuition of modern physics, nor in any dubious relevance for contemporary religion. He had already become an anachronism in the eighteenth century. His value for us is historical; he put together the most complete picture of the Puritan faith at the very time that the doctrines of Calvinism were disappearing from the educated American mind. Between Edwards's writing of *Religious Affection* in 1746 and the completion of his *Original Sin Defended* in 1758, many of the influential books of the Enlightenment were published. Writers like Hume, Voltaire, and Montesquieu were all active in spreading the basic assumptions of scientific rationalism, and explaining its incompatibility with revealed religion. But

Edwards continued undisturbed in his grand construction of a Puritan synthesis. Only an untimely death cut short his labor. The writings of Jonathan Edwards are an extraordinary monument to a lost cause. With his own experience of divine grace, Edwards was in the tradition of Saint Augustine; but with his abstract summary of a disappearing religious system, Edwards was in the position of Saint Thomas Aquinas.

Shortly after he was called to the presidency of a new college at Princeton, a smallpox vaccination caused the end of Edwards's life. It was the final irony of his tragic career to be cut down by an intended medicine offered by the natural scientists. Earlier in the century when Cotton Mather recommended that Christians allow themselves to be vaccinated against smallpox, the controversy had nearly ruined his career. When Jonathan Edwards followed Mather's good advice, he left unfinished the Summa Theologica of American Puritanism. And who was left to complete it, or even to read it, in the new world of Benjamin Franklin and Thomas Jefferson?

4

THE ECLIPSE OF GOD

At the same time that Jonathan Edwards was striving to prepare men for the knowledge of God available through regeneration, Alexander Pope was writing in his *Essay on Man:* "Know then thyself, presume not God to scan;/The proper study of Mankind is Man." Although the words of the poet may have been intended merely as a typical warning to man not to overreach his "middle state," they do imply a revolution in eighteenth-century thought. Among the writers and philosophers of the Enlightenment, theology was no longer the queen of the sciences. For hundreds of years the goal of Western philosophy had been to gain knowledge of God. In the words of Saint Augustine it had been assumed that "if God, through whom all things are made, is Wisdom, as the divine truth declares, the true philosopher is a lover of God."[1] But the philosophers of the Enlightenment, men like David Hume, Voltaire, and Benjamin Franklin, proceeded with a different and more secular assumption. In the same year that Jonathan Edwards preached his warning about hell-fire to the congregation at Enfield, David Hume wrote on the other side of the Atlantic:

> There has been a sudden and sensible change in the opinions of men . . . by the progress of learning and of liberty. Most people, in this island, have divested themselves of all superstitious reverence to names and authority: The Clergy have entirely lost their credit: Their pretensions and doctrines have been ridiculed; and even religion can scarcely support itself in the world.[2]

Although Edwards continued for another seventeen years to publish treatises on the fundamental doctrines of Puritan theology, the new philosophy coming from Europe would render his conclusions largely irrelevant. While Edwards was still defending the doctrine of original sin, other writers on both sides of the Atlantic were beginning to expose the story of the Fall of Man as a primitive fable. Emphasis was shifting from a belief in the depravity of man to an optimistic faith in man's goodness and perfectibility. While Edwards held fast to Calvin's principle of limited atonement, which permitted only a few Puritan saints to expect salvation through the sacrifice of Christ, many of Edwards's contemporaries were ready to abandon this narrow doctrine. Some churches in America were advocating a policy of total redemption— "Christ died for all mankind." Other churches at the same time were denying the basic need for any redemption. If the biblical story of the Fall is discredited, then what original sin does man have to be saved from? As the general belief in man's own goodness grew stronger, the purpose and necessity of divine grace declined in proportion. As a result the divinity of Christ was called into question. First the Deists, and later the Unitarians, found no need to recognize the life and death of Christ as a supernatural reordering of human affairs. The Trinity was then reduced to a single, abstract, and impersonal Deity.

While Edwards continued to believe in the Bible as the undeniable word of God, the new critical philosophy in Europe was encouraging anthropological speculation and the study of comparative mythology. Gradually the Enlightenment began to understand the Bible as the work of many authors and the recorded history and superstition of a primitive people. While Edwards still counted upon the ministers of the established churches to interpret and preach the Scriptures, many of his contemporaries were declaring their independence from such authority. Benjamin Franklin explained in his *Autobiography* that he did not bother to go to church because Sunday was his "studying day."[3] And he wasn't studying theology.

While Edwards continued to believe above all else in the sovereign power of God to reveal His anger or grace, other men in the eighteenth century began to think of God merely as the remote Creator of the universe, an impersonal Power bound by the laws of natural philosophy. A rational universe precludes the existence of miracles. After proving to his own satisfaction that miracles are inconceivable, David Hume wrote ironically: "The Christian Religion not only was at first attended with miracles, but even at this day cannot be believed by any reasonable person without one."[4] Such skepticism itself was inconceivable to Jonathan Edwards, who always thought that nothing was more reasonable than the miraculous presence of God.

What caused the Puritan vision to become obsolete at the very time that Edwards was providing its most intelligent theological synthesis? Recent historians of the Enlightenment, especially Ernst Cassirer and Peter Gay, have answered that question by describing a revolution in Western thought, a change from "mythical" to "critical" thinking. The true believer in any religion cannot see beyond the mythology that controls his particular allegiance. He gives exclusive credit to one myth, one Holy Scripture, one true God. But critical thinking introduces comparative mythology, studies various claims for scriptural authority, and discovers how men have invented many gods. In the light of critical thinking myths become fictions, miracles are refuted, and faith is challenged. The brightening sun of the Enlightenment meant the eclipse of God.

But what precisely do the historians of the Enlightenment mean by "critical thinking"? The phrase is often used interchangeably with the word "reason," and that can be very misleading. Reason, logic, order, intelligence, all of these can be associated with either mythical or critical thinking, and thus will not serve to distinguish among them. Saint Thomas thought that the existence of God could be demonstrated by reason; David Hume thought that the non-existence of miracles could be proved by reason; but the debate can never be resolved in such terms.

Critical thinking may be distinguished by two principal characteristics: it empirically tests hypotheses, and it is democratic or anti-authoritarian in its tolerance of all evidence. The development of both characteristics had been accelerating in the past century, and both together emerged to dominate and define the Enlightenment.

The steady growth of natural science throughout the seventeenth and eighteenth centuries helped to establish the value of empiricism. Any knowledge gained by careful observation and repeated experiment must depend upon sensory experience and not supernatural intervention. Critical thinking therefore precludes divine revelation, incarnation, scriptural authority, and all forms of mystical apprehension. The empirical testing of hypotheses demands that attention be focused upon the natural evidence rather than upon a supernatural explanation. The career of Benjamin Franklin as a practical inventor and scientist is an outstanding example of the success of the empirical method in the eighteenth century.

The growth of democratic ideas and institutions throughout the eighteenth century encouraged the second characteristic of critical thinking—the tendency to challenge authority with the spirit of equalitarianism and tolerance. Revolutions in the name of democracy helped to destroy the power and authority associated with the very idea of sovereignty. When kings can be sent to the guillotine, what happens to the concept of sovereign power so important for defining the Puritan God? Mythical thinking implies that all human conduct is ruled by supernatural will. Jonathan Edwards believed fully in the Bible as the authoritative Word of God; the foundation of his faith was complete submission to divine power. But critical thinking allows man to choose for himself how he shall be ruled. The democratic spirit killed more than kings. It is no coincidence that Thomas Jefferson wished to be remembered as the author of the Statute of Virginia for Religious Freedom as well as the Declaration of Independence.

EMPIRICAL PHILOSOPHY

Francis Bacon is often cited as the "prophet of empiricism."[5] It was Bacon who wrote early in the seventeenth century that mankind must undertake nothing less than "a total reconstruction of sciences, arts, and all human knowledge, raised upon proper foundations."[6] The extraordinary scope of his vision proved subversive to narrow dogmas and provincial beliefs. But even more subversive was the mode of "reconstruction" that he proposed. Henceforth knowledge was to be gained by an empirical study of all available evidence. Hypotheses would prove useful only if they could be verified by the experiments of disinterested observers. Bacon was recommending the systematic acquisition of knowledge with a built-in method for checking and improving the system; he was recommending what later became known as the "scientific method." And he knew the revolutionary force of his proposal. "The true and lawful goal of the sciences," he wrote, "is none other than this: that human life be endowed with new discoveries and powers."[7]

At the beginning of the seventeenth century, the scientific method was strengthened in a different way by the philosophy of Descartes. Although the followers of Descartes often proved antagonistic to the disciples of Francis Bacon, contrasting their mathematical and rational deduction with Bacon's more inductive method, the differences were less important than their common goal. Both were ready to announce a revolution in learning. Just as Bacon called for a "total reconstruction of sciences, arts, and all human knowledge," Descartes surveyed the curriculum of the schools and churches and declared "that nothing solid could have been built on such unstable foundations."[8] While he advocated a new rationalism of clear and distinct ideas, he also knew that "observations are the more necessary the further we advance in knowledge."[9] In the great French *Encyclopédie* of the eighteenth century—the chief gathering of Enlightenment judgment—both Descartes and Bacon were justly recognized for having "introduced the spirit of experimental science."[10]

The rhetoric of Bacon and Descartes represents an early but strong challenge in the revolutionary battle to turn attention from God to man. In his *Novum Organum,* 1620, Bacon called for the "kingdom of man, founded on the sciences." And soon thereafter Descartes predicted in *Discours sur la méthode* that men will "render themselves the masters and possessors of nature." A century later Alexander Pope would be able to write with some complacency that "the proper study of Mankind is Man."

Neither Bacon nor Descartes considered his recommendations for a new learning to be at all unchristian. Although both philosophers advocated a scientific revolution, both continued to allow for the independent existence of religious truth, and neither could foresee how damaging scientific habits of thought would prove to religious dogma. Bacon and Descartes merely wished to separate theological argument from their empirical and rational design for learning. Bacon's pious acknowledgments of faith were undoubtedly sincere, but the thrust of his scientific thought, nevertheless, was in the direction of secular materialism.

By shifting man's attention to natural experience, utility, invention, and progress, the prophets of the scientific method in the early seventeenth century encouraged new hopes for the future. Heretofore the vision of a bright future had been reserved by Christianity for some possible redemption in a supernatural life, while here on earth the presence of original sin meant a downward progression to death. Paradise had been lost because of man's disobedience, and it could not be regained without God's mercy. But now Bacon and Descartes were telling men how to become "the masters and possessors of nature," and thereby obtain "new discoveries and powers." The new positive image of the future helped to give exceptional value to the idea of progress. In Bacon's *New Atlantis* the golden age was transferred from the imaginary past to the possible future. Perhaps no idea has achieved greater popularity since the Renaissance than the idea of progress; and no idea has proved more unsettling to the dogmas of Puritan theology. If a utopia can be built scientifically by men here on earth, then who needs Heaven, Christ, or God?

Galileo was the contemporary of Bacon and Descartes who was most active in practicing the new empirical philosophy. While his attempts to prove the Copernican theory with his recently invented telescope earned for Galileo the harassment of the Inquisition, his systematic inventions and discoveries helped to demonstrate how the scientific method could be successfully applied. Galileo's scorn for the academic astronomers who refused to look through his telescope was a sign of the pride and confidence of the new empiricism. His famous difficulties with the censors of the church merely dramatized the futile battle of religious authority to turn back the tide of experimental science. Galileo was forced to recant his "heretical" theories before the Inquisition in 1633, but their empirical truth was already being confirmed by other scientists throughout Europe.

Thomas Hobbes had the good fortune to be born in England where he was at least free from the extreme harassment of the Inquisition. But in the early seventeenth century he still acquired a notorious reputation. Although his writings were scorned and despised, they were also studied. It was Hobbes who paid tribute to Galileo as "the first that opened to us the gate of Natural Philosophy Universal, which is the knowledge of the Nature of Motion."[11] Hobbes wanted to accomplish for psychology and moral philosophy what Galileo had done for astronomy and physics; he expected to provide empirical evidence in the place of groundless speculation. He included in *Leviathan* a brief psychological account of the religious impulse. Hobbes argued that the "natural seed of religion" can be found in "ignorance of second causes" and "devotion toward what men fear." Such heretical claims proved to be an enormous stimulus to the study of the origin of religion that proceeded rapidly in the next century.

Despite a few concessions to the Christian faith, Hobbes remained throughout his very long life just as convinced as Galileo in the basic truth of scientific principles. Hobbes argued in *Elements of Philosophy*, 1655, that nothing exists except matter, and that matter has two qualities: dimension and motion. The only function left for God in such a materialistic universe was to receive credit for having originally designed the physical world and for having set it in motion. But no divine guidance was necessary to keep the natural mechanism operating; Galileo had already proved that motion does not require the continuous application of force. Thus Puritan teleology was replaced by a mechanical system of cause and effect, and God was reduced to the status of the first inventor and engineer.

The advances in natural philosophy near the end of the seventeenth century were dominated by the two great figures of John Locke and Isaac Newton. Locke's study of human nature followed the empirical lead of Francis Bacon, but Locke went further in separating psychology from dogma and metaphysics. "What we know of the works of nature," Locke wrote, "is only by the sensible effects."[12] In his famous *Essay*

Concerning Human Understanding the mind is described as a "white paper" which only receives ideas through the experience of sensation or reflection—"our observation employed either about external sensible objects, or about the internal operations of our minds, perceived and reflected on by ourselves."[13] If all knowledge must be acquired in this way, then some of the fundamental assumptions of Puritan theology are jeopardized. If the mind does not contain innate ideas, then how can original sin be inherited? If man does not inherit the guilt of Adam and Eve, then why is any divine redemption necessary? If the human mind is at first a tabula rasa, how does the idea of God develop? If truth can be obtained only by sensation and reflection, what happens to the supposed authority of Holy Scriptures?

Despite the secular implications of his empirical psychology, Locke remained a sincere member of the Anglican church. He continued to believe that Christ was the Messiah foretold by the prophets of the Old Testament. But in *The Reasonableness of Christianity,* 1695, Locke tended to discount many of the other miracles and dogmas of the traditional faith. When he described revelation as an exalted form of reason, his compromise was soon attacked from both sides. Those more inclined to traditional piety accused Locke of radically diminishing their religious truth; while those more inclined to secular enlightenment found the terms "revelation" and "reason" simply incompatible. The objections of both sides were finally summarized in Voltaire's scoffing remark: "Mr. Locke's reasonableness of Christian religion is really a new religion."[14] Neither the pious Anglicans nor the secular philosophes wanted a new religion. Nevertheless the empirical psychology of John Locke proved extremely useful to the emerging English Deists. Although Locke himself continued to believe in the divinity of Christ, his psychology laid much of the groundwork for a post-Christian view of human nature.

The patron saint of the Enlightenment was Isaac Newton. His application of the scientific method to astronomy and physics became a model of natural philosophy for the eighteenth century. Although many could not follow the mathematics which led to Newton's explanation of planetary motion or his principles of optics, few remained unimpressed or unconvinced by the scope and intelligence of his natural theories. Extraordinary praise for Newton became a standard feature of much eighteenth-century writing. Voltaire thought Newton to be the greatest man who had ever lived. Newton was made president of the Royal Society in 1703, and two years later he became the first English scientist to be honored with knighthood.

As an empirical scientist Newton modestly refused to speculate beyond the reach of available evidence. "I do not feign hypotheses," he solemnly repeated. The ultimate nature of gravitational force he was willing to leave a mystery. But as an Anglican with strong convictions he accepted much of the dogma and authority of Protestant theology. He saw no conflict between science and religion. His discoveries in natural philosophy were interpreted by many people, himself included, as proof of the supreme and rational intelligence of God. Men of various religious persuasions joined together in praising Newton for having demonstrated that the universe, though a mighty maze, was not without a plan. John Locke wrote with conviction that "the works of nature in every part of them sufficiently evidence a Deity."[15] Even Jonathan Edwards could read Newton with real pleasure and satisfaction.

Newton believed in a God who "governs all things . . . as Lord over all."[16] He also accepted the authority of Scripture, and spent many years attempting to fix the systematic order of Old Testament prophecies. Newton's prolonged research into biblical chronology may have embarrassed many future scientists, but to his contemporaries it just served as more evidence that natural philosophy and religion were still in harmony. Nor did Newton's mechanical system of planetary motion rule out the possibility of divine intervention. He found some irregularities in the system that would require, he believed, adjustment by special providence. It was not until later in the eighteenth century that a more sophisticated mathematics developed by Laplace and Lagrange was able to provide a naturalistic explanation for the "irregularities" of planetary motion. It was also in the second half of the eighteenth century that philosophers of the Enlightenment learned to accept Newton's science without Newton's theology. Next to his discoveries in physics and mathematics, his religious conjectures gradually began to seem irrelevant.

The growth of natural philosophy throughout the seventeenth and eighteenth centuries was followed with great interest in the American colonies. Some of the second generation Puritans in the Massachusetts Bay Colony kept in fairly close contact with scientific developments in England. Increase Mather, for example, traveled across the Atlantic on official business from the Bay Colony and maintained a friendship with Robert Boyle, the most prominent English chemist in the late 1600s. But the chief scientific interest of Increase Mather was in the new astronomy. Despite the fact that Martin Luther had dismissed Copernicus as "an ass who wants to pervert the whole art of astronomy and deny what is said in the book of Joshua,"[17] the theories of Copernicus had become part of the curriculum at Harvard College as early as 1660. Increase Mather was an avid student of the new cosmology, and he developed a particular interest in the meaning and prediction of comets. He carefully read the work on comets by Robert Hooke, secretary of the Royal Society. Mather also studied the astronomy of Tycho Brahe and Kepler. In 1683 he published his own contribution to the subject, a strange mixture of natural and supernatural philosophy entitled *Kometographia*. Mather assumed that science and revelation were in complete agreement; he was interested in the empirical determination of a comet's precise orbit; but he was more interested in interpreting the appearance of comets as divine messages or "ensigns." Mindful of the star announcing the birth of Christ, Mather admitted that some comets might signify good news, but he was more apt to believe in comets as signs of God's wrath and omens of disaster. Although he was intrigued by the work of the natural philosophers, Increase Mather remained too much of a Puritan to accept the premises of the scientific method. He was still convinced that God's world must be "very mysterious and beyond human capacity."[18]

Cotton Mather went further than his father in the study of natural philosophy. He learned the new astronomy as a student at Harvard, and the more he understood about the design of the solar system, the more he wanted to praise the glory and intelligence of the Creator. When he first looked through a microscope as a young man and discovered a world of small living things in a drop of water, his admiration for the "wonders" of God was also magnified. He was convinced that the lowest form of created life was sufficient evidence to prove the existence of an intelligent Deity. "There is not a Fly," he wrote, "but what may confute an Atheist."[19]

Many of Cotton Mather's ideas about the agreement of science and religion were acquired from a book published in the year of his birth, 1663, by his father's English friend Robert Boyle. *The Usefulness of Experimental Natural Philosophy* lives up to its title in a rather pious manner. Robert Boyle wanted to show how his studies in physics and chemistry might serve to illustrate the infinite skill of the Creator. Cotton Mather probably read this book before he was twenty years old; it left a lasting impression upon him. More than three decades later in *The Christian Philosopher,* he still based his argument for the compatibility of science and religion upon the analogies drawn by Robert Boyle.

But with his tendency to feel or imagine persecution, Cotton Mather became more conscious of the dangers and contradictions of Boyle's "natural theology." There was nothing new, of course, in seeing the natural world as an image or symbol of the divine. Saint Augustine had been a good Platonist as well as a Christian. Mather's grandfather, John Cotton, had described nature as "a mappe and shaddow of the spirituall

estate of the soules of men."[20] But as the empirical philosophers of the
seventeenth century began to describe the circulation of the blood in
the human body, or to plot the orbits of the planets in the solar system, the map of nature gradually became a mechanical model. Cotton
Mather was especially alert to the threat of a total mechanistic
philosophy. When he read Descartes *Discourse on Method,* he was
alarmed by the hypothesis that the universe might be self-regulating.
It was not enough for God to have set the universe in motion; Mather
also had to believe that God had the sovereign power to influence its
direction. Mather suspected that much natural philosophy, despite its
frequent Christian affirmations, might be little more than a new version
of the materialism originally formulated by Epicurus two thousand
years before. Although Mather was always intrigued by the new science,
and was certainly very proud to become a member of the Royal Society, he strongly opposed any natural philosophy that seemed to him
to reduce the world to "meer blind material causes."[21] He took great
satisfaction in Isaac Newton's acknowledgment of the need for an
omnipotent God to regulate and sustain the gravitational system. He was
also very pleased to learn that Newton was devoting much of his time
to the study of biblical chronology.

Mather's double reaction to the new science, his attraction and suspicion, can be measured in his use of the word "reason." At first he
wanted the Puritan dogmas to be accepted as rational, and in 1700
he published a tract entitled *Reasonable Religion.* He hoped to attract
converts to his church by describing the Holy Scripture as "reason in
its highest elevation."[22] The word "reason" was thus given a double
meaning; it was the human instrument for comprehending the design of
God's world; it was also the revelation of God's will. The apparent contradiction of human initiative and divine power had been supported
five years earlier by John Locke in *The Reasonableness of Christianity.*
But already Cotton Mather began to have misgivings about this easy
alliance of reason and revelation. Were not Christians discounting the
divine authority of their faith in order to accommodate the claims of
reason? Cotton Mather's suspicions were confirmed in the following
year by the appearance of a book by one of the English Deists, John
Toland's *Christianity Not Mysterious.* Toland asserted that faith must
be "entirely built upon ratiocination."[23] The ensuing Deist controversy
that engaged clerics on both sides of the Atlantic greatly dismayed
Cotton Mather. He did not want to abandon reason, which he continued
to call an "excellent faculty," but he knew that it must be made subordinate to revelation, or else the sovereignty of God would be compromised. Therefore the limitations of reason were stressed by Mather

in his 1712 tract *Reason Satisfied and Faith Established.* And in *The Christian Philosopher* written a few years later Mather continued to argue that reason is helpful to man, but certainly not as helpful as the saving grace of the Lord—"Reason forms an imperfect Idea of this incomprehensible Mystery."[24]

While Cotton Mather was warning against the dangers of natural philosophy in America, some Christians in England were following the implications of rational, empirical thought and were setting forth the basic principles of Deism. In John Toland's *Christianity Not Mysterious,* 1696, and Anthony Collins's *A Discourse of Free-Thinking,* 1713, the outlines of a new religion took shape. Deism was the logical consequence of natural philosophy. As new rational designs began to dominate man's understanding of astronomy, chemistry, and physics, the value of mystery and revelation began to decline. As the limits of human knowledge expanded, the capricious authority of God was reduced. The Deists wanted to rescue Christianity from ignorance and superstition. They wanted a rational God.

The emergence of the Deists at the beginning of the eighteenth century represents a decisive change from mythical to critical thinking—a change from the devout acceptance of supernatural power to the skeptical analysis of dogma. Cotton Mather's worst fears were eventually realized. How much of the Christian faith could survive if its doctrines had to be put to the rational and empirical tests of natural philosophy? The Deists were hopeful that Christianity could be purified from unnecessary superstition. But once men were embarked on the critical mode of thinking, the questions and doubts would continue to multiply. At first only "insignificant miracles" were discarded as unworthy of intelligent religion, but soon all miracles were under attack. If the parting of the Red Sea is recognized as a natural impossibility, why believe the virgin birth or the resurrection of Christ? Either the universe conforms to natural laws or it does not, and if the first assumption is correct, then the majority of the Christian myth must be recognized as false. Once revelation was submitted to critical thought, it was reduced to the status of an unproved hypothesis. The Holy Scriptures were then seen to contain a bewildering number of contradictory hypotheses. Even the simple accounts of creation were in disagreement with the natural laws of the new science. There was no place in a rational system for an earth "without form." Attempts to pick and choose among the claims of Scripture only led to further questioning and doubt. Either the Bible was the authoritative word of God, or it was untrustworthy. In their desire to free Christianity from mystery, irrationality, and superstition, the Deists succeeded, beyond their expectations, in sabotaging the authority of revelation. They ended up with a Christianity without Christ.

The natural theology of the Deists transformed the sovereign God of the Puritans into the rational Creator of the Newtonian universe. Consequently most of the doctrines maintained by Calvin were abandoned. Once men became convinced of their ability to be the "masters and possessors of nature," the guilt of original sin was neglected, and the need for any redemption disappeared. The prospect of steady moral improvement in the natural world replaced the Puritan expectation of supernatural grace. As the power of judgment was shifted from God to man, the Puritan dread of future reckoning was replaced by an optimistic faith in human perfectibility. The myth of Christ as a divine Savior was exchanged for the figure of Jesus as a moral teacher. Piety surrendered to moralism. Instead of communities of visible saints anticipating their glorious reception into Heaven, the eighteenth century, spurred by the assumptions of the Deists, produced numerous societies dedicated to improving the conditions of this world. Benjamin Franklin refused to become a member of any particular religious congregation, but he was forever organizing clubs and societies for civic improvement. Without the doctrines of original sin and divine grace, what remained of the Puritan faith? The Deists continued to believe in a Creator, and most continued to call themselves Christians, but the Puritan belief in a sovereign God was replaced by the simple acknowledgment of a rational Deity. Responding to the influence of natural philosophy, the Deists were determined to submit at least some of their theology to empirical and rational tests. The authority of the old God was thus preempted by critical knowledge. The image of Benjamin Franklin conducting electricity from the sky may indicate the Promethean success of the revolution.

The Deists of course were resented and attacked by the more orthodox clergy. Cotton Mather began to withdraw his support of "reasonable religion" as soon as he realized some of the long-range implications of Deism. Jonathan Edwards was more enraged in his protest: "The Deists wholly cast off the Christian religion, and are professed infidels." Edwards was appalled to discover that the Deists "deny any revealed religion, or any word of God at all; and say that God has given mankind no other light to walk by but their own reason."[25] Many of Edwards's own theological writings, especially his study of predestination, *A Careful and Strict Enquiry into the Modern Prevailing Notions of That Freedom of Will, Which Is Supposed To Be Essential to Moral Agency,* and his account of innate depravity, *The Great Christian Doctrine of Original Sin Defended,* were written in partial response to the

heretical claims of the Deists. Edwards's defense of revealed religion
does include some knowledge of Locke and Newton, but Edwards
could not successfully steal the lightning from the natural philosophers.
He did attempt to refute some of the conclusions of the Deists by
accepting a few of their rational premises. Edwards argued that the
laws of nature are proof that the universe is predetermined, and he
offered empirical data to prove the existence of original sin. Thus he
hoped to trap the Deists with their own assumptions. But Edwards's
defense of revealed religion was in vain. The Deists enjoyed their freedom from the yoke of a sovereign God; life was more comfortable and
promising with a remote and rational Deity; no argument from Jonathan
Edwards, no matter how ingenious, could bring them back to superstition and slavery.

At the beginning of the eighteenth century, the Deists were greatly
outnumbered in England and America. All the powerful church positions were held by more traditional Christians. The writings of the
Deists were therefore received with hostile criticism, and the efforts to
refute their arguments started a great debate on the question of natural
versus revealed religion. Before long the debate escalated into polemical
warfare. Puritans on both sides of the Atlantic had had considerable
practice in casting out heretics and thus proceeded with confidence to
expose the errors of the Deists. After three or four decades of controversy, the debate appeared on the surface to have been won by the
orthodox clergy. The radical voices of Deism—Toland, Woolston, and
Tindal—were silenced by death, madness, or exhaustion. But the triumph
claimed by the established churches proved to be a hollow victory. The
trend supported by the Deists in the direction of secular humanism was
irreversible. Many Puritans had misunderstood the nature and extent of
the controversy, failing to realize that the Deists represented more than
just another form of heresy that could be put down by citing the truth
of Scripture. It was precisely such revealed "truth" that the Deists
wanted to question. Even Jonathan Edwards, who did recognize that
the Deists had "cast off the Christian religion, and are professed infidels," did not know how to respond except by reaffirming the fundamental doctrines of Calvinism. Unable in his own mind to doubt the
truth of Holy Scripture, Edwards could not fully understand the new
questions posed by the Deists.

While Edwards continued to describe human psychology in terms of
divine intervention, the Deists began to analyze superstition as if it were
a mental and emotional disease. While Edwards could only explain the
Great Awakening as an unexpected outpouring of God's grace, the
Deists were prepared to regard such religious enthusiasm as a psychological

aberration. In 1709 the English Deist John Trenchard in *The Natural History of Superstition* raised many significant questions about religious passion. Why do men frighten themselves with the specter of an angry God? Why do men deceive themselves with the myth of supernatural providence? How could the human race have allowed itself for so long to be victimized by priestcraft, dogma, and superstitition? How could mere enthusiasm have been accepted as divine grace? How could the primitive stories recorded in the Bible have been mistaken for the wisdom of God? Trenchard's method for answering all such questions was to submit human nature to rational and empirical analysis—"to examine into the frame and constitution of our own Bodies, and search into the causes of our Passions and Infirmities."[26]

Interest in the psychopathology of religious behavior had been intensified late in the seventeenth century by the witchcraft hysteria, and again a generation later by the emotional violence of the awakening. On the continent the writings of Pierre Bayle and Bernard Fontenelle explored the psychology of pagan religions and exposed the motives of fear and hope at the root of demonology and idol worship. Bayle and Fontenelle both followed the ancient leads of Democritus and Lucretius in trying to find natural explanations for religious behavior. Their skeptical analysis of pagan rituals, faith in miracles, and primitive mythology sent waves of recognition and shock throughout the Christian world. Bayle wrote sarcastically that "there is no absurdity from which the human mind is immune."[27] The Deists recognized the need to separate Christianity from the crude rituals and dogmas inherited from the primitive imagination. John Trenchard's *Natural History of Superstition* was an attempt to repudiate the errors of the Puritan experience in order to recover the simple truth of a rational and intelligent faith. But the Deists could not strip Calvinism of primitive superstition without destroying the powers of the sovereign God. Jonathan Edwards was prophetically right when he recognized the Deists as "infidels." Their faith, however sincere, was a halfway station on the road to secular humanism. But Jonathan Edwards and his disciples were wrong in thinking that the Deists were common heretics. The Puritans knew how to argue forever about different interpretations of Scripture, but they did not know how to confront the form of intelligence that finds the Bible simply irrelevant. It was not just controversy over this or that doctrine which separated the Puritans from the Deists; it was the difference between mythical and critical modes of thought.

The study of anthropology and comparative mythology increased steadily throughout the eighteenth century. John Trenchard's *Natural History of Superstition* was followed almost fifty years later by David

Hume's *The Natural History of Religion.* The bold development of critical thought during the first half of the eighteenth century can be measured by the difference between these two books. John Trenchard was careful to separate superstition from Christianity. Although many of his arguments by implication criticized the fundamental doctrines of Puritan theology, Trenchard left the central miracle of Christ's resurrection unexamined. David Hume was not so timid. Hoping to free his countrymen from "the Christian superstition," Hume followed the empirical and rational principles of natural philosophy to their logical end: "We may conclude, that the Christian Religion not only was first attended with miracles, but even at this day cannot be believed by any reasonable person without one."[28] By studying religious behavior as a psychological and social phenomenon, Hume reduced the status of religion to the natural development of primitive hopes and fears.

In the middle of the eighteenth century, Hume was joined by many of the French philosophers in the attack on Christianity as a primitive form of superstition. The cautious arguments of Bayle, Fontenelle, and the English Deists were boldly extended by many voices of the Enlightenment, especially by Condorcet, d'Holbach, and Voltaire. Generous praise for "the progress of philosophy and the sciences" was voiced by Condorcet in his *Sketch for a Historical Picture of the Progress of the Mind.* He rejoiced in the advances of the physical sciences, especially those which tended to expose the errors of religion. "There is not a religious system," Condorcet wrote, "nor a supernatural extravagance that is not founded on ignorance of the laws of nature."[29] The writers of the Enlightenment often took pride in declaring war on the twin enemies ignorance and superstition. The exhilaration of victory is unmistakable in the voice of Condorcet:

> At last man could proclaim aloud his right, which for so long had been ignored, to submit all opinions to his own reason and to use in the search for truth the only instrument for its recognition that he has been given. Every man learned with a sort of pride that nature had not forever condemned him to base his beliefs on the opinions of others; the superstitions of supernatural religion disappeared from society as from philosophy.[30]

Condorcet was a great optimist. But he died in prison, probably by suicide, when the hopes of the French Revolution turned into the Reign of Terror. Other voices of the Enlightenment were just as strong in their equation of Christianity with superstition and ignorance. Baron d'Holbach wrote in 1768: "Man is superstitious only because he is afraid. He is afraid only because he is ignorant."[31] The ancient fear theory expounded by Democritus and Epicurus enjoyed a considerable revival in the eighteenth century as a principal explanation for man's invention of terrible gods. For d'Holbach there was no longer any distinction between primitive superstition and Christianity. All forms of religious behavior were recognized as irrational and unhealthy. D'Holbach thus set out to cure his fellow man of such "malades imaginaires."[32] Liberation from the mental illness of religion would lead men to the confident mastery of nature. No degree of wit, sarcasm, or hyperbole was spared by the philosophes in their campaign against superstition. The master of calculated outrage was Voltaire, who never wearied of dissecting pious behavior and prescribing strong medicine for the religious disease. "Every sensible man," Voltaire wrote, "every honorable man, must hold the Christian sect in horror."[33]

How could the Protestant clergy on either side of the Atlantic respond to the increasing torrent of abuse? The followers of Jonathan Edwards continued to echo his reaffirmation of the fundamental doctrine of Puritan theology. And revivalism, especially on the American frontier, continued to be a popular force. Although the ranks of the Presbyterians and Congregationalists gradually declined, the numbers of Baptists and Methodists increased dramatically. Many churches were split after the Great Awakening and many new congregations formed. But Jonathan Edwards would not have been happy. Even his most devoted followers, men like Joseph Bellamy and Samuel Hopkins, had to dilute his theology in order to appeal to the new spirit of revolution. For the emerging world of Franklin and Jefferson, the reactionary doctrines of Puritanism were no longer relevant. Frequent attempts to revive the corpse of Puritanism by artificial respiration, sporadic doses of messianic hope, only demonstrated the futility. While large numbers of poor and uneducated people, white and black, continued to practice a caricature of the Puritan faith in the South and West, the founding churches of New England moved through various forms of liberal Christianity toward Unitarianism. By the end of the eighteenth century, more than three-quarters of the oldest churches in Massachusetts had abandoned their original Puritan covenants.

If most attempts to reaffirm Puritan doctrines in the face of the Enlightenment proved futile, attempts to liberalize the faith in order to accommodate the claims of natural philosophy offered shallow consolation and often proved to be self-deceptive. The faith of the fathers was largely abandoned by the many compromises of their children. The movement within the established church toward liberal Christianity had been underway for a long time. The tolerant piety of Erasmus had not been totally submerged by the passions of the Reformation, and a small number of scholars and mystics continued to affirm a simple form of Christianity unmarred by the twin forces of righteousness and persecution. Voices of reason and tolerance were often difficult to hear during the great religious upheavals of the sixteenth century, but in the rising Dutch Republic the words of Jacobus Arminius attracted a popular following. The optimistic piety of the Arminians was rejected by the strict Calvinists, but still the simple idea that all men might deserve Heaven by virtue of their good deeds here on earth proved very appealing to many Christians. By the eighteenth century the comfortable faith of the Arminians had combined with Enlightenment notions of progress and tolerance to produce a more liberal form of Christianity.

A small but influential group of English churchmen in the seventeenth century, the Cambridge Platonists, also helped to design a moderate piety. In their attempt to find the philosophical unity of the Christian faith, the Cambridge Platonists tended to discount the more rigid doctrines of Calvinism. Belief in such dogmas as original sin and predestination was discouraged in favor of a more optimistic faith in human goodness and freedom. The Cambridge Platonists also distrusted "enthusiasm," and sought to establish the rational principles of religious virtue.

The liberal tendencies of the Arminians and Cambridge Platonists were developed more fully by the clergymen who dominated the Church of England toward the end of the seventeenth and the beginning of the eighteenth century. The sermons of John Tillotson, the powerful and influential Archbishop of Canterbury, pictured a benevolent Deity accessible to all men of decency and good will. The awesome features of the Puritan God were compromised in order to appeal to reason and hope.

A similar move in the direction of a more liberal and humanistic faith was marked in New England in 1699 by the formation of the Brattle Street Church according to "broad and catholick" principles. By relaxing the traditional requirements for membership in their new church, the progressive merchants of Boston opened the door to many of the reforms prompted by the enlightened attitudes of the new century. A few decades later clergymen in Boston like Charles Chauncy were extolling the good sense of rational Christian piety, and warning against the fanatical extremes of the Great Awakening.

Many of the clergy who shared in the long development of liberal Christianity could not foresee how completely their accommodation of enlightened philosophy would erode the authority and substance of

Puritanism. When John Tillotson in England, or Charles Chauncy in Boston, preached a comfortable, optimistic, rational faith, both men were highly regarded as orthodox and respectable, and neither could suspect or admit that he was compromising the essential power of the Calvinist vision. Many sincere and well-intentioned Christians on both sides of the Atlantic would have been shocked to discover that their compromises would lead eventually to Deism and Unitarianism. It is ironic that even the respected voices of the established churches contributed to the eclipse of the Puritan God. They succeeded so well that by the end of the eighteenth century the founders of the new American republic could demonstrate their adherence to natural philosophy and remain just nominal Christians. Benjamin Franklin abandoned the Puritanism of his birthplace and adopted the basic principles of Deism. Thomas Jefferson discarded most of the doctrines of the Anglican faith and came at the end of his life to confess a minimal form of Unitarianism.

BENJAMIN FRANKLIN

The empirical philosophy of the Enlightenment was dramatized for a wide audience by the extraordinary career of Benjamin Franklin. The editors of the recent Yale edition suggest that Franklin's *Autobiography* should be viewed as "a landmark in the secularization of Western thought: a lay sermon, delivered after Puritan religious ardor had declined, preaching a utilitarian morality and recommending an industrious asceticism directed toward earthly rather than heavenly ends."[34] There are moments in his familiar career when the events of Franklin's life appear to symbolize the progress in America from religion to science. His boyhood migration from Boston to Philadelphia, for example, may suggest the historical change from John Winthrop's "city upon a hill," where the Puritans felt "the God of Israel is among us," to William Penn's city of brotherly love, where Franklin was ready to accept the challenges of business, politics, and science. Although he had been brought up in a Puritan household, and no doubt had been forced to listen to more than one sermon by Cotton Mather, when Franklin became a free citizen of Philadelphia he attended no church. Franklin's chief reason for leaving Boston had been to escape the tyranny of his older brother, but he also hoped to avoid the public censure of his own growing skepticism. "My indiscreet Disputations about Religion," Franklin wrote many years later, "began to make me pointed at with Horror by good People as an Infidel or Atheist."[35]

As a young man Franklin had discovered the writings of the English

Deists, and years later he explained how the encounter left him "a real Doubter in many Points of our Religious Doctrine."[36] Attempts to reconstruct a spiritual biography of Franklin are untrustworthy, because most of the evidence comes from Franklin's own recollections of his youth which were not written down until many decades after the events described. Although it is true that Franklin's *Autobiography* is neither always candid nor accurate, it does provide an unusual witness to the growth of his opinions. Franklin dates the beginning of his skepticism from a few years before his flight from Boston. "My Parents had early given me religious Impressions, and brought me through my Childhood piously in the Dissenting Way. But I was scarce 15 when, after doubting by turns several Points as I found them disputed in the different Books I read, I began to doubt of Revelation itself."[37] In the very same year that such doubts came to young Franklin in Boston, the converting experience of divine grace overwhelmed young Jonathan Edwards in Connecticut. There is no greater irony in American history than the simultaneous start of these two men of genius in opposite directions.

Although Franklin's conversion to Deism was swift and complete— "In short I soon became a thorough Deist"—he also recognized that his radical convictions might cause him some public embarrassment. After observing the behavior of a few close friends with whom he shared his philosophy of Deism, Franklin "began to suspect that this Doctrine, tho' it might be true, was not very useful."[38] When considering these words from his *Autobiography*, allowance must be made for the way in which the diplomacy of Franklin's mature years moderated the confident opinions of his youth. To the sixty-year-old smiling public man, the bright ideas of his adolescence no doubt seemed rather distant and vain, and therefore "true" doctrines could be lightly set aside if they proved "not very useful." But it was always characteristic of Franklin to measure experience by the standard of utility. Perhaps when he converted his best friends to the principles of Deism, and then saw his friends betray his confidence, he learned something about the necessary connection of ideas and action. Although his ideas about religion were formed in the midst of the Deist controversy, he soon recognized the futility of continuing the debate. Once he had learned that principles must be tested in action—the guiding assumption of empiricism—Franklin had placed himself above the endless controversy about religious doctrine that consumed so much time and talent in the eighteenth century.

Franklin's only contribution to the polemical crossfire was a small tract on metaphysics printed while he was working in London. He was just nineteen when he wrote *A Dissertation on Liberty and Necessity, Pleasure and Pain.* It was a response to Wollaston's *The Religion of Nature Delineated* which Franklin was required to set in type for his London employers. In bold language Franklin asserted the principles of Deism, and attempted to refute such Puritan doctrines as original sin and predestination. He later came to believe that his youthful book was "not so clever a Performance as I once thought it," and he burned the remaining copies except for one. Franklin decided that his "printing this Pamphlet was another Erratum," not because he came to reject the content of his publication, but rather because he doubted the utility of exposing his radical opinions.[39]

Franklin's youthful contact with the Deist controversy left him with a permanent distaste for any form of dogmatic argument. After years of successful diplomacy Franklin observed how "a positive dogmatical Manner in advancing your Sentiments, may provoke Contradiction and prevent a candid Attention." This lesson is often repeated in the *Auto-biography,* and much of Franklin's success in persuading other people to action was due to his skill in pretending to be the helpful and friendly adviser rather than the convinced spokesman for any particular dogma. It is not surprising that *Poor Richard's Almanack* eventually reached the largest eighteenth-century audience, nor that his countrymen depended upon Franklin's skill to negotiate their most important treaties.

Once Franklin accepted the utilitarian notion that ideas must lead to action, he avoided further abstract religious argument. His program for the American Philosophical Society, which he helped to create, placed the most emphasis upon applied science, technical inventions, and civic improvement. While Jonathan Edwards was writing *A Treatise Concerning Religious Affections,* Franklin issued his *Proposal for Promoting Useful Knowledge.* The lists of his own inventions, contributions to civic improvement, and discoveries of useful knowledge need no rehearsal. What is of interest here is Franklin's application of utilitarian standards to religious theory. As a young man he had concluded that only a few of the doctrines taught to him in his childhood could withstand any practical test. Franklin was no more willing to humble himself beneath the sovereignty of the Puritan God than he was later willing to submit to the intolerable rule of King George. His skeptical intelligence rejected most a priori authority—"Revelation had indeed no weight with me as such."[40] When he measured the dogmas of his childhood by the standard of usefulness, Franklin was convinced that much Puritan theology was either irrelevant or injurious to the successful pursuit of life, liberty, and happiness. He knew, of course, that the doctrines of Calvin had not been designed to accommodate such worldly goals. The business of a Puritan was ideally to prepare for the supernatural life to come. But Franklin believed in taking one world at a time, and he found much business to detain him in this natural world.

Although Franklin cared far more about success in this life than about salvation in some hypothetical future life, he was neither a complete materialist nor a convinced atheist. Despite his remarkable contribution to the advance of secular humanism, Franklin stopped short of affirming a full natural vision. In his old age he still held firm to the religious principles of Deism. He believed in a rational, benevolent God and the hope of immortality. Franklin's concept of divine power made very few demands upon men. The prophet of worldly success had no use for the strict piety of Jonathan Edwards. But there is no reason to doubt the sincerity of Franklin's profession of Deism. An account of his religious principles appears twice in his *Autobiography*. In the first version Franklin describes the progress from the Calvinism of his early childhood to the basic tenets of Deism that remained with him for almost seven decades:

> I had been religiously educated as a Presbyterian; and tho' some
> of the Dogmas of that Persuasion, such as the Eternal Decrees of
> God, Election, Reprobation, etc. appear'd to me unintelligible,
> others doubtful, and I early absented myself from the Public
> Assemblies of the Sect, Sunday being my Studying-Day, I never
> was without some religious Principles; I never doubted, for in-
> stance, the Existence of the Deity, that he made the World, and
> govern'd it by his Providence; that the most acceptable Service
> of God was the doing Good to Man; that our Souls are immortal;
> and that all Crime will be punished and Virtue rewarded either
> here or hereafter; these I esteem'd the Essentials of every
> Religion. . . .[41]

The ease with which Franklin could dismiss some of the Puritan dog-mas as "unintelligible" or "doubtful" reveals his distance from Ed-wards's belief in divine grace. And Franklin's sly mention of "Sunday being my Studying-Day" dramatizes his happy and confident recognition of that distance. He would not obey any commandment to keep the Sabbath holy. His optimistic vision of human nature left him unconcerned with the typical Puritan anxiety about sin and damnation. Although he often refashioned his worldly roles, the *Autobiography* itself being a late revision of his life's drama, Franklin apparently never felt the need for the regeneration promised by the faith of his fathers. Instead of yielding himself to an all powerful Deity, Franklin asserted confidently that "the most acceptable Service of God was the doing Good to Man."

There were few vestiges of Puritanism left in Franklin's statement of religious principles. Totally missing was any active commitment to the sovereignty of God, any recognition of original sin, any anticipation of Christ's return, any belief in the authority of Holy Scripture, any will to participate in the rituals and sacraments of an organized church, or any need to join a congregation affirming a special covenant with God. Franklin was neither afraid of damnation nor especially eager to join the saints in Heaven. He did believe that "Crime will be punished and Virtue rewarded," but he hesitated to say if that judgment will come "here or hereafter." He objected to the ministers of Philadelphia who merely advocated their particular dogmas—"their Aim seeming to be rather to make us Presbyterians than good Citizens."[42] What statement could better reveal the priority Franklin gave to secular concerns? Although tension between the demands of church and state had been present from the very beginning of the Puritan experience in the New World, Franklin was remarkably unconcerned with the conflict; his enlightened religious principles allowed him to perform the business of a good citizen of Philadelphia without apology.

Franklin rejected the dogmas of Puritan theology, but he did retain the habit of introspection encouraged by the Puritans in America. But instead of searching his soul for hints of sin or grace, Franklin was more concerned with judging his conduct by ethical standards. Instead of worrying about where he stood in relationship to God, Franklin was more interested in his standing with his fellow citizens. Therefore he replaced the stern piety of Jonathan Edwards with his famous "Plan for Self Examination." He wanted to measure his own performance of secular virtues—frugality, industry, moderation, etc. Franklin's "Project for arriving at moral Perfection" has been widely imitated and often ridiculed. A modern reader is apt to wonder how much humility Franklin learned by striving every day to "imitate Jesus and Socrates." Extreme distaste for his ethical pragmatism and also for Franklin's smug recommendation of his own virtues inspired the passionate denunciation issued by D. H. Lawrence: "And now I, at least, know why I can't stand Benjamin. He tries to take away my wholeness and my dark forest, my freedom."[43] But Franklin's plan for moral improvement was more revolutionary than his recent critics have admitted. By replacing the Puritan concern about sinful behavior with a more secular account of practical virtues, Franklin helped to free his contemporaries from the fear and anxiety of being judged by some arbitrary power. Instead of surrendering to the will of a sovereign God, Franklin was ready to assume responsibility for his own actions. Franklin's bold rejection of Puritan judgment helped to make "wholeness" and "freedom" possible.

Late in his life Franklin acknowledged that many of his ideas about moral improvement had been influenced long before by the sermons and writings of Cotton Mather. Franklin even took the trouble to write Mather's son to confirm his gratitude. Franklin claimed that the words of Cotton Mather, especially those in the *Essays To Do Good,* produced "such a turn of thinking, as to have an influence on my conduct through life."[44] A similar confession appears in the *Autobiography,* and there is no reason to doubt Franklin's sincerity. But it would be a mistake to accept Franklin's admission as wholly accurate. Cotton Mather was the leading clergyman in the Boston of Franklin's youth, and no doubt Mather's words left their mark on the boy's imagination. When Franklin returned briefly to Boston in his eighteenth year, he paid a memorable visit to the aged Puritan minister. Sixty years later Franklin recounted the visit in his letter to Mather's son. But from the very beginning Franklin's spirit had been at odds with the rigid piety of Cotton Mather. Franklin's first publication, printed under the pseudonym of "Mrs. Silence Dogood," was a satire on Mather's recently published *Essays To Do Good.* Franklin's youthful venture in satire was sufficiently provocative to help cause his brother's newspaper to be officially suppressed. If Cotton Mather had discovered the identity of the author, the visit a few years later from young Franklin probably could not have taken place. Few men have suffered more from public ridicule, real or imagined, than Cotton Mather. And Franklin, from his youthful satire on Mather's writing to his mature political exposure of Thomas Hutchinson's private letters, never underestimated the advantage of public ridicule. It is an ironic coincidence of history that the career of Cotton Mather, plagued by the frequent mistrust of his contemporaries, troubled by his own neurotic conscience, and haunted by the shadow of defeat, should have briefly crossed paths with the career of Benjamin Franklin, the model of self-confidence, public approbation, and political success. And it is greater irony that Franklin, or anyone else, should believe that the fretful Puritan minister could teach the young satirist and future politician lessons in moral improvement. What could the aged lion say to the young fox? Mather was the dying champion of mythological vision. Toward the end of his life he looked daily for the descent of angels from Heaven—"They are coming! They will quickly be upon us; and the World shall be shaken wonderfully!"[45] Franklin was the advocate and hero of the growing critical mode of thought. When lightning came down from the sky, he gathered it with the help of a piece of string.

Franklin's plan for moral improvement was revolutionary in two ways: it was secular and utilitarian. His catalog of virtues does not include holiness. The central theme of Puritan theology, anticipation of divine grace, is completely missing. All his chosen qualities serve to promote order and success in this life; none is concerned with any preparation for a future life. And that is what gives Franklin's plan such utilitarian value. Puritan attempts at introspection had been doomed to uncertainty because the individual could never be sure where he stood in the eyes of God. Even the most saintly Puritans were often troubled by guilt for imaginary sins. But Franklin removed the uncertainty by focusing his introspective questions on practical conduct that could be known and measured. At the end of each day Franklin knew where he stood. He could enter his marks on his moral chart, and even enjoy "seeing on my Pages the Progress I made in Virtue."[46] Moreover his progress in the virtues of industry, frugality, etc., produced tangible rewards of material and political success. Franklin was thus able to set an example for generations hoping to rise from "Poverty and Obscurity . . . to a State of Affluence and some Degree of Reputation in the World."[47] And for men like D. H. Lawrence, who felt nothing but scorn for Franklin's utilitarianism, the high degree of his success offered a ready target for protest: "And this is all the God the grandsons of the Pilgrim Fathers had left. Aloft on a pillar of dollars."[48]

A partial explanation of Franklin's success in many different fields can be found in his reliance upon the empirical method. His early and rather embarrassing defense of Deism may have taught him to look more closely at the connection of ideas and action. He learned very early in the Junto Club, a group of his friends organized for conversation, to be wary of just scoring argumentative points. Much theological discussion seemed to him merely irrelevant. The important test of language, he knew, was how it moved people to action. His diplomatic and political success at the court of Louis XVI and later at the Constitutional Convention followed the same empirical design as his ventures into business and writing. He always studied human nature in order to discover what his contemporaries would accept and how it could be accomplished. *Poor Richard's Almanack* was purchased by more Americans in the eighteenth century than any other book with the exception of the Bible. Franklin was able to retire from the active management of his business affairs when he was forty-two. The same empirical discipline was the coherent force behind his plan for moral improvement. By setting aside the metaphysical questions of sin and salvation, Franklin was able to measure and celebrate his secular progress.

The modern implications of Franklin's empirical method are evident when his response to lightning is contrasted with the reaction of Jonathan Edwards. While Edwards felt the majesty of God revealed in a flash of lightning, Franklin merely confirmed his scientific hypothesis about electrical energy. Edwards had been especially fascinated by thunderstorms. Before his conversion experience, he had been "uncommonly terrified with thunder," but after his experience of grace thunder and lightning gave him unusual pleasure: "And scarce any thing, among all the works of nature, was so sweet to me as thunder and lightning. . . . I felt God at the first appearance of a thunder storm. And used to take the opportunity at such times to fix myself to view the clouds, and see the lightnings play, and hear the majestic and awful voice of God's thunder."[49] Franklin's critical mind simply ignored any mythological associations; he looked instead for natural causes. A simple experiment could direct the path of electricity from the clouds. Nature was then no longer a holy temple; it had become a modern laboratory.

Franklin's contemporaries were probably right in praising his scientific accomplishments as his chief empirical success. Throughout Europe and America he was recognized for his experiments with electricity. The Royal Society elected him to its membership and honored him with the award of a special medal. Besides the scientific value of his famous experiments, his more enlightened contemporaries recognized the symbolic value of Franklin stealing fire from the gods. Immanuel Kant was the first to compare Franklin to Prometheus. The motto designed for Franklin's portrait was soon echoed throughout Europe: "He snatched the lightning from the sky and the sceptre from tyrants."[50] The success of the American Prometheus, and the international acclaim for his bold achievements, implicitly mark the passing of the Puritan God into intellectual disrepute and permanent eclipse.

DEMOCRATIC REVOLUTION

The progress of scientific thought in the eighteenth century was paralleled by the rise of democratic expectations. The protest of the natural philosophers against theological dogma was matched by political revolt against the claims of absolute monarchy. In each case established authority was being challenged by new ideals of truth and equality.

And in both revolutions the image of God suffered a decline of power and importance. Thomas Jefferson's interest in the growth of science was as strong as his belief in the value of democracy, and both together prompted his distaste for any form of religion based on authoritarian habits of thought. He looked with special disfavor on the remnants of the Puritan faith. It is appropriate that Jefferson wished to be remembered as the author of the Statute of Virginia for Religious Freedom as well as the author of the Declaration of Independence. He had no more use for bishops than he had for kings.

The founders of the Puritan religion in New England were outspoken in their rejection of democratic ideas. "I do not conceive," wrote John Cotton, "that God did ever ordain [Democracy] as a fit government for either church or commonwealth." Governor Winthrop agreed that "democracy has always been accounted the meanest and worst of all forms of government." The repeated warnings indicate that some democratic tendencies were already threatening to disturb the balance of dogmatic power. While still on their way to the New World the Puritan saints had to be reminded by Governor Winthrop that authoritarian habits should not be abandoned. Winthrop began his famous sermon on board the *Arbella* by telling his congregation that inequality is a necessary part of God's design: "God Almighty in His most holy and wise providence hath so disposed of the condition of mankind as in all times some must be rich, some poor; some high and eminent in power and dignity, others mean and in subjection."[51] In the next century the same assumptions of permanent inequality and arbitrary power became the favorite targets of enlightened skepticism. But almost 150 years had passed before Jefferson could formally proclaim the revolutionary idea that all men are created equal and possess the right to establish their own government.

Winthrop and Cotton believed that the function of civil government in Massachusetts should be to protect the community of Puritan saints from all disruption. No heresy in thought or deed could be tolerated. Hence the swift action taken against the mild differences of opinion represented by Anne Hutchinson and Roger Williams. Religious freedom was unthinkable in the Massachusetts Bay Colony. Any appearance of heresy could discredit the vision of a community of saints, and might affect their special covenant with the Lord. All clerical and civil power therefore served the same purpose—to promote the kingdom of God in the wilderness of the New World. The leaders of the Massachusetts Bay Colony were deliberately intolerant, dogmatic, and authoritarian. Theirs was a narrow version of the structure of religious and political authority that had prevailed in medieval and Renaissance

Europe. All power was assumed to flow down from a sovereign God
to the kings and bishops, who were acknowledged to be His deputies
on earth. But in the New World there were no kings and bishops;
therefore the first Puritans in America believed themselves to be directly
at the mercy of their absolute God.

The strong protest of Winthrop and Cotton against any suggestion
of democratic equality was an indication of their awareness of the
potential threat to religious authority. The Puritan fear of democratic
expectations may paradoxically have grown from the initial Protestant
revolt against the authority of the prince of Rome. By rejecting the
sovereignty of the pope, the leaders of the Reformation started down
the long road toward freedom of conscience. But to compensate for
the boldness of the first revolt against papal authority, the followers
of Luther and Calvin demanded a still more excessive submission to
dogma and Scripture. (Hence the paradoxical nature of the reformed
faith: revolutionary in its origin but fiercely reactionary in its outlook.)
But the idea of rebellion tested by Luther and Calvin was bound to
multiply in the imagination of their followers. Winthrop and Cotton
could not forever protect the fortress of Puritan dogma against new
reformers. In the beginning was the end.

Once the authority of the pope had been challenged and it became
possible for a secular prince like Henry VIII to proclaim himself the
head of a national church, the splintering of religious authority further
encouraged the Protestant reformers to discount secular power and
anchor their faith in the authority of Holy Scripture and the sovereignty
of God. If the original separation from the prince of Rome had been a
difficult break from traditional obedience, the skeptical denial of Tudor
and Stuart sovereignty followed more readily. Only six generations
passed between the publication of Luther's *On Christian Liberty* and
the decision of English Puritans to take the liberty of beheading their
king.

Two decades earlier the great migration of Puritans across the Atlantic had demonstrated a practical transfer of allegiance from the crown
of England to a special covenant with a sovereign God. If the Puritans
in Massachusetts were doubly aware of the revolutionary steps that
separated them from Rome and England, it is not surprising that men
like John Winthrop feared that any more freedom might destroy all
sovereign authority. The first generation of Puritans in the New World
therefore magnified the power of God in order to compensate for their
disobedience and to disguise their guilt.

Freud offered a psychological explanation for the appearance of a
jealous God that may help to explain the fear and guilt of the early

Puritans. In *Moses and Monotheism* he described original sin as the consequence of primitive man killing the tribal father. Freud accepted the hypothesis of Atkinson that human tribes were ruled by a tyrannical father until the sons united together and revolted against the tyrant. (Freud knew that the hypothesis was generally regarded as untrue, but he refused to abandon his speculation.) Freud then argued that the invention in the human mind of images of divine power might have been the psychological compensation necessary to cope with the guilt stemming from the murder of the tribal father. When this primal situation was echoed in recorded history, with the death of Moses for example, the psychological need to deify a father image was dramatically increased. Hence the worship of a sovereign, jealous, punishing Jehovah. If Freud's theory is at all correct, the early Puritans may have been stirred by the rejection of pope and king to a heightened recollection of primal guilt, which prompted them to elevate original sin to a leading position among their dogmas, and then worship with extraordinary zeal a strong and threatening God. Historians of the Puritan experience have been unable to explain the tremendous outpouring of guilt in Puritan sermons and diaries. Augustine and Calvin notwithstanding, what prompted the extraordinary vogue of original sin in the seventeenth century? Freud's theory at least suggests a coherent answer. The feeling of guilt was further heightened by the second and third generation Puritans in America because they so often suffered the additional remorse of not matching the expectations of their own fathers. Fear and guilt were the familiar themes of the jeremiads preached by Cotton Mather and so many of his contemporaries. Whatever the validity of the anthropological theory about the killing of the primal father, it is true that the shadow of regicide extended from the murder of the English king in 1649 to the guillotining of Louis XVI in 1793, and it was during the same period that the Puritan image of a sovereign God was exalted and then suffered decline. Likewise the power of original sin was greatly magnified in the seventeenth century and then gradually diminished in the eighteenth.

The transition from primitive guilt to popular rebellion was marked by the rise of democratic impulses. At the beginning of the period men like Winthrop and Cotton were anxiously worshiping their supernatural God, and warning against the horrors of democracy. At the end of the period men like Jefferson and Paine were advocating democratic rebellion and watching with pleasure the decline of sovereign authority both political and religious. The guilt experienced by the early Puritans was finally overcome when their descendants in the next century learned to accept their democratic motives. What occurred in psychological terms was a shift from an anxious defense of the father image to an aggressive commitment to the role of rebellious son. The fears of the superego were replaced by the bold confidence of the ego. The Puritans had been convinced that man must be dependent upon God; the contemporaries of Franklin and Jefferson declared their independence. The worst apprehensions of Governor Winthrop were eventually realized.

The progressive rise of democratic assumptions could only occur with the gradual weakening of the old habits of thought which supported hierarchical order and authority. For centuries, of course, challenges to the structure of religious and political authority had been appearing. The writing of Machiavelli spread considerable skepticism throughout Renaissance Europe concerning the claim of rule by divine right. Many of Shakespeare's history plays test the theory of divine right monarchy against the practical demands of secular power. When the forced abdication of a king was dramatized by Shakespeare in *Richard II*, even Queen Elizabeth had good reason to be fearful of the precedent. In Shakespeare's play King Richard depends upon God to defend him, while his opponent plays a successful game of power politics and gains the general support of the people. The forced abdication and murder of a king was a scene that haunted the imagination of the Renaissance. Queen Elizabeth did not want to take any chances; she claimed the power of divine right, but she also felt obliged to win and hold the popular support of her subjects. In the next generation the instability of political order increased. John Donne wrote in 1611: "And new philosophy calls all in doubt . . . 'Tis all in pieces, all coherence gone;/All just supply, and all relation:/Prince, subject, father, son, are things forgot."[52] Donne's words were extreme, but a few decades later the English king was executed. The conscience of the seventeenth century remained troubled by the instinct of rebellion. In England the monarchy was restored; in America the Puritans inflated the power of original sin and the sovereignty of God. The habit of thinking in terms of hierarchical order was hard to outgrow. It was only in the next century that the shadow of guilt diminished, and then the philosophers of the Enlightenment were free to challenge all the father images: kings, bishops, popes, and God. The independent republic declared in America with ideals of democratic equality and tolerance was a true creation of the Enlightenment.

The shores of the New World provided a suitable testing ground for democratic impulses. Merely by crossing the Atlantic the immigrants to America were able to leave behind much of the civil and ecclesiastical power inherent in the old hierarchical order. No wonder Governor Winthrop was concerned that class distinctions might be ignored and all authority destroyed. In the wilderness of the new continent, the distinctions were bound to decrease. Some democratic actions were necessary for the very survival of the first settlers. Although Governor Winthrop did attempt to maintain strict authority, and often warned against the forbidden taste of liberty, the distrusted principle of democracy still informed many of the practices of the young colony. Some limited elections were held. When new churches were formed in the wilderness, many decisions were generated by the people and not imposed by a higher power. Gradually the habit of independent decision replaced the traditional obedience to hierarchical authority. The seeds of democracy thus took root in the very practice of congregational polity. In some colonies the vestiges of authoritarianism were much stronger than in others. While religious persecution was still vigorously practiced in Massachusetts, the spirit of tolerance grew with less difficulty in Rhode Island and Pennsylvania. But even the Puritans in Massachusetts could not long maintain autocratic power in a New World that could do better without it.

As long as the Puritans in New England were convinced of their mission to build a City of God in the wilderness, they were intolerant of all thought and action that appeared to interfere with that objective. The growth of tolerance in the eighteenth century is a symptom of the decline of religious conviction. Tolerant action follows from the assumption of democratic equality; it is the natural enemy of authority and hierarchy. As long as the Puritans could regard themselves as a chosen people, any dissenters could be persecuted with zeal. But when the covenant with the Lord was compromised by succeeding generations, the Puritan hope of building a City of God was replaced by the ideal of a democratic republic.

The creation of the United States was a disconcerting event for many of the established churches in the New World. The revolutionary period shifted attention to the immediate concerns of politics, diplomacy, and war. Although the clergy in New England, except for the Anglican, generally supported the goals of the Revolution, all denominations suffered from the controversy and distraction. Often church facilities were appropriated for military purposes. The meeting house of the Old South Congregation in Boston, for example, was turned into a riding school by the British army. The shift of attention from religion to politics caused a rapid decline in church membership. By the end of the revolutionary period less than ten percent of the population could be counted as church members.

The physical disruption of the churches proved less significant than their philosophical disarray. While the followers of Jonathan Edwards tried to resist the tide of the Enlightenment by holding fast to their reactionary and impractical theology, other ministers in New England preferred to drift with the times and try to adapt their faith to the increasing democratic expectations. Neither strategy was successful. The disciples of Edwards could only preserve the remnants of his Puritan vision, while the liberal clergy compromised away the substance of their faith. The latter process of disintegration accelerated during the second half of the eighteenth century and achieved its full destructive momentum during the years of the revolutionary war. Although the beginnings of a liberal movement had been visible early in the century with the formation of the Brattle Street Church along "broad and catholick" lines and the installation of John Leverett as the president of Harvard, the full effect of the Enlightenment was not felt until the emergence of Unitarianism at the end of the eighteenth century.

The gradual drift away from Puritan theology was reflected in the long ministry of Charles Chauncy at the First Church in Boston. His warning against the enthusiasm of the Great Awakening, *Seasonable Thoughts on the State of Religion in New England,* appeared in 1743, and then for more than forty years he helped to shape the liberal Christianity emerging in New England. After his rejection of the Great Awakening, Chauncy placed little value upon the crucial Puritan experience of regeneration. The ideals of human progress and a reasonable faith were more appealing to his temperament than the old Puritan insistence upon a jealous God and the dogma of original sin. Chauncy also discarded the belief in predestination, preferring instead the Arminian confidence in the value of good works. Mystical piety was replaced by rational morality. The democratic expectations of the century were accommodated by opening the covenant of the church to accept all who wished to join. The sacraments were no longer reserved for the regenerate. The communion of saints, who once stood together in anticipation of divine grace, was transformed into a congregation assembled to hear polite sermons about moral progress. While the democratic ideals of equality and tolerance were advanced, the authority of the clergy diminished, the rule of dogma lessened, and the sovereignty of God declined.

Near the end of the eighteenth century, the drift toward liberal Christianity led to the emergence of Unitarianism. King's Chapel in Boston became the first Unitarian church in America in 1787. Within two or three decades many of the prominent churches in New England, including the First Church of Boston, followed the revolutionary example of King's Chapel. Influenced by the popular ideals of the Enlightenment—reason, progress, tolerance, and equality—Unitarianism abandoned many of the dogmas of the Puritan faith. Most significantly, the divinity of Christ was compromised. The idea of the Trinity seemed to the

Unitarians both irrational and unnecessary. Why believe in the redemptive power supposedly generated by the sacrifice of Christ, if human nature is credited with enough reason and goodness to effect its own improvement? The disappearance of original sin had removed the need for any divine redemption. To compensate for abandoning the divinity of Christ, the Unitarians emphasized his value as a moral teacher. While the miracles of Christ were set aside, the moral lessons of the New Testament were studied as a guide for human progress. Benjamin Franklin would have approved.

The triumph of democratic expectations during the revolutionary war, and the challenge of national independence that followed, were both reflected in the confidence and optimism of the Unitarian vision. Just as the political idealism of the young republic was inspired by the idea of a new beginning and the dream of a great destiny, the Unitarian faith pictured the new America as a reincarnation of Adam, innocent and free, blessed with the chances of an earthly paradise. The political and religious ideals were almost interchangeable; both were incarnations of the popular Enlightenment belief in progress. In the vision of William Ellery Channing, the most important Unitarian minister in Boston for almost four decades: "Christianity should now be disencumbered and set free. . . . It should come forth from the darkness and corruption of the past. . . . It should be comprehended as having but one purpose, the perfection of human nature, the elevation of men into nobler beings."[53] The goal of religion had thus become moral progress. In the words of Channing there was no hint of the mystery and miracle of salvation. In place of the Puritan wish to exalt the sovereignty of God, the Unitarians merely hoped to elevate men into "nobler beings." In his old age Thomas Jefferson rejoiced in the growth of Unitarianism. "I trust," Jefferson wrote in 1822, "that there is not a young man now living in the United States who will not die an Unitarian."[54]

THOMAS JEFFERSON

The talents of Jefferson—philosopher, diplomat, politician, scientist, architect—defy any single pattern of intellectual history. When President Kennedy was hosting a dinner for Nobel Prize winners at the White House, he reminded all of them that so much talent and intelligence had not been assembled in the East Room since the days when Jefferson dined there alone. The success of Jefferson as a revolutionary spokesman, diplomat, and democratic leader was a triumph for many principles of the Enlightenment. Although he was born and raised in Virginia as a nominal Anglican, Jefferson was always receptive to the more advanced and skeptical thoughts imported from Europe. While the followers of Edwards in New England were trying to preserve the remnants of the Puritan vision, Jefferson was reading the philosophy of Locke, Hume, Voltaire, Montesquieu, Condorcet, and Rousseau. Eventually his religious thinking passed beyond an acceptance of Deism to the full approval of Unitarianism. It is not surprising that many of his contemporaries, especially those living in New England, regarded the third president of the new republic as a probable "infidel" and "atheist."

Jefferson spent two important years of his adolescence in the home of an aggressive and self-righteous Anglican minister. The experience helped to inspire his lifelong hostility to the established clergy. "The grand purpose of life," preached the Anglican minister, "is to prepare for death, and that is preparing for eternity." But Jefferson preferred to echo the slogan of the Enlightenment: "The earth belongs to the living." Jefferson saw the established clergy as messengers of fear and superstition. What could be done, he asked, to reduce their authority and power? His answer was to guarantee the separation of church and state. Jefferson never lost an opportunity to remove and prohibit any government support of religious activity. When he became the governor of Virginia, he used his power to transform the College of William and Mary—replacing clergymen with professors of science, mathematics, and modern languages. When Jefferson introduced a bill in the Virginia assembly to force the independence of church and state, his language was strong: "To compel a man to furnish contributions of money for the propagation of opinions which he disbelieves and abhors, is sinful and tyranical. . . . Our civil rights have no dependence on our religious opinions. . . ."[55] Jefferson was dismayed by the legal code of Virginia which allowed a punishment of three years in prison for the crime of denying the Trinity. Unitarians could even be declared unfit parents and deprived of their children. Heretics could be executed. Jefferson agreed with John Locke that "the care of every man's soul belongs to himself."

Jefferson was familiar with much of the European speculation about the sources of God in the human imagination. One theory identified fear and superstition as the principal motives leading to the worship of divine power. The classical account of the fear theory could be found in the Latin poem *De rerum natura* by Lucretius. Once the manuscript of the poem was discovered during the Renaissance, the power of its skepticism and the scope of its religious criticism spread inevitably to philosophers throughout Europe. David Hume in Scotland and Voltaire in France were both fascinated by the skeptical analysis of religious motives. Attempts to refute the theories of the Latin poet were made by pious Christians in the middle of the eighteenth century. Cardinal Polignac published his *Anti-Lucretius* in 1747, but the resulting controversy served only to publicize the radical ideas of *De rerum natura*. Jefferson later obtained eight copies of the heretical book for his library at Monticello.

Lucretius argued repeatedly in his long poem that religion is prompted by fear and supported by ignorance. *De rerum natura* was a dramatic attack upon mythological thinking, and a passionate challenge to the human mind to replace fear with critical knowledge. "This dread and darkness of the mind therefore need not the rays of the sun," Lucretius wrote; "only knowledge of nature's forms dispels them."[56] Such words had special appeal to the natural philosophers of the eighteenth century, who saw the forms of nature revealed in the scientific light of Isaac Newton. "We are living," wrote Immanuel Kant in 1784, "in an Age of Enlightenment."[57] The image of dispelling darkness, so often dramatized in *De rerum natura*, also appealed to the skeptical and revolutionary minds of men like Voltaire and Jefferson. In many of Jefferson's notes and letters the image of darkness is associated with priestcraft, superstition, and Puritan dogma, while the image of light is reserved for the ideals of the new republic, political freedom, and democratic equality.

Although the defiance of religion in the writing of Lucretius sparked controversy among his own contemporaries—Cicero found it politically advantageous to feign ignorance of *De rerum natura*—the strongest praise for the radical philosophy of Lucretius came from no less a poet than Virgil: "Happy the man who can know the causes of things, and has trampled underfoot all fears, inexorable fate, and the clamor of greedy hell."[58] Jefferson may have discounted much that he read in his eight editions, but what American has ever welcomed more fully the happiness that comes from gaining a scientific knowledge about "the causes of things," taking part in a successful revolution against "inexorable fate," and proclaiming religious freedom from the dogma of "greedy hell"? In the days of the dying Roman republic, Lucretius spoke as a prophet of light; at the dawning of the American republic, the ideals of the Enlightenment were tested by the mind and action of Thomas Jefferson.

There are many assumptions in the Declaration of Independence that stand in direct contradiction to the beliefs and goals of the Puritan vision of Christianity. Neither Winthrop nor Edwards would have agreed with Jefferson's idea of the Creator endowing men with "certain inalienable rights." Either representative of the Puritan conscience would have dismissed Jefferson's "self-evident" truths as dangerous examples of heresy. The assumption that "all men are created equal" was a direct challenge to the hierarchical order which most Puritans in the New World continued to support. Winthrop had argued that it was the wise providence of God to make some men "high and eminent" and others "mean and in subjection." Only with such differences in degree, Winthrop believed, could any political and religious structure be maintained. The principle of equality was also in conflict with the important Puritan belief in predestination. If a sovereign Judge has already chosen the few men who will be granted salvation, then the idea of equality is impossible. The crucial task for the Puritans was to distinguish the regenerate from the unregenerate; the radical inequalities of the Puritan community—restriction in church membership, citizenship, economic rights, etc.—often followed from that distinction. But Jefferson was a determined enemy of the old vision of hierarchical authority, and he boldly dismissed the idea of predestination as one of "the demoralizing dogmas of Calvin."[59]

The assumption that man is endowed with inalienable rights would have been seen by the Puritans as an attack upon the power of the Almighty. "Absolute sovereignty," wrote Edwards, "is what I love to ascribe to God."[60] The list of human rights suggested by Jefferson—life, liberty, and the pursuit of happiness—would not have impressed Edwards. If the descendants of Adam and Eve inherit the burden of original sin, then life is a pilgrimage through the valley of the shadow of death. If a jealous God may let the spider fall at any moment into the burning pit, then liberty is no more than a naive illusion. If accommodation with the Lord requires a humble denial of self, then the pursuit of happiness is no better than the worship of golden idols. Edwards preferred to be "humbled to the dust." But Jefferson believed that the Puritans were "mere usurpers of the Christian name, teaching a counter-religion made up of the *deliria* of crazy imaginations."[61] Jefferson wanted the American colonies to secure their liberty from the dogmatism of John Calvin as well as the tyranny of King George.

Jefferson's revolutionary campaign against "kings, nobles, and priests" often aroused the fear and anger of the established clergy. Especially in New England the attacks upon the "infidel" and "atheist" president were extremely bitter. "I am not afraid of the priests," Jefferson wrote, "they have tried upon me all their various batteries, of pious whining, hypocritical canting, lying and slandering, without being able to give me one moment of pain."[62] When the attacks upon his character and philosophy became more vehement, Jefferson's own bitterness, expressed in private letters, also increased. He was inclined to denounce all Puritans as a "band of dupes and impostors."[63] Nevertheless Jefferson did not abandon what he liked to refer to as the true "religion of Jesus." Instead he reserved his scorn for the historical churches, both Catholic and Protestant, condemning Saint Paul for being the "first corrupter of the doctrines of Jesus," and castigating John Calvin for being among the "impious dogmatists . . . , the false shepherds . . . teaching a counter-religion." It is the common strategy of men who want to promote a revolution to accuse their opponents of having betrayed the true faith. Thus Jefferson frustrated his pious critics by accusing them of "blasphemies" and "infidelity."

Setting aside the rhetorical warfare, what was Jefferson still willing to accept as the "religion of Jesus"? Late in his life he summed up his religious philosophy in a letter to a friend. "The doctrines of Jesus are simple," Jefferson wrote, "and tend all to the happiness of man."[64] There was no mention of the jealous, threatening God of the Puritans. Although nearly half a century had passed since Jefferson had first described the pursuit of happiness as an inalienable right, his religious philosophy was still in harmony with his revolutionary politics. Among the "doctrines of Jesus" that Jefferson was willing to accept, he did include the simple confession: "There is one only God, and He all perfect." Any vision of the Trinity was dismissed as impossible. The perfection of the single Deity was revealed in the rational order of the physical universe and the moral order of human nature. Although the divinity of Christ was rejected, and the miracle of resurrection was simply denied, the value of Jesus as a moral teacher was still retained. When Jefferson boldly rewrote the New Testament to suit his own religious philosophy, omitting any reference to miracle and superstition, he typically called the result *The Life and Morals of Jesus of Nazareth.*

The religious philosophy described by Jefferson in the letter to his friend did not require any faith in "the demoralizing dogmas of Calvin." Some reference was made to "a future state of rewards and punishments," but the vision of immortality was not defined, and the Puritan idea of a sovereign Judge was not mentioned. While the Puritans had mixed their love for God with fear and anxiety, Jefferson was convinced that "the Being who presides over the world is essentially benevolent."[65] How characteristic of Jefferson to reduce the jealous God of the Puritans to a single, impersonal, abstract "Being"!

Jefferson lived for exactly fifty years after signing the Declaration of Independence. Although he saw the later revolution in France lead to a reign of terror, he never doubted the justice of the republican battle against "kings, nobles, and priests." He remained true to the ideals of the Enlightenment: the critical attack of free inquiry upon the power of dogma, and the challenge of democratic equality to all political and religious tyranny. In the New World, at least, Jefferson hoped that the battle had been won. He regarded the creation of the American republic as the "last, best hope of man." The covenant with a high and powerful God had been exchanged for a social contract among free and equal men. In the final letter of his life, Jefferson proclaimed the victory of the Enlightenment over established religion: "The general spread of the light of science has already laid open to view the palpable truth, that the mass of mankind has not been born with saddles on their backs, nor a favored few booted and spurred, ready to ride them legitimately, by the grace of God."[66]

The success of the Revolution led to the vision of the American as a new Adam, taking paradise into his own possession, throwing off the rule of foreign masters both natural and supernatural, and then celebrating his new freedom and confidence. The aim of the Enlightenment had always been to reverse the Fall of Man. The progress of natural science and the rise of democratic expectations were two fronts in the campaign to free the human imagination from the bonds of original sin. No one appreciated the triumph of the Enlightenment in America more fully than Jefferson. "It is a part of the American character," he wrote, "to consider nothing as desperate—to surmount every difficulty by resolution and contrivance."[67] When man assumes the confidence and power to accomplish anything, paradise on earth becomes his goal, and the Puritan image of a sovereign God is then dismissed as improbable and unnecessary.

At the end of his life Jefferson believed that "there is not a young man now living in the United States who will not die an Unitarian." At the very same time young Ralph Waldo Emerson was preparing in New England to become a Unitarian minister. He started preaching in the year of Jefferson's death. Soon he was ordained junior pastor at the Second Church in Boston—the same church instructed in Puritan dogma for sixty-four years by Increase and Cotton Mather. But Emerson did not fulfill the prophecy of Jefferson. Instead he left the pulpit of the Second Church and began a long career of writing and lecturing that would add another chapter to the religious imagination in America.

5

TRANSCENDENTAL PROPHET

The blood of Puritan ministers was in the veins of Ralph Waldo Emerson. For generations his family had preached the Word of God in New England. His father, who died when Emerson was a young boy, had become the Unitarian minister of the First Church in Boston. Following the example of his father, Emerson was educated at Harvard College, and in 1829 he was ordained to preach as a Unitarian minister. But after three years he presented his resignation. "It is the best part of the man," he confided to his journal, "that revolts most against being a minister." Emerson's rebellion against the established clergy had been growing in his mind for a number of years. Two important public gestures dramatized his defiance: his resignation from the pulpit in 1832, and his strong attack on the preaching of historical Christianity in his Divinity School Address in 1838. Both gestures served notice that Emerson had come to believe that the goal of vital religious experience could best be achieved independently of established Christianity. Even the most liberal faith of the Unitarians was rejected as too cold and restrictive. The boldness of Emerson's break from organized religion inaugurated a new stage in the history of the religious imagination in America.

Emerson's revolt was inspired by three different philosophical sources: the idealism which he learned from Plato and Immanuel Kant, the worship of nature which he recognized in the writings of Carlyle and the English romantic poets, and the concept of self-reliance which came to Emerson as a mixture of democratic self-confidence and Yankee independence. All three influences came together in Emerson's mind to form the complex design of Transcendentalism. The origin of the term is uncertain, and its meaning, to say the least, is ambiguous. The term first gained recognition among the followers of Immanuel Kant. Although the label was often used derisively by unsympathetic observers, Emerson and some of his friends accepted the title as if it were a badge of honor. After leaving the Unitarian ministry Emerson devoted the majority of his long career to writing and lecturing on the principal themes of his new religion. Speaking to audiences from Maine to California, he became known as the leading philosopher and prophet of Transcendentalism. His essays soon gained recognition on both sides of the Atlantic. Matthew Arnold once praised Emerson as the author of the most important English prose written in the nineteenth century, and John Dewey cited Emerson as the only American philosopher worthy of being compared to Plato.

PLATO AND KANT

Emerson's study of Platonic idealism at Harvard provided him with a philosophical basis which he never abandoned. Emerson shared with Plato the sadness of a poet recognizing the mutability of nature, and the visionary desire of a philosopher wanting to affirm the permanence of beauty and truth. Plato had learned from Heraclitus to look at the world of sensible phenomena as a constant flux. "All is changing save the law of change," Heraclitus had said; "you cannot step in the same river twice." But Plato had also learned from Parmenides that the world of sensible phenomena may be apprehended as a mere shadow of the unchanging world of absolute Being, the unified and eternal One. Hence Plato speculated on the metaphysical nature of perfect "forms" or "ideas." Beautiful things in nature are subject to mutability, but the "idea" of beauty is immortal—"Time is a moving picture of eternity."

Emerson's first book, *Nature,* is an adaptation of Plato's basic dualism. "Nature," Emerson insisted, "is the symbol of spirit." An individual may transcend the flux of time if he becomes "conscious of a universal soul within or behind his individual life, wherein, as in a firmament, the natures of Justice, Truth, Love, Freedom, arise and shine."[1] Just as Plato transformed Socratic definitions into metaphysical "ideas," all the capitalized abstractions in Emerson's sentence become stars in the transcendental firmament of his imagination. The education of a philosopher, Plato said, requires "turning the eye of the soul" from the changing shadows of the natural world to the "universal light." This is the act of transcendent vision that informs the prophetic tone of Emerson's *Nature.* In one notorious paragraph Emerson compared himself to a "transparent eyeball" capable of seeing or feeling all "the currents of the Universal Being." In Plato's *Republic* the philosophers "come at last to their consummation . . . at which they must raise the eye of the soul to the universal light which lightens all things and is the absolute good."

Plato's rather vague and ambiguous definitions of the transcendent realm have baffled commentators for centuries. At times his "absolute ideas" are merely logical concepts, and at times they assume a metaphysical existence as transcendent realities. Emerson also had difficulty in naming and describing whatever was revealed to him in the act of transcendent vision. He used abstract nouns with capital letters— "Justice, Truth, Love"—without distinguishing them. At times he referred to the higher reality as the "Over-Soul" or the "Universal Being." Occasionally he used the word "God." Only then did Emerson reveal to what extent he was remaking some of Plato's philosophical ideas into a new religion. Whereas Plato had been content to describe the goal of education as "the vision of truth," Emerson wrote that "the intellect searches out the absolute order of things as they stand in the mind of God."[2]

Christianity, of course, from the very beginning had contained influences of Platonic mysticism. "The first and last lesson of religion," Emerson liked to remind his audience, is summarized in the words of Saint Paul: "The things that are seen, are temporal; the things that are unseen, are eternal."[3] In any system of philosophical or religious dualism, some rules must be defined for movement between the natural and supernatural. The novelty of Emerson's Transcendentalism resides in the accessibility of "the eternal One." All men, Emerson believed, may awaken their spirits to "apprehend the Absolute." In Plato's *Republic* only a few men ever receive the education required for a true philosopher, and even the select few are not ready for a "vision of the truth" until they reach the age of fifty. Writing in his early thirties, Emerson ignored Plato's emphasis upon preparation and maturity. Instead he associated the power of vision with the innocence and purity of youth. Emerson followed the Christian precedent: "Except ye be converted, and become as little children, ye shall not enter into the kingdom of heaven" (Matthew 18:3). According to Puritan doctrine, only the sovereign God may decide when to allow such a conversion. Emerson, however, believed that "a man is a god in ruins." He claimed that the failure of vision is the responsibility of man—"the ruin or the blank that we see when we look at nature, is in our own eye." The goal then for Emerson and other Transcendentalists was "to look at the world with new eyes." But how could that be possible?

Plato had described in the *Republic* the education required for a "vision of truth," but Emerson regarded that process as too long and exclusive. The Puritans had maintained that sinful man was powerless to effect his own redemption, that vision might only come as a divine gift; but Emerson refused to surrender himself to the whim of a sovereign God. The Unitarians could offer no assistance at all. They had accepted the psychology of John Locke and his picture of the human mind with all knowledge based upon the reception of sense impressions. The Unitarians were trying to defend historical Christianity with a rational analysis of biblical evidence. Professor Andrews Norton worked for years writing *The Evidence of the Genuineness of the Four Gospels.* But Emerson had no patience with Unitarian scholarship. He rejected the preaching of historical Christianity that "comes out of the memory, and not out of the soul." Emerson also recognized the limitation of the Lockean psychology. If the human mind is like a mirror which receives the sense impressions that are all determined by the properties of nature, what agency or power is available for transcendent vision? It is not possible "to look at the world with new eyes" if the act of seeing is determined mechanically by the properties of sense impression. Emerson required a model of human perception in which the mind itself could play a larger role in determining the nature of what is seen. He found his solution in the philosophy of Immanuel Kant.

In his *Critique of Pure Reason* Kant studied the scientific rationalism of the eighteenth century and attempted to state its shortcomings. Empirical science, Kant asserted, may describe the phenomenal world of sense impressions, but it cannot reveal the world in all its completeness. Knowledge of absolute reality would require a perfect mind unrestricted by human methods of perception and reflection. It is therefore necessary to rely upon intuition and faith for any hint of a reality beyond the reach of rational knowledge. "I have," wrote Kant, "found it necessary to deny *knowledge* of *God, freedom,* and *immortality,* in order to find a place for *faith.*"[4] The door was thus opened for men like Carlyle, Coleridge, and Emerson to promote a religion based on personal intuition rather than on reason and traditional authority. For almost a hundred years theologians had been trying to follow the thesis found in Locke's *Reasonableness of Christianity.* The Unitarians in New England had been in the vanguard of liberal Christianity by attempting to make their religion conform to rational statements. Many of the dogmas of Calvin had been abandoned in order to accommodate the demands of reason. But once Kant was able to demonstrate the limits of rational knowledge, men like Emerson could break openly from the Unitarians and celebrate once again the mystical resources of human nature.

Kant successfully challenged the mechanical design of human perception which was still accepted by the followers of Locke. The human mind is more than just a mirror, Kant argued; it has power of its own to affect experience. Where does the power come from? The mind, Kant answered, has its own spiritual resources. His claim was hardly original. Mystics of all kinds had suggested for centuries that the mind resembles a burning lamp, a soul alive with light and inspiration, rather than a passive reflector of sense data. By showing the limits of rational perception, Kant merely helped to revive interest in the old psychology of human faculties—the picture of the mind that had long predated the empiricism of John Locke. Hence in the philosophy of Kant a distinction was maintained once again between the rational faculty for perceiving the evidence of the phenomenal world, and the spiritual faculty for experience beyond the scope of reason. Whenever the spiritual faculty is enjoyed, claims are typically made about mystical contact with a higher reality, and the experience is often described with metaphors of light and fire. In the *Republic* Plato compared the illumination of soul to the eye beholding the light of truth—"The soul perceives and understands, and is radiant with intelligence." Emerson preached a "doctrine of inspiration" in his Divinity School Address; he recommended a "faith" that would "blend with the light of rising and of setting suns."

Kant was more cautious in identifying the inherent power of the mind than were many of his followers. While the professor at Königsberg used his logical ability to demonstrate the limits of rational knowledge, his disciples celebrated the increased significance of intuition and faith. While Kant attempted a systematic analysis of human consciousness, his followers showed their disdain for systems of thought and indulged their preference for mystical experience. It was also among Kant's followers—Herder and Jacobi in Germany, Coleridge and Carlyle in Britain, and Emerson in America—that the word "Reason" with a capital letter was used frequently in place of "intuition" or "faith." This intentional confusion of language occurred first in the writing of Jacobi. After identifying the spiritual faculty as "Faith" (Glaube), he substituted the word "Reason" (Vernunft), and then assigned the traditional use of reason for logical analysis to a lower faculty of the mind which he labeled the "Understanding" (Verstand). By using the word "Reason" to identify the inherent mystical power of the human mind, romantic philosophers were able to enjoy the best of both worlds—the natural and the supernatural. But the subordination of "Understanding" to "Reason," so popular among the followers of Kant, had been suggested long before in Plato's *Republic.* "Let there be four faculties in the soul," Socrates argued; "reason answering to the highest, understanding to the second," etc.[5] By adapting the old distinction to a new purpose, Emerson was able to describe the human mind as a double force, creative and reflective, capable of transforming the world as well as merely perceiving it. With all physical reality thus subordinate to the power of vision, Emerson was able to conclude his book on nature with amazing confidence: "Build therefore your own world. . . . A correspondent revolution in things will attend the influx of the spirit." The challenge of looking at the world with new eyes was advanced by the faculty of "Reason." With this power of transcendental vision, Emerson predicted, man will be "restored to perfect sight."

Emerson's idealism was shared and enjoyed by other members of the Transcendental Club, which met periodically in Boston and Concord. The club was organized in 1836, the same year as the publication of Emerson's *Nature,* and it consisted largely of young Unitarians like George Ripley and Orestes Brownson who were ready to spread the new gospel of Transcendentalism. Ripley defended Kant from "the charge of mysticism and obscurity," and Brownson praised Emerson as a "friend of truth, freedom, piety, and virtue."[6] But when Emerson brought his philosophy of inspiration to the graduating class of the Harvard Divinity School in 1838, the older generation of Unitarian ministers and scholars responded with outrage and condemnation. Andrews Norton, who had ruled the Divinity School when Emerson and Ripley were students at Harvard, felt obliged to publish his criticism of Emerson in a Boston public newspaper. Norton attacked Emerson's idealism as "the latest form of infidelity," and worried openly about "the disastrous effect upon the religion and moral state of the community."[7] Ironically, it had been Norton who had worked for years to establish a liberal Christianity independent of the harsh dogmas of Calvin. He was praised by Orestes Brownson for having "demolished Calvinism," and for having "made an end in all thinking minds of everything like dogmatic Protestantism."[8] But when Brownson went on to say that "Unitarianism itself satisfies nobody. It is negative, cold, lifeless, and all advanced minds among Unitarians are dissatisfied with it," the revolution against traditional Christianity was being carried further than Norton himself could understand or tolerate. Nothing surpasses the wrath of a liberal theologian who discovers that the next generation is ready to dismiss his opinions as old-fashioned and conservative. Norton complained bitterly that the truths of Christianity were being "abused in modern times by infidels and pantheists." The older generation of Unitarians rallied with Norton to defend their orthodoxy. The editors of the *Christian Examiner* declared that Emerson's idealism was "neither good divinity nor good sense." One polite critic encouraged all good Christians "to abhor and abominate R. W. Emerson as a sort of mad dog."

Much of the outrage was caused by Emerson's criticism of historical Christianity and his suggestion that the organized churches were responsible for the "universal decay and now almost death of faith in society." Stung by such charges, the older generation of Unitarians led by Andrews Norton attempted to assail the character and substance of the young Transcendentalists. "The characteristics of this school," wrote Norton, "are the most extraordinary assumption, united with great ignorance, and incapacity for reasoning." Emerson's Divinity School Address was dismissed as an "incoherent rhapsody." The foreign influences upon Emerson—"a strong infusion of German barbarisms"— were singled out as an easy target for scorn and censure. In all this rhetoric Andrews Norton could neither freely express nor fully disguise his acute sense of betrayal. Many of the young rebels had been his students at Harvard. The liberal challenge of Unitarianism had encouraged the translation of foreign books. Emerson's own father had helped to establish the Boston Athenaeum which made available the latest books and periodicals from abroad. Norton must have recognized with bitterness and chagrin at least some truth in the old charge that Unitarianism was a halfway house on the road to infidelity.

What had gone wrong? When the older generation of Unitarians had encouraged the study of literature and helped to establish libraries, they expected their children and students to read the philosophy of Locke and the literature of Augustan England. The poetry and philosophy of German and English romanticism had not been anticipated. When the next generation turned with enthusiasm to Carlyle and Goethe, when Emerson brought the "doctrine of inspiration" into the very citadel of Unitarian education, the editors of the *Christian Examiner* could only pray in vain: "Defend us from the wordiness and mysticism, which are pretending to be a better literature, a higher theology, and almost a new revelation."[9]

All efforts by men like Norton to turn back the tide of "infidelity" were doomed to failure. How could the older generation of Unitarians defend their rational theology and organized faith against the disdain of the Transcendentalists who placed inspiration above logical argument and independence above conformity to established religion? The Unitarians had learned how to use the philosophy of Locke to argue against the dogmas of Calvin. There is "no mode of establishing religious belief," Norton had written, "but by the exercise of reason, by investigation, by forming a probable judgment upon facts."[10] But the followers of Kant were claiming a spiritual faculty capable of witnessing divine truth without the help of rational study or scriptural authority. The logical arguments of the Unitarians were powerless to refute the Transcendental idealism of Emerson. Because the new inspiration was not limited to a systematic theology, and because it was not bound to any particular church, its influence could spread rapidly through the body of New England religion. Opponents did not know where to attack or how to stop its growth. Voices rose from the Harvard faculty warning of "a diseased admiration" of German philosophy, and a "sheer midsummer madness" of Transcendental enthusiasm. But attempts to ridicule "the unstable quagmire of mystic conjecture" only served to spread its influence. Gradually the generation of Andrews Norton passed away. After many years Emerson would be invited to speak again at Harvard. By then younger ministers were taking his heresies for granted.

Emerson never realized to what extent his Transcendental idealism might sabotage the authority of traditional Christianity. When he preached his "doctrine of inspiration" to the divinity students at Harvard, Emerson spoke as a prophet of visionary light—"Through the transparent darkness the stars pour their almost spiritual rays."[11] He meant to awaken his young audience to a mystical appreciation of "the light of rising and of setting suns." Emerson meant well. But he underestimated the heresy of his position. The reaction of older Unitarians like Andrews Norton was stronger and more abusive than anything Emerson had expected. Although they did not know how to confront Emerson's claims for the power of intuition and insight, the older Unitarian ministers sensed correctly that his idealism posed a direct threat to the order and authority of the established faith. They feared the consequence of replacing the rational psychology of Locke with the philosophy of Kant. If all men are allowed to rely upon their own intuition of divine power, Norton argued, the result will be confusion and anarchy.

When Emerson accepted the distinction between Reason and Understanding, he did not foresee how it would prove to be a two-edged sword. If the spiritual faculty may be exercised independently of any rational control, the reverse is also possible. Scientific analysis is then free to pursue its logical ends without any religious apology. For centuries traditional Christianity, Protestant and Catholic alike, had attempted to bring faith and reason together in harmony. The Unitarians in particular had been influenced by Locke's *Reasonableness of Christianity*. For more than a hundred years few people had followed Pascal's suggestion that the heart has its reasons which the mind cannot know. It was therefore a revolutionary strategy for Kant and Emerson to promote the separation of faculties. While it granted independence to faith and reason, it deprived both of the power that only a harmony of the two might produce. Given independent status, faith was set free to indulge any vision of mystical experience. Emerson could become a "transparent eyeball" and report within himself the "currents of the Universal Being." By separating faith and reason the many excesses of nineteenth-century evangelical religion were made possible. The appetite for visionary experience, unchecked by any rational control, could project Emerson and his followers to the dubious height of Shelley— "pinnacled dim in the intense inane"—while the power of rational understanding, released from any partnership with spiritual concerns, was free to extend its empirical control over the natural world. Emerson's attempt to breathe new life into the religious imagination of his contemporaries therefore enjoyed an ironic success. One supporter of Emerson declared that "no man who writes the English tongue has now so much influence in forming the opinions and character of young men and women."[12] But the more he inflated visionary expectations, the more the hopes of Transcendentalism lost any rational moorings and drifted away toward the improbable heaven of idealism. "He that has never doubted the existence of matter," Emerson liked to quote from Turgot, "may be assured he has no aptitude for metaphysical inquiries." The more Emerson inflated the claims of Transcendentalism, the less matter his new religion seemed to contain. The Christian God, affirmed by Puritans and Unitarians alike, melted away in the vapors of Emerson's Transcendentalism.

DIVINE NATURE

After separating religious experience from any basis in rational understanding, not to mention scriptural authority, Emerson did recognize the need to provide some empirical foundation for his Transcendental vision. He turned to the deification of nature so prevalent in the writings of Carlyle and the English romantic poets. Emerson followed Wordsworth in finding the joy of elevated thoughts in the "light of setting suns,/And the round ocean and the living air,/And the blue sky." After resigning as a Unitarian minister, Emerson traveled in Europe for almost a year. There he met and talked with Carlyle and Wordsworth. Plans for a book began to appear in Emerson's journal early in the year of his departure for Europe. But in listing the subject matter for nine different chapters, Emerson did not mention the word "nature." Although the proposed

topic for his first chapter was "the mind is its own place," Emerson
apparently had not yet located that place in nature. But after some
months of travel in Europe, and conversations with Wordsworth among
the lakes and mountains of Cumberland, Emerson began to refer in his
journal to a prospective "book about nature." Three years later five
hundred copies of *Nature* were published.

The influence of Carlyle and Wordsworth upon the philosophy of
Emerson has been the subject of considerable study. Emerson acknowledged in 1840 that "the fame of Wordsworth is a leading fact in modern literature." Of the many things that Emerson admired in the work
of Carlyle and Wordsworth, the sense of a divine presence in nature
left the strongest impression upon him. From the opening paragraph
of *Nature* to the close of his long career, Emerson continued to write
and lecture about the immanence of a divine power in the natural world.
At times the presence of divinity in meadow, grove, and stream inspired
the writer with an immediate visionary delight. At times Emerson confessed more difficulty in awakening the faculty of vision. But he never
entirely lost sight of the goal expressed by Wordsworth—"The earth,
and every common sight . . . Appareled in celestial light."

But was there anything dramatically new or different in the pantheism
affirmed by Emerson? Had it not been common a century earlier for
Jonathan Edwards to look for "images or shadows of divine things"
among the sights of nature? Was it not a basic tenet of the Christian
faith to look upon the natural world as the creation of God? Why
should nature not reveal signs of divine power? If Emerson was merely
discovering the force of God in nature, why were his critics so concerned that "an undisguised pantheism shall spread its poison through
our literature"? Still many of the established clergy in Boston were convinced that Emerson's talk about the presence of God in nature could
do nothing but compromise the traditional power of the Christian Deity.
Jonathan Edwards may have looked upon nature as a reflection of divine
power, but he never forgot the great distance which separated his infinite God from the natural creation. When that separation began to
disappear in the visionary enthusiasm of Emerson, his critics had cause
to be alarmed. They scoffed at what they took to be his equation of
the "religious sentiment" with "mountain air." They laughed at Emerson's attempt to proclaim "the identity of the law of gravitation with
purity of heart." But their ridicule was serious. Intelligent critics like
Andrews Norton saw clearly that Emerson was reshaping the image of
God in a superficial manner. The equation of divine power with the
natural world might inspire some to see the earth appareled in celestial
light, but what would happen to any remaining belief in the authority

and power of a sovereign Judge? Norton also wanted to know what would happen to the authority of Scripture and the rule of any established church. Emerson's willingness to abandon both elements of historical Christianity provoked the strong reaction to his Divinity School Address. Instead of depending upon the words of Scripture, Emerson told his audience to obey "the eternal revelation in the heart." Instead of spending time in church, Emerson encouraged his listeners to awaken their faith with "the flying cloud, the singing bird, and the breath of flowers." Wordsworth might have listened to the Divinity School Address with pleasure and approval; the Unitarian leadership of Boston could only respond with shock and outrage.

The promises of Transcendentalism were appealing to many people who did not know, or did not care, that they were accepting heresy. In his essay "Nature's Nation" Perry Miller wryly exclaims how many Americans in the nineteenth century turned to the enthusiastic worship of nature, and yet still insisted on calling themselves "Christians." After two centuries of defending their holy settlements against the wilderness of a new continent, Americans were ironically ready to make nature itself a principal source of religious experience. The early Puritans in Massachusetts would have been appalled. They had regarded the natural world as a trial that must be endured in order for the City of God to be created in the wilderness. The reevaluation of nature in the nineteenth century indicated a basic change in spiritual goals. The "city upon a hill" envisioned by Governor Winthrop was replaced with the vision of a natural paradise.

The heightened appreciation of nature dramatized in so much nineteenth-century art and literature represented more than a change in religion. It also meant a new recognition and acceptance of psychological impulses long repressed in the Puritan mind. The full revolutionary thrust of Emerson's recommendation of nature is evident when man's image of nature is understood to be a projection of his own inner wilderness of irrational desires. The Puritans had recognized the need to control and suppress such impulses if the image of a sovereign God was to be sustained. When Emerson called for the satisfaction of natural impulses, the result was a celebration of the ego and id at the expense of the superego. As more Americans in the nineteenth century moved toward a religion of nature, the psychological base for the sovereign God of the Puritans gradually disappeared.

The new psychological freedom implicit in Emerson's revolt against what he called "historical Christianity" was soon represented in the literature of his contemporaries. One immediate consequence of Emerson's reevaluation of nature was the burst of freedom, sensuality, and sheer blasphemy dramatized in Whitman's "Song of Myself." Even Emerson must have been slightly amazed at Whitman's striking irreverence—"I believe in the flesh and the appetites ... The scent of these armpits aroma finer than prayer,/This head more than churches, bibles, and all the creeds." But the complete acceptance of physical nature celebrated in Whitman's poetry was a logical consequence of Emerson's philosophy. His turning away from the psychological restraints and fears of the Puritan mind was a bold step toward the greater freedom of the twentieth century, and a significant advance in man's escape from the image of a threatening God.

SELF-RELIANCE

Is there a power in nature that causes men to report the experience of vision? Or does the power rest within the human sensibility itself? Can the experience of Transcendental vision be initiated and controlled by individual will? The romantic poets typically hedged their answers. Wordsworth, for example, described how the eye and the ear respond to nature in a double manner—"both what they half-create,/And what they perceive." Emerson likewise had difficulty in labeling the source of his inspired moments. "Yet it is certain," wrote Emerson in *Nature*, "that the power to produce this delight does not reside in nature, but in man, or in a harmony of both."[13] Despite the confident beginning of that sentence, Emerson concluded, like Wordsworth, by affirming some combination of man and nature. But the emphasis was usually upon man. In the Divinity School Address it was boldly declared that "man is the wonder-worker." The virtues of individuality, self-reliance, and non-conformity were all predicated by Emerson upon the divine spirit that may be awakened within each man and woman. The emphasis upon self-reliance was an integral part of Emerson's Transcendentalism.

Together with his philosophical idealism and his romantic vision of nature, Emerson's insistence upon individuality also disturbed the guardians of historical Christianity. Andrews Norton publicly assailed the arrogance and pride of the Divinity School Address. Other critics could not tolerate the way Emerson calmly placed his own intuition above the commands of Holy Scripture. One critic wrote scornfully that "he knows no more of the religion of the New Testament than Balaam's ass did of the principles of Hebrew grammar."[14] Emerson, however, refused to moderate his revolutionary claims for the power of individuality. Three years after the Divinity School Address he published a collection of essays which included "Self-Reliance." Again the importance of individuality was emphasized—"Nothing is at last sacred but the integrity of your own mind." Again the ministers of historical Christianity were put on the defensive.

Emerson's belief in the power of individuality may have been derived in part from romantic attitudes dramatized in England and Germany; Emerson gave some credit to Carlyle and Goethe, but nowhere did the virtue of self-reliance find a more enthusiastic welcome than in America. Emerson's doctrine of self-reliance was firmly rooted in the soil of democratic equality and nourished by the pioneer tradition of independent— "do-it-yourself"—enterprise. Emerson could also appeal to the native egotism and pride that had recently been strengthened by the success of the new republic. It is not surprising that leaders of American industry later in the nineteenth century often selected quotations from Emerson's "Self-Reliance" to decorate their office walls. Even his contemporaries hailed Emerson as "the most American of our writers" and praised him for representing the American "idea of personal freedom."

Emerson preached the virtue of individuality because he believed that an awakening to Transcendental vision could only occur as a result of personal inspiration. Each man must discover his own potential divinity. Emerson rejected all intermediaries. No organized church was necessary; none should be allowed to stand between man and his own divine power. No social regulation was necessary; none should be allowed to interfere with private inspiration. "Society everywhere," declared Emerson, "is in conspiracy against the manhood of every one of its members." Emerson knew that his stress upon individuality might pose a revolutionary threat to the law and order of the community. If all members of a society should act upon the principle that "no law can be sacred to me but that of my nature," the logical result would be division and anarchy. Emerson, however, discounted that possibility, because he felt that all men would discover within themselves the same divine force. Self-reliance would therefore lead to a general spiritual harmony. There was no real danger of social disintegration, Emerson declared, because the awakening to Transcendental vision would promote moral behavior. The essential goodness of man could be trusted. Puritan concern with original sin could be set aside, Emerson optimistically thought, because he believed instead in the idea of innate divinity.

Emerson thus completed a process of separation that had begun with the Reformation. Luther and Calvin had launched a determined attack against many of the intermediaries placed by the Catholic Church between man and God. The idols were broken and the saints abandoned. But the leaders of the Reformation had no confidence that man could find God by himself. The authority of Scripture was still necessary to establish the law of God, and a strong church was still required to administer the law to the world of sinful men. Emerson continued the thrust of the Reformation by challenging the authority of the last remaining intermediaries. He discounted the special revelation of Scripture, and disowned the command of any organized church. He declared instead the spiritual independence of all men to realize their own divine potential.

The possibility of direct contact with God, independent of church or Bible, had been strongly condemned by the original Puritans in New England. Vigorous attempts were made to suppress any form of the Antinomian heresy. When Anne Hutchinson claimed the mystical guidance of a private revelation, she was condemned as a heretic and banished to Rhode Island. When the Quakers claimed obedience to an "inner voice," they invited the fate of a public hanging. Such individuality could not be tolerated by a community of saints determined to uphold the authority of a sovereign and supernatural Judge.

But how could the heresy of private revelation be distinguished from the true reception of divine grace? The central Puritan experience of regeneration was not very different in appearance from the experience reported by Anne Hutchinson and the Quakers. The Puritans, nevertheless, saw that some distinction had to be maintained if the authority of their faith was to be preserved. Hence their vigilant attempt to protect the community of saints from the disruptive threat of heresy. But the attempt was doomed to failure. The appeal of private revelation was stronger than the authority of Scripture or the power of the organized churches. Two hundred years later Emerson could preach the doctrine of personal inspiration without fear or apology; he could almost make it sound respectable! The critical voices still opposed to the Antinomian heresy in the nineteenth century were outnumbered by the many individuals ready to accept the freedom of personal inspiration. Emerson should have been banished or hanged. Instead he was merely forbidden to speak at Harvard for a number of years.

His critics tried in vain to expose his errors, and to warn the public against the danger of his infidelity. Accusations of "nonsense and impiety" failed to stop the growing tide of interest in the ideas of Transcendentalism. Andrews Norton argued that Emerson's doctrine of personal inspiration was false and impossible. "There can be no intuition," Norton wrote, "no direct perception, of the truth of Christianity." But still Emerson spoke and wrote in tones of prophecy. The arrows of rational criticism failed to counteract the effect of his inspired rhetoric. Norton saw clearly that the rational basis of religion was threatened.

"There is," he stubbornly insisted, "no mode of establishing religious belief, but by the exercise of reason." But still Emerson continued to preach the divine power of man's intuition.

Even the calm voice of William Ellery Channing was finally raised in protest. Channing warned that all who followed Emerson in affirming the divine potential of man were "in danger of substituting private inspiration for Christianity." As minister of the Federal Street Church in Boston for almost forty years, Channing was a leading spokesman of Unitarianism in New England. The younger members of his church who joined with Emerson to form the Transcendental Club still continued to hold Channing in very high esteem. It was ironic that Channing felt obliged to warn against the religious claims of the Transcendentalists, because Emerson and his friends were often just developing hints of theology that were implicit in Channing's own sermons. As early as 1828 Channing had asked "how we obtain our ideas of God," and he answered in a sermon: "We derive them from our own souls. . . . In ourselves are the elements of the Divinity."[15] It was ten years later when Emerson expanded the same idea in his address to the graduating class of the Harvard Divinity School and the guardians of the Unitarian establishment expressed shock and outrage. Surely their dismay was mixed with some guilt. Channing also must have been haunted by the old charge that Unitarianism was a halfway house on the road to infidelity.

Emerson continued to preach "the eternal revelation in the heart" until his critics fell silent, and his radical individualism was taken for granted. The result was a further disintegration of the Puritan faith. "Nobody, who can help it," wrote a friend of Emerson's after the appearance of *Nature,* "preaches the old-fashioned doctrine of God's Sovereignty."[16] What would Jonathan Edwards have thought? Both the Puritan theologian and the Transcendental prophet reported the enjoyment of mystical experience. But Edwards never failed to acknowledge a supernatural God as the source of his inspiration, while a century later Emerson seldom looked beyond the divine potential of man and nature. "The beams of glory," Edwards always affirmed, "come from God, and are something of God, and are refunded back again to their original."[17] Emerson, however, described the visionary experience as a moment of personal omniscience. The individual becomes a "transparent eyeball" endowed with total vision—"Man is the wonderworker."

Centuries of tradition, both Catholic and Protestant, which identified human pride as a cardinal sin, were ignored by the optimistic vision of Transcendentalism. The doctrine of self-reliance transformed pride into a virtue. When the conceit of Satan prompted him to challenge the authority of God, the consequence was expulsion from Heaven. When Prometheus stole the heavenly fire to give to man, his punishment was endless torment chained to a rock. When Faustus exchanged his soul for godlike power, the end of his life was a dramatic exit through the jaws of Hell. But when Emerson recommended the divine potential of human nature to his willing contemporaries, his popularity as a lecturer and essayist continued to increase. Chastisement was limited to some angry controversy in the public journals. The threatening God of the Western imagination was no longer potent. The voice of the superego was almost silent. In its place reigned the new power of ego, the new respectability of pride. Emerson helped to turn the eternal damnation of Satan, Prometheus, and Faustus into a vision of Heaven on earth.

The impact of Emerson upon the religious imagination of his countrymen has not always been fully recognized. Some critics have attempted to dismiss Transcendentalism as a small local phenomenon only affecting a few intellectuals in Massachusetts. Others have attempted to limit Emerson's influence merely to his impact upon American literature. But the truth is suggested by Sydney Ahlstrom in his recent *A Religious History of the American People:* "The Emersonian message was not a mere softening of traditional doctrines, but a dramatic and drastic demand for a complete recasting of religious life and thought. . . . Emerson is in fact the theologian of something we may almost term 'the American religion.'"[18] Transcendentalism, of course, was never intended to be a coherent religion, but Emerson's idealism, his deification of nature, and his emphasis upon self-reliance attracted many followers among the descendants of Puritans and Unitarians alike. Many forms of mysticism received greater popularity thanks to the example set by Emerson. Evangelical revivals that occurred throughout the nineteenth century often owed more to Emerson's vision of personal inspiration than to Christian ideas of regeneration. Popular acceptance of the Kantian separation of faith and reason, the romantic attitude toward nature, and the doctrine of self-reliance did come together to form a new "American religion." Many of Emerson's contemporaries who adopted the principles of Transcendentalism, without much concern for logic and less knowledge of history, still continued to call themselves Christians.

Although Emerson modified his optimism somewhat in later essays, he never withdrew his support from the basic doctrines which had been announced in his early writings. Nor did he ever fully recognize the revolutionary impact of his own philosophy. He cheerfully recommended the worship of divine force in man and nature, without thinking much about the outraged ghosts of his own Puritan ancestors. It took the mind of Emerson's friend and neighbor Nathaniel Hawthorne to weigh the full implications of religious change. Hawthorne lived for awhile among the Transcendentalists at Brook Farm; he also lived in his imagination among the shades of seventeenth-century New England Puritans. In his short stories and novels he dramatized the tensions of the American religious imagination, the contrast of Puritan guilt with Transcendental optimism, the tensions that developed over two hundred years as Governor Winthrop's City of God was gradually replaced by Emerson's vision of a natural paradise. No author in the middle of the nineteenth century thought more deeply about his Puritan inheritance; no writer cast a more skeptical eye upon the Transcendental visions of his contemporaries. The next chapter in the history of the religious imagination in New England belongs to Nathaniel Hawthorne.

6

PURITAN ROMANCE
Nathaniel Hawthorne

Nathaniel Hawthorne is the first writer in this study of the religious imagination in America who was fully committed to the practice of literature. Although his short stories and romances often dramatize religious experiences, Hawthorne did not recommend any particular religious opinion. Types of behavior, both Puritan and Transcendental, are held up in his fiction for dramatic scrutiny. The complexity of Hawthorne's vision implies a skeptical temperament, a constant questioning of man's limited knowledge, rather than any confident resolution. Hawthorne possessed a very large measure of the "negative capability" which Keats attributed to Shakespeare—"capable of being in uncertainties, mysteries, doubts, without any irritable reaching after fact and reason."[1] Hawthorne brought to American literature a critical and psychological fascination with the very roots of religious behavior. He provided a skeptical and tragic analysis of the forbidden impulses, the secret guilts, the tormented pleasures of both the Puritan and Transcendental faiths.

Herman Melville was the first to see that "the world is mistaken in this Nathaniel Hawthorne. . . . He is immeasurably deeper than the plummet of the mere critic."[2] Hawthorne traveled to the heart of darkness before Conrad and Freud, and he was often embarrassed by what he saw there. Many of his friends and relatives were even less prepared to accept his symbolic projections. His wife responded to *The Scarlet Letter* with a "grievous headache" and Emerson simply lamented, "Ghastly, ghastly." Hawthorne sometimes tried to relieve his own anxiety by keeping from himself the full significance of his discoveries. What novel about the desires and guilts of forbidden passion is more

chaste than *The Scarlet Letter?* How could Hawthorne acknowledge
the themes of incest and patricide claimed by recent psychological
critics to be implicitly dramatized in the symbols of his fiction? But
Hawthorne did not frequently deceive himself. He knew that the
romance of Hester Prynne and Arthur Dimmesdale was a "hell-fired
story." He may have regretted the impossibility of softening the gloom
with at least a hint of "cheering light," but he did recognize the extent
of the darkness.

Although Hawthorne wanted to follow the truth of his own imagination, and usually could not help but do so, he also wanted to win and
hold a popular audience. Thus he sometimes made concessions to the
sensibility of his readers. He adopted artistic strategies of compromise,
indirection, and irony. His symbolic method allowed much to be implied that was not explicitly stated. His deliberate use of ambiguity
invited multiple interpretations. And sometimes his use of a naive story-
teller allowed the inclusion of a popular although inappropriate moral
ending. The voice near the end of *The Scarlet Letter* that tells us to
"Be true! Be true!" is an example of a naive commentator whose moral
conclusion does not begin to do justice to the complex story.

D. H. Lawrence suggested years ago that "the proper function of a
critic is to save the tale from the artist who created it." He encouraged
critics to look beyond the conventional moral in order to see the implicit direction of the story itself. Writing about *The Scarlet Letter,*
Lawrence warned, "You *must* look through the surface of American
art, and see the inner diabolism of the symbolic meaning."[3] The critics
who follow Lawrence's advice may sometimes act as if they are con-
fusing psychoanalysis and literary criticism; their discoveries of "inner
diabolism" may seem bizarre and eccentric; but without psychological
interpretation, without the drama of symbols, what is left of Hawthorne's
art? The critics who ignore Lawrence's advice and remain content with
the pointed moral conclusions, reduce Hawthorne's fiction to a single
dimension of minor interest. If Hawthorne is important to us, it is because he looked beyond the language of religious dogma and conventional morality. He wondered, for example, if the idea of original sin
had not been invented by man in order to allow for the masochistic
enjoyment of guilt. He dramatized the unholy pleasure of Dimmesdale's penance and the sexual jealousy in Puritan justice. For two centuries the best minds in New England had been arguing about matters
of religious belief. Hawthorne rendered much of the argument superfluous. With his dramatic fiction he cut through the level of controversy
to the underlying roots of motivation and psychological consequence.
Calvinist? Unitarian? Transcendentalist? What could such labels possibly

mean to a man who recognized how piety may be generated by sexual energy and conscience may be a mixture of fear and hypocrisy? Hawthorne was the first American writer to see how the reality of Heaven and Hell must be located merely in the human mind. He saw all religions as myths that are lived in secular time: fascinating, deceitful, and tragic.

Despite the evidence of psychological knowledge dramatized in so much of Hawthorne's fiction, a number of critics still want to attribute to Hawthorne a few simple and conventional beliefs. A choir of pious commentators all maintain that Hawthorne enjoyed an "unquestioned belief in God," that he also "believed in immortality," and that he had a "sure faith in Providence."[4] Nothing of the sort can be substantially demonstrated. His fiction does not reveal what beliefs he may, or may not, have possessed. "The man and the writer," commented Hawthorne's son, "were as different as a mountain from a cloud."[5] His many letters and journals play with various points of view without resolving the contradictions. His friends and family suggested differing visions of the man, often admitting the impossibility of knowing him well. A close friend at college, for example, wrote: "I love Hawthorne; I admire him; but I do not know him. He lives in a mysterious world of thought and imagination which he never permits me to enter."[6] When Hawthorne's only son read *The Scarlet Letter* after his father's death, he found himself "constantly unable to comprehend how a man such as I knew my father to be could have written such books."

Hawthorne's dramatic imagination was never without a sense of audience. His words and ideas were always selected and adapted to suit their expected readers. His short tales which appeared in the contemporary magazines were those most apt to have a conventional and inadequate moral which may well have been added to satisfy and deceive the popular audience. Melville was the first to recognize that Hawthorne "takes great delight in hoodwinking the world,—at least, with respect to himself." Even in his private journals Hawthorne often sketched observations in a dramatic manner as if the seeds of fiction were springing to life. His temperament was experimental and skeptical. Even his earliest letters to his family suggest a mind that plays with words and avoids commitment. Only when writing to his fiancée did Hawthorne indulge himself in religious language, and then he surely knew and enjoyed the very old tradition of praising a secular woman in terms of religious idolatry. That Hawthorne deeply loved his wife cannot be doubted; that he shared her churchgoing piety cannot be accepted.

Before entering college Hawthorne wrote to his mother about choosing a possible career: "I have not yet concluded what profession I shall have. The being a Minister is of course out of the Question. I should not think that even you could desire me to choose so dull a way of life."[7] After dismissing lawyers and doctors with the same impatience, Hawthorne went on to ask: "What do you think of my becoming an author, and relying for support upon my pen? . . . But authors are always poor devils and therefore Satan may take them." This early letter is remarkable, not only because it reveals Hawthorne's deep-rooted contempt for the ministry, but also because it shows that Hawthorne already at seventeen knew that he was damned to be a writer. His only god would be the muse of his imagination.

As a young child Hawthorne had been forced to attend church with his mother and sisters. The East Salem Church at the time was drifting toward Unitarianism. Religious services at college were also compulsory. Besides morning and evening chapel on weekdays, all Bowdoin students were required to attend three church services on Sunday. The minister was a pedantic and zealous Calvinist. The unpopularity of Parson Mead led to a minor rebellion among the students in which the Calvinist minister was hanged in effigy. Hawthorne's strong negative reaction to evangelical piety was expressed in many of his college letters. He was repeatedly fined and disciplined for "unnecessary walking on the Sabbath." In order to avoid attending church services he cynically developed the art of feigning "Sunday sickness." It was an art that he perfected during the rest of his life. Years later when his wife and daughters would go off to church, Hawthorne would prefer to go walking with his son. Non-attendance at religious services became a habit and a principle.

Hawthorne's aversion to ministers also remained strong and permanent. Even as a small boy he so disliked a bust of John Wesley that he tried to break it apart by freezing water inside. Neither "variety of the black-coated tribe," Calvinist or Unitarian, escaped Hawthorne's scorn. In 1842 he wrote: "I find that my respect for clerical people as such, and my faith in the utility of their office, decreases daily." When Hawthorne eventually became a distinguished consul in England, he took vengeance upon an American clergyman who appeared at the consulate in an advanced state of debauchery. Hawthorne preached to the reprobate until the poor sinner trembled with fear. It was one of the few sermons that Hawthorne ever enjoyed.

Hawthorne's abiding distrust of churches and clergymen was a symptom of his independence and skepticism, but it did not guarantee a total absence of religious faith. Emerson after all had just been recommending the virtue of private inspiration. He had complained that the churches were an obstacle to faith; open worship in the temple of nature was preferable. Hawthorne also asked why anyone should expect to find God's presence in the "pent-up nook" of a Puritan church instead of "kneeling beneath the awful vault of the firmament." But Hawthorne felt just as uncomfortable with the inspiration preached by Emerson as he did with the Calvinist faith of his ancestors. He saw the spiritual pride and self-delusion of both public and private worship. His skeptical mind could not draw confidence from any religious creed. "We certainly do need a new revelation," he wrote, "for there seems to be no life in the old one." Hawthorne still made no attempt to discourage the churchgoing piety of his wife and daughters, perhaps because he saw the futility, even the cruelty, of disturbing their customary ways. Furthermore he recognized and feared the unhappy consequence of imposing one human will upon another. He dramatized such domination in tales like "The Birthmark" and "Endicott and the Red Cross." Hawthorne was therefore careful not to impose his own thoughts upon his family. His son recalled that the common words of religion—"God, Christ, salvation"—were hardly ever mentioned in the home. Religious discussion was avoided to such an extent that Julian Hawthorne was unable to say for sure what denomination of faith the family was supposed to profess. "Unitarian seems the most likely," wrote Julian after his father's death, "but what Unitarianism I was never told, or asked, or knew, except that it was good Bostonian."

Hawthorne understood and accepted the fact that his family and most of his friends could not share his skepticism. He gave to them whatever he could without compromising the integrity of his tragic vision, and he enjoyed in return their love and support. But few American writers have recognized more fully the essential solitude of the creative imagination. Only one man in the middle of the nineteenth century had the unique credentials to probe the disguises of Hawthorne's mind. Herman Melville was able to know Hawthorne as a friend and as a fellow writer. Their lives crossed briefly during the strategic center of both careers, and Melville recorded the following observation:

> There is a certain tragic phase of humanity which, in our opinion, was never more powerfully embodied than by Hawthorne. We mean the tragicalness of human thought in its own unbiassed, native, and profounder workings. We think that into no recorded mind has the intense feeling of the visable truth ever entered more deeply than into this man's. . . . There is the grand truth about Nathaniel Hawthorne. He says NO! in thunder; but the Devil himself cannot make him say *yes*.[8]

Hawthorne was dismayed by the centuries of theological debate that had consumed so much of the spirit of New England. The portraits of Puritan divines stared down at him from the walls of the Old Manse which he rented in Concord—the very same house in which Emerson had written his "Essay on Nature." Hawthorne also loved the woods and fields surrounding the Old Manse, but he could not escape from history, he could not turn optimistically to the natural surroundings. Instead he confronted the faces of the past, including his own ancestors; he wanted to understand the roots of their passion, the dark secrets of their cruelty and strength. Hawthorne doubted the existence of their God; he was indifferent to their dogma of salvation; he did not share their belief in the presence of the invisible world of devils, witches, and angels; to all dogma he said "NO! in thunder"; but he recognized the common roots of such fantasies in human nature, and he was fascinated by their power. Hawthorne did not want to add another chapter to the theological debate of his ancestors. Unlike Emerson he did not come forward with a new faith. Instead the author of *The Scarlet Letter* had the imagination and the art to dramatize the psychological forces of conscience: the fear, piety, vengeance, repression, and spiritual pride.

Hawthorne's understanding of human nature was supported by three habits of thought: introspection, observation, and historical study. Each form of analysis served to reinforce the others, and all three together supplied Hawthorne with the images and characters for the dramatic speculation at the heart of his fiction.

Introspection had been of central importance to the education of the early Puritans in New England. It was still common at the beginning of the nineteenth century for educated men and women to keep a private record of their thoughts and feelings. Like many of his ancestors and contemporaries, Hawthorne also kept a personal journal. But he did so with a difference. The Puritans were required to keep a diary in order to record their transactions with a sovereign God. They were instructed to watch their souls for hints of grace or signs of damnation. In the nineteenth century the Transcendentalists also filled their private journals with the hopeful progress of their inspiration. But Hawthorne wandered further into the dark labyrinth of mind. His journals offer little consolation; they are descriptive and analytic. Uncertainty, paradox, irony, all tend to replace the traditional praise for the growth of a faltering soul. Hawthorne's introspection should be recognized as a form of dramatic speculation. He was not just a moralist looking at the virtues and faults of human nature. He was not just a psychologist trying to understand their motives and consequences. He was more importantly an artist finding in the depths of his own mind the themes and images of his fiction.

Hawthorne was especially familiar with the value and danger of introspection. For almost a dozen years after college he devoted himself to the lonely mastery of his own creative skills. Many of his short stories dramatize the curse of solitude. But it could not be avoided. Hawthorne understood, like Freud some generations later, that knowledge of human psychology begins with deliberate self-analysis. Hawthorne also recognized, like Freud, the terrible price of such knowledge. "No one," wrote Freud, "who, like me, conjures up the most evil of those half-tamed demons that inhabit the human breast, can expect to come through the struggle unscathed."[9] Hawthorne's best-known picture of that struggle is the drama of Hester Prynne accepting and suffering her own solitude: "Thus, Hester Prynne . . . wandered without a clew in the dark labyrinth of mind; now turned aside by an insurmountable precipice; now starting back from a deep chasm. There was wild and ghastly scenery all around her, and a home and comfort nowhere."[10] Translate the gothic scenery into psychological terms, and what becomes evident is a portrait of Hawthorne's introspective struggle.

The second habit of thought that supported Hawthorne's analysis of human nature was his practice of close observation. He filled his notebooks with detailed accounts of men and events. Despite the time required for the solitary quest of his art, Hawthorne also maintained a number of social and political contacts. At college Hawthorne made friendships that lasted throughout his life. The political patronage jobs that came his way then enabled Hawthorne to observe the contemporary world of commerce and politics. His introduction to *The Scarlet Letter* is a notorious result. Time spent at Brook Farm enabled Hawthorne to see first hand the aspirations and mistakes of the Transcendentalists, and to gather detailed material for *The Blithedale Romance.* During his years in Europe Hawthorne developed into an indefatigable sightseer. Whole sections of *The Marble Faun* are borrowed from observations recorded minutely in his journals. Although Hawthorne did not think of himself as a novelist bound to standards of realism, his creation of psychological romance could not have been possible without his deliberate power of observation.

And finally Hawthorne studied history. He devoted himself in particular to the records of New England. He read such books as Cotton Mather's *Magnalia Christi Americana* and Felt's *Annals of Salem.* He confronted the shadows of his Puritan ancestors, and he discovered common psychological designs. In the drama of Puritan justice he recognized the disguised enjoyment of repressed desires. The magistrate who whips the back of a Quaker woman smiles with the pleasure of sexual appetite poorly disguised as righteous punishment.

The minister who torments himself with guilt secretly enjoys the pleasure of his martyrdom. The Puritans and the Quakers are locked together in a vicious cycle of punishment and masochism. For Hawthorne the history of the early Puritan colonies in New England provided a microcosm of human behavior. The more extreme the behavior—persecution, torture, hanging—the better for Hawthorne's dramatic and tragic art. All the evidence of human depravity needed by any writer could be found in the records of Boston and Salem. Hawthorne dramatized the repressed instincts; he explored the roots of Puritan strength and righteousness; he wrote the psychological history of those early colonies established to glorify the Puritan God.

PURITAN HERITAGE

Hawthorne added to the religious imagination in America by altering its history. In the middle of the nineteenth century while many Americans were ready to ignore their Puritan ancestors, others with foolish pride were at work creating the sentimental legend of the first Pilgrims and the Mayflower—a fake temple was built on Cape Cod in 1867 to hold the meaningless Plymouth Rock. Hawthorne was almost alone with his tragic vision of the past. He was neither indifferent nor sentimental as he confronted his prominent ancestors. He knew they would not approve of him: "No aim, that I have ever cherished, would they recognize as laudable; no success of mine . . . would they deem otherwise than worthless, if not positively disgraceful" (*Scarlet Letter,* p. 10). But Hawthorne returned their disapproval. He saw the terrible "cruelties" inherent in their "mode of glorifying God." He granted them a lasting notoriety, not quite the Heaven or Hell they had anticipated, when he turned their dark history into his own dramatic art.

The first Hathorne to come to America crossed the Atlantic with John Winthrop in 1630. He may have been in the congregation to hear Winthrop's sermon about the building of "a city upon a hill." William Hathorne served the Bay Colony as a major in the Salem militia and a legislator in the Massachusetts House of Delegates. He contributed to the building of Jerusalem in the wilderness by acting as a strict prosecutor "with informers ever moving among the people in search of criminals."[11] Any symptom of crime was treated with sadistic punishment. Among the available legal tortures were burning, maiming, branding, and hanging. William Hathorne became the most dreaded magistrate in the Bay Colony, and before long even Governor Winthrop and John Cotton felt obliged to restrain his zeal for promoting moral rectitude.

While his civil and religious sadism was practiced against all sinners, whose crimes varied from manslaughter to "wanton dalliance," his special torture was reserved for Quakers. One woman of the "accursed sect," found guilty of walking naked on the streets of Salem, was sentenced by William Hathorne to be tied to a cart's tail and whipped through the towns of Salem, Boston, and Dedham. Two hundred years later Nathaniel Hawthorne studied the accounts of his first American ancestor with fascination and horror. "The figure of that first ancestor, invested by family tradition with a dim and dusky grandeur, was present to my boyish imagination, as far back as I can remember. It still haunts me, . . . this grave, bearded, sable-cloaked, and steeple-crowned progenitor,—who came so early, with his Bible and his sword. . . . He had all the Puritanic traits, both good and evil (*Scarlet Letter*, p. 9).

Hawthorne was appalled by Puritan injustice. His books often display — the instruments of torture and persecution: whipping post, stocks, scaffold, and gallows. All this cruelty in the service of God intensified Hawthorne's sense of dramatic irony. He recognized the terrible union of religious dogma and civil power—the righteous strength of his first ancestor who came "with his Bible and his sword." Hawthorne also recognized that much of the harsh punishment was actually a way of vicariously enjoying the very passions that were condemned. Consider his description of how the Quaker woman was whipped in public:

> And there a woman,—it is Ann Coleman,—naked from the waist upward, and bound to the tail of a cart, is dragged through the Mainstreet at the pace of a brisk walk, while the constable follows with a whip of knotted cords. A strong-armed fellow is that constable; and each time that he flourishes his lash in the air, you see a frown wrinkling and twisting his brow, and, at the same instant, a smile upon his lips. He loves his business, faithful officer that he is, and puts his soul into every stroke, zealous to fulfil the injunction of Major Hawthorne's warrant, in the spirit and to the letter. There came down a stroke that has drawn blood! Ten such stripes are to be given in Salem, ten in Boston, and ten in Dedham; and, with those thirty stripes of blood upon her, she is to be driven into the forest.[12]

The smile upon the lips of this faithful officer who loves his business and puts his soul into every stroke (What kind of faith, love, and soul?) is Hawthorne's way of dramatizing the sadistic pleasure of the Puritan constable. Hawthorne never underestimated the degree of implicit sadism in the image of the vengeful Puritan God. He saw how the early Puritans had magnified the image of supernatural power in order to enjoy their own cruel delight in punishment. The abuse of the flesh, whether inflicted by the constable upon the Quaker woman, or, in the case of Dimmesdale, by the guilty minister upon himself, was required to satisfy the demands of a jealous God. Hawthorne revealed the exercise of punishment as a mixture of sexual fear and vicarious satisfaction. That is why a frown crosses the brow of the constable and "at the same instant" there is a smile upon his lips. Hawthorne wondered if man's fear of his own potency does not encourage him to create the threatening image of an omnipotent God. Fear and passion, guilt and pleasure—Hawthorne continued to dramatize their strong combination in the Puritan soul.

If William Hathorne was a "bitter persecutor," his son John Hathorne inherited his Puritan zeal. He served as one of the three judges in the Salem witchcraft trials in 1692. "He made himself so conspicuous in the martyrdom of the witches," Hawthorne wrote of his great-great grand-father, "that their blood may fairly be said to have left a stain upon him" (*Scarlet Letter,* p. 9). It was a family tradition that one of the poor victims had pronounced a curse upon Judge Hathorne and his posterity. "God will give you blood to drink!" shouted the condemned witch from the gallows.

Hawthorne knew that he could not escape "the deep and aged roots" which his family had struck into the soil of New England. "I felt it al-most as a destiny to make Salem my home." The witches had all been hanged more than a hundred years before Hawthorne's childhood in Salem, but the shadow of Gallows Hill still captured his imagination. In one of his earliest short stories, "Alice Doane's Appeal," Hawthorne dramatizes the madness of witch hunting. "I strove to realize," declares the narrator of Hawthorne's story, "the deep, unutterable loathing and horror, the indignation, the affrighted wonder, that wrinkled on every brow, and filled the universal heart." Hawthorne first describes the frightened victims of the persecution on the way to their execution at the top of Gallows Hill:

> . . . here tottered a woman in her dotage, knowing neither the crime imputed her, nor its punishment; there another, distracted by the universal madness, till feverish dreams were remembered as realities, and she almost believed her guilt. One, a proud man once, was so broken down by the intolerable hatred heaped upon him, that he seemed to hasten his steps, eager to hide himself in the grave, hastily dug at the foot of the gallows.[13]

Hawthorne's sympathy for these pathetic victims is tempered with an understanding of their own weakness and delusion. They are being hounded to death with terrible injustice, but they cannot escape sharing to some extent the "madness" of their persecutors. The first victim is lost in dotage and ignorance; the second cannot distinguish reality and feverish dreams; the third is ready to hasten his own death. Complete innocence is rarely presented in Hawthorne's fiction. He knew too much about the complementary nature of sadism and masochism, too much about the shared guilt of persecutor and victim; he knew the ignorance, feverish dreams, and madness of the human imagination.

Hawthorne next describes the false witnesses who have claimed to be afflicted by the sorcery of the witches:

> Behind their victims came the afflicted, a guilty and miserable band; villains who had thus avenged themselves on their enemies, and viler wretches, whose cowardice had destroyed their friends; lunatics, whose ravings had chimed in with the madness of the land; and children, who had played a game that the imps of darkness might have envied them, since it disgraced an age, and dipped a people's hands in blood.

Hawthorne's ancestor was one of the three judges who listened to the false testimony of these villains, cowards, and lunatics. He never doubted the existence of witches, and he never regretted the sentences of death that he righteously pronounced. If the Devil was active in Salem, as the Puritan judges devoutly believed, then God's justice had to be done—the witches had to be executed on Gallows Hill. But whose side was the Devil on? Hawthorne turned the charge back upon the judges themselves. There is much that Hawthorne could not explain about persecution, scapegoats, and human sacrifice, but he did understand that the Devil is merely a way of describing certain impulses of human nature, and that the Puritan judges, unable to recognize or to admit the evil in themselves, acted out their destructive instincts by sacrificing their helpless victims. Hawthorne saw how a dogmatic belief in the supernatural existence of devils could allow the real demons of human nature to hold power in disguise. Puritan justice was more than the pleasure of sadism; it was the punishment of sexual instinct dictated by the tyranny of the superego. And the instincts being punished were simultaneously being enjoyed. The Puritan judges held an orgy of witch hunting to purify the land.

After describing the sad procession up Gallows Hill, Hawthorne adds a harsh portrait of Cotton Mather:

> In the rear of the procession rode a figure on horseback, so darkly conspicuous, so sternly triumphant, that my hearers mistook him for the visible presence of the fiend himself; but it was only his good friend, Cotton Mather, proud of his well-won dignity, as the representative of all the hateful features of his time; the one blood-thirsty man, in whom were concentrated those vices of spirit and errors of opinion that sufficed to madden the whole surrounding multitude.

Why did Hawthorne attach all the responsibility for the public hysteria to this one figure of Puritan authority? Hawthorne must have known that his bitter picture of Cotton Mather was not accurate as history. In fact Cotton Mather did not play a central role in the hanging of the accused witches. But Hawthorne singled him out for special blame, because Mather could symbolize all the zealous qualities of the Puritan tempera-ment, and it was the union of religious dogma with political authority that Hawthorne identified as the worst evil. Cotton Mather is therefore presented as the Devil himself. Hawthorne altered the details of history in order to reveal the psychological design. The delusions of the crowd, victims and false witnesses alike, are inspired by the "vices of spirit and errors of opinion" at the heart of Puritan orthodoxy. Cotton Mather is placed on a horse, "darkly conspicuous" and "sternly triumphant," to demonstrate how the devilish father of Puritan authority presides over the saturnalia of violent repression. The tormented procession of sinners and persecutors on its way to the top of Gallows Hill is a ritualistic pro-logue to the most familiar scene in Christian mythology. The Puritan judges in this case have decreed the sacrificial murders—"pouring out sanctified blood as an acceptable sacrifice upon God's altar." Hawthorne did not hesitate to indict the God of the Puritans for demanding human blood. The excuses of Cotton Mather are reported by Hawthorne with ironic scorn—"for listen to wise Cotton Mather, who, as he sits there on his horse, speaks comfortably to the perplexed multitude, and tells them that all has been religiously and justly done."[14]

After describing the persecution of the Quakers and the hanging of the witches, Hawthorne proceeds to offer a grotesque vision of the funeral of Governor Bradstreet. Punishment, sacrifice, and death thus form a dark trinity of Puritan obsessions. If Hawthorne revealed with bitter irony the pleasure his ancestors took in whipping Quakers and hanging witches, he increased his scorn for the "grisly jollity" of Puritan funerals. The obsequies of Governor Bradstreet are described in terms of satanic revelry. The pallbearers are drunk and stagger with the coffin. The mourners enjoy many a draught of spiced wine and "tread on one another's heels." Even the nose of the Puritan minister, "through which he has just been delivering the funeral discourse," appears to glow "like a ruddy coal of fire." Hawthorne turns history into black comedy in order to dramatize the ironic deceits of the Puritan conscience. The salvation of Governor Bradstreet is the public excuse for the funeral celebration, but the violence of human appetite is the private explanation. The tyranny of justice built upon severe repression forces all physical desire to adopt various self-righteous disguises. Beyond the rituals of persecution and sacrifice is the ultimate celebration of death. Dimmesdale in *The Scarlet Letter* is another Puritan more than half in love with easeful death. His favorite medicine is made of dark weeds grown in a graveyard. Beyond his self-inflicted punishment is the goal of martyrdom. His legacy—"the law we broke!—the sin here so awfully revealed!"—is summed up at the end by the symbol on a dark gravestone. The dance of death at the funeral of Governor Bradstreet is also far from a celebration of immortality; it is a revelry of morbid desire, a drunken expression of forbidden pleasure. "New England must have been a dismal abode for the man of pleasure," Hawthorne concludes sarcastically, "when the only boon-companion was Death!"

Why should any god smile upon the rituals of punishment and sacrifice conducted in his name? What kind of god would be honored by the human celebration of death? In Hawthorne's account the God of the Puritans is a jealous parent who will not suffer the independence of his offspring. Self-assertion is a crime; sexual knowledge is guilt; life's only enjoyment is preparation for death. Hawthorne was appalled by the negative force of the Puritan morality. His stark psychological vision of the "vices of spirit" practiced by his own ancestors helped to blacken the image of the Puritans passed on to our century.

Persecution, sacrifice, death—Hawthorne's description of the early Puritans in America is narrow and relentless. And given Hawthorne's habit of calling "Puritanic" or "Calvinistic" most character traits—bigotry, righteousness, cruelty—which he found repugnant, it is highly ironic that some critics have seen fit to call Hawthorne in turn a "Puritan." The charge is not altogether mistaken. Hawthorne certainly did not share the dogmas and the delusions of the people he condemned, but after describing the repressive deeds of his ancestors Hawthorne does admit that "strong traits of their nature have intertwined themselves with mine." The similarity was first drawn in a famous comment by Herman Melville:

Whether Hawthorne has simply availed himself of this mystical blackness . . . or whether there really lurks in him, perhaps unknown

to himself, a touch of Puritanic gloom,—this, I cannot altogether
tell. Certain it is, however, that this great power of blackness in
him derives its force from its appeals to that Calvinistic sense of
Innate Depravity and Original Sin, from whose visitations, in some
shape or other, no deeply thinking mind is always and wholly free.[15]

Hawthorne, who possessed little interest and less belief in abstract doctrines, shunned theological debate. But his imagination was drawn
repeatedly to the subjects of temptation, guilt, and shame. Without
believing literally in the biblical story of the Fall of Man, Hawthorne
recognized the "great power of blackness" in human nature. In searching
the labyrinth of spirit for marks of secret guilt, Hawthorne was as relentless and anxious as the seventeenth-century Puritans. But he saw the
dark charade of human passion rather than the rigid imprint of supernatural fate. He saw adultery, torment, and masochistic pleasure rather
than the abstract doctrine of original sin. Hawthorne was not a Puritan;
he merely understood the psychological truth condensed in some of the
Calvinist dogmas. Hawthorne was remembered at his funeral, Emerson
later reported, for having "shown a sympathy with the crime in our
nature," and for having "done more justice than any other to the shades
of life."[16]

The tragic errors of human nature are dramatized repeatedly in Hawthorne's fiction; he knew how Paradise had been lost; but he did not
share the Puritan faith that it could ever be regained. The Puritans, who
followed the theology of Calvin, were able to balance the doctrine of
original sin with the hope of Christian atonement. But the public and
private writings of Hawthorne almost never include a reference to Christ.
Hawthorne explored the subtle passions and deceits of the human spirit
without anticipating any divine redemption. When Hester Prynne, at the
climax of *The Scarlet Letter,* asks the dying minister to look into eternity,
Dimmesdale talks instead about the sin they have committed on earth.
The heart of Hawthorne's tragic vision is the irreversible loss of Paradise.
His characters are unable to find happiness in this existence or any other.

TRANSCENDENTAL CONTEMPORARIES

Hawthorne's abiding sense of evil set him apart from the majority of his
contemporaries. He could not share the optimism of the present because
he knew so much about the shared darkness of the past. His skeptical
understanding saw through the self-deceptions of the Transcendentalists.

The cool relationship of Emerson and Hawthorne is a familiar story. Although the two men, almost the same age, lived near one another at times in Concord, and talked to one another upon many occasions, a sharing of deep intellectual concerns never developed. Emerson was unable to fathom the reticence of Hawthorne. "He said so little," Emerson complained after Hawthorne's death, "he gave no indications." Hawthorne, from his point of view, probably thought that Emerson talked too much. When offered a free ticket to one of Emerson's lectures, Hawthorne politely but firmly declined the gift.

Hawthorne's marriage to Sophia Peabody tempted him to make closer ties with the Transcendentalists. His wife had once believed that "Mr. Emerson is the greatest man—the most complete man—that ever lived." Her sister operated a bookstore which circulated the latest Transcendental literature. But Hawthorne resisted the pressure. He did invest in Brook Farm during his engagement to Sophia, but life at the utopian community soon confirmed his skepticism. The social gospel of the Transcendentalists seemed just as naive to Hawthorne as their religious enthusiasm. The other participants at Brook Farm believed in human progress toward the realization of a utopian community; they were convinced that man could redeem himself. But Hawthorne, with his understanding of inherited guilt, remained skeptical of human improvement. "There is no instance," he wrote, "in all history, of the human will and intellect having perfected any great moral reform by methods which it adopted to that end."[17]

Hawthorne's cynical indifference to the gospel of progress is dramatized in "Earth's Holocaust"—a brief story that serves as a satire of typical reform movements. The narrator of the story tells how a great bonfire was built in the middle of America to consume at once all of the obstacles to human perfection. Democratic reformers tossed into the bonfire all symbols of aristocracy and royalty. Temperance leaders added to the flames great barrels of liquor and bales of tobacco. Advocates of universal peace witnessed the destruction of weapons and munitions. But the success of all the reformers does not result in the dawning of paradise. Instead the zeal for purification leads to wanton destruction. Soon the best achievements of civilization are sacrificed on the bonfire. Literature and art and constitutional laws are turned into smoke and ashes. What began as a celebration of human improvement concludes as a riot of ignorance and vengeance. Thus Hawthorne dramatizes the hidden vice, the human pleasure in destruction, that often masquerades as the ideal of progress.

At the end of "Earth's Holocaust" the narrator offers another reason for the impossibility of significant reform. Even if the visible signs of guilt could all be eliminated, without a fundamental change in human nature, the progress would soon be undone. The heart itself must be transformed, Hawthorne's narrator implies, otherwise it will produce again "all the shapes of wrong and misery." And the "heart," one of Hawthorne's terms for the unconscious, is described as a "foul cavern . . . wherein existed the original wrong, of which the crime and misery of this outward world were merely types."[18] The psychological journey into the heart's darkness, a typical Hawthorne theme, heads in the direction of the "error at the very root of the matter."

Hawthorne's distance from his optimistic contemporaries is measured further in "The Celestial Railroad"—his nineteenth-century imitation of Bunyan's *Pilgrim's Progress.* Hawthorne satirizes his fellow country-men who expect their faith in progress to smooth the way to Paradise. In "The Celestial Railroad" Hawthorne ridicules "the traveller of liberal mind and expansive stomach," the modern pilgrim, who counts upon reaching Paradise without effort or inconvenience. Hawthorne was scorn-ful of easy routes to salvation, either the individual redemption suggested by the Transcendentalists or the conventional formula for salvation preached by the evangelical descendants of the Puritans. All clergymen who believed that a person can effect his own salvation seemed to Haw-thorne to be appealing to man's vanity and delusion. "The reverend clergy," says the narrator of Hawthorne's satire, "are nowhere held in higher respect than at Vanity Fair."[19] Hawthorne especially distrusted the romantic notion of the Transcendentalists that private inspiration could serve as the power of redemption. After suffering ample exposure to the Kantian metaphysics of Emerson and Thoreau, Hawthorne took his revenge in "The Celestial Railroad" by introducing a great monster, a German by birth, called "Giant Transcendentalist." This "ill-proportioned figure, . . . a heap of fog and duskiness," reports Haw-thorne's narrator, "makes it his business to seize upon honest travel-lers, and fat them for his table with plentiful meals of smoke, mist, moonshine, raw potatoes, and saw-dust." Small wonder that Hawthorne and Emerson could never enjoy full confidence with one another.

While Emerson and the Transcendentalists were pouring new op-timism into the religious imagination of America in the 1830s and 1840s, Hawthorne was already at work on his tales of psychological insight and religious satire. The bright confidence of the Transcenden-talists merely inspired black doubts in the skeptical mind of Hawthorne. What separated him profoundly from his optimistic contemporaries was his knowledge of sin and evil. "I have never been able," Emerson con-fessed, "to make evil seem real to me." But the shadow of evil, Hawthorne believed, like the black veil over the face of the Puritan minister in one of his stories, could not be ignored or removed. Hawthorne was able to praise Emerson as a poet of beauty and tenderness, but "sought nothing from him as a philosopher." Emerson likewise wrote in his journal that Hawthorne's fiction was "not good for anything." The inability of these two neighbors in a small New England town to come to any mutual understanding of their revolutionary ideas amounts to more than just an irreconcilable difference of temperament; it indicates a fundamental division of the religious imagination in the middle of the last century. From Emerson and Thoreau descend a host of modern visionaries, nature enthusiasts, and individualists, ready to save themselves, if not the world, with their own inspiration. From Hawthorne descend the existential philosophers of guilt and passion, unable to spare themselves, or the world, from the dark knowledge of psychological insight and skepticism.

RENAISSANCE TRAGEDY

Hawthorne should be recognized as America's first author of tragic literature. Unable to share the optimistic vision of the Transcendentalists, and unable to believe in the divine redemption expected by the Puritans, Hawthorne dramatized fictional characters trapped in a cycle of sin and guilt. If tragedy requires a conflict or dilemma that is incapable of resolution, neither the Transcendentalists, believing in the innate goodness of human nature, nor the Puritans, believing in the possibility of supernatural grace, were able to imagine a tragic conflict. But Hawthorne was prepared to meet the requirements of tragedy: his characters neither ignore the reality of evil, nor can they possibly escape from it.

Tragic literature is apt to come in the evolution of a culture when the religious imagination of a people is disturbed by skepticism or doubt, when the quest for truth has moved away from dogmatism and toward a dramatic analysis of human psychology. The best example is Shakespearean tragedy. When the religious certainties of the Middle Ages were challenged by the new knowledge of the Renaissance; when the dogmas of medieval Catholicism were unsettled by the skepticism of Machiavelli and Montaigne; then Shakespeare could dramatize a tragic hero like Hamlet caught in a world of corruption and doubt where nothing is certain and "readiness is all." Hamlet wants to believe in the "special providence" which determines the "fall of a sparrow," but his world has suddenly become unsettled by questions that he cannot resolve. Even the relative value of life and death is uncertain. Hamlet's discovery of sexual corruption and ambitious murder—the source and consequence of original sin—fundamentally disrupts his faith in any special providence. The shock to his conscience tends to paralyze his will, and Hamlet can only purge evil from his corrupt world by following the commands of his ghostly father. After the seeds of vengeance issue forth as multiple murder, Horatio may piously hope that "flights of angels" will sing the Prince of Denmark to his rest, but Hamlet's own curiosity about death has caused him to ask the gravedigger: "How long will a man lie i' th' earth ere he rot?" When mortal knowledge of this kind is able to cancel religious expectation, the result is the vision and drama of tragic literature.

Hawthorne's position at the religious crossroads of the American imagination corresponds to the position of Shakespeare in the English Renaissance. Both authors could reveal the psychological depths of human nature by dramatizing contemporary skepticism against a background of religious certainty. Hamlet's questions about the relative value of life and death render problematical a thousand years of Catholic dogma. Hester Prynne's thoughts about the "consecration" of her adulterous passion contradict the seventh commandment and thus disturb the basic certainty of Puritan law. Both characters are trapped in the hopelessness of a tragic dilemma. Hamlet cannot escape the corruption of his world; the poisoned weapon is waiting for him at the end. Likewise Hester Prynne cannot leave behind the shadow of her guilt; the black gravestone with the scarlet letter becomes her final symbol. Although both characters are conscious of how the world is fatally marred—"The time is out of joint"—such tragic knowledge cannot save them.

Melville was the first to compare Hawthorne to Shakespeare. In a review of Hawthorne's work in the *Literary World* in 1850, Melville emphasized the psychological depth of both writers:

> Now it is that blackness in Hawthorne, of which I have spoken, that so fixes and fascinates me, . . . this blackness it is that furnishes the infinite obscure of his background,—that background, against which Shakespeare plays his grandest conceits, the things that have made for Shakespeare his loftiest, but most circumscribed renown, as the profoundest of thinkers.[20]

It was Melville's almost simultaneous discovery of the tragic literature of Shakespeare and Hawthorne that supercharged his own imagination for the writing of *Moby-Dick.* The renaissance of American literature in the middle of the nineteenth century, as F. O. Matthiessen knew, was more than just a special flowering of native genius; it was the rebirth of tragic vision in the consciousness of the New World.

A full example of tragic literature appeared first in New England with the publication in 1850 of Hawthorne's *The Scarlet Letter*. The story has been variously interpreted by critics who often neglect its place in the history of America's religious imagination. Hawthorne's own contemporaries were puzzled by the book. Some, who read beyond the bitter satire of the introduction, simply joined Emerson in shaking their heads and murmuring, "Ghastly, ghastly." Other readers praised the book for dramatizing Puritan morality and confirming the righteous punishment of sin. Still others, with Transcendental opinions, allowed themselves to sympathize with the natural passion of Hester Prynne, and praised her as an early martyr for the liberation of women. Such contradictory interpretations, both Puritan and Transcendental, still exist in twentieth-century criticism. A reading of the novel as a tragic drama depends upon their ironic combination—"ironic" because the two points of view are religious opposites, and "tragic" because they are, according to Hawthorne, inseparable.

The true Renaissance character in the book, the only figure to achieve full tragic stature, is Hester Prynne. Although she lives among seventeenth-century Puritans in the fictional world of Hawthorne's romance, she was created in the middle of the nineteenth century for an audience far removed from the righteous bigotry of early New England. The group of Puritans awaiting Hester's appearance at the beginning of the book exchange comments of such harsh intolerance that readers are quickly moved to sympathize with the helpless victim. The sympathy turns to curious admiration when Hester mounts the scaffold with the infant in her arms and reveals the scarlet letter embroidered with "so much fertility and gorgeous luxuriance of fancy." Hester then stands on the scaffold as a mixture of pride and shame. The audience of Puritans is startled to see how "her beauty shone out, and made a halo of the misfortune and ignominy in which she was enveloped" (*Scarlet Letter*, p. 53). Hawthorne was probably the first American author to suggest a possible halo around the head of a beautiful adulteress. Is she a sinner or a saint? Or paradoxically has she saved herself by the advantage of a fortunate fall? Is it fair to punish her for having violated the seventh commandment? Is it right to honor her for believing that her passion has a "consecration" of its own? Such questions echo throughout the book. Critical answers tend to divide between Puritan and Transcendental points of view. The former critics side with Dimmesdale and praise his ultimate rejection of Hester. The latter critics sympathize with Hester and blame an intolerant society for persecuting a heroine of nature.

The central ambiguity of Hawthorne's book is the meaning of the adultery committed by Hester Prynne and Arthur Dimmesdale. Among the records of the early New England colonies, Hawthorne may have noticed that at least one helpless woman was branded with the letter *A* as a punishment for adultery. At the beginning of *The Scarlet Letter* some of the Puritans waiting around the scaffold recommend that the "brand of a hot iron" be put to Hester Prynne's forehead. Still others wish that Hester could be put to death. They feel certain that her sin is a crime against God and a threat to the order of the community. From the Puritan point of view there is no question about her guilt; the only argument is about the severity of the punishment. Some part of Hester's nature must accept the Puritan judgment against her. "She knew that her deed had been evil," reports the narrator of the story; "she could have no faith, therefore, that its result would be for good" (*Scarlet Letter,* pp. 89-90). She was enough of a Puritan herself to live and die at the edge of that righteous community.

But from the beginning of the book it is also clear that her shame is mixed with pride. Her token of punishment has been changed with gold thread into a badge of defiance. She stands upon the scaffold with a "natural dignity and force of character" that set her above the meanness of her persecutors. With the child in her arms, the narrator remarks, one might even mistake her for the "image of Divine Maternity." What is the nature of Hester's superiority? Is she presented as a fatal temptress or a beautiful fertility goddess? When Hester Prynne is together with Dimmesdale in the dark forest, she casts off the scarlet letter, removes her Puritan cap, and with the appearance of her long dark hair, there comes a moment of natural splendor. Her smile appears to shine from "the very heart of womanhood," and it is matched by a sudden flood of sunlight that breaks through the dark woods. The central strength of Hester's character is her impulsive and passionate nature. She is the wild rose condemned to grow and die in the black earth of the Puritan community.

Hester is a divided character: her intelligence has been conditioned by Puritan training to accept the moral judgment that is made against her, but her emotions remain impulsive and passionate. The romantic part of her nature continues to believe in the value of her relationship with Dimmesdale. Hester stays for seven years within range of her persecutors, to some extent because she accepts their punishment, and to some extent because she wants to remain close to her secret partner in adultery.

The division within Hester's character represents in dramatic form the crossroads of the religious imagination. Although her ego and id together are resolved upon independence and passion, her conscience cannot permanently escape the moral commands of the Puritans. Two centuries of changing attitudes are condensed into Hawthorne's story. The Puritans in New England had attempted to exalt the superego to a position of absolute tyranny. The voice of a sovereign God was supposed to be heard in the individual conscience giving commands—"Thou shalt not commit adultery!"—that could be ignored only at the cost of damnation. But the Puritans had gradually discovered that no degree of exhortation or punishment could enforce the complete tyranny of the superego. After thousands of sermons, repeated trials, and too many executions, the evidence of sin continued to increase. Puritan ministers eventually grew weary of predicting the end of the world. In the meantime the vision of a New Jerusalem in the wilderness fell victim to its own prosperity. As the temptations of this world became more attractive, the negative voice of the superego began to wane. By the middle of the nineteenth century, the Transcendentalists were able to complete the shift of religious value away from the Puritan conscience with its strict moral restraints and sovereign God. By promoting the ego under the banner of self-reliance, and by liberating the forces of the id in order to celebrate nature, the Transcendentalists effectively sabotaged the control of the superego. Hester's act of adultery could then be seen by Transcendental readers as an heroic defiance of the antiquated and repressive moral code of the Puritans.

The conflict of forces within Hester creates the intensity of tragic drama. Hester yearns for a greater freedom, she even travels abroad for a while, but she returns to live out her days by the edge of the Puritan community. The symbol of her guilt is inescapable. Hawthorne did not imagine, like some of his neighbors in Concord, that freedom from guilt could be found in a hopeful future. He recognized, fifty years before Freud, that the psyche may be understood as a battleground of conflicting forces. Hawthorne saw how the Puritan attempt to subordinate all impulses to the superego had been futile and perverse. He also saw that the contemporary celebration of the ego and id was vain and dangerous. The Puritans hoped that strict obedience of their sovereign God might give them a future in Heaven. The Transcendentalists believed that Paradise could be found on earth. But Hawthorne saw the psychic battle as unending. Hence the tragic vision of *The Scarlet Letter.*

Hawthorne was careful to place Hester Prynne at the crossing point of the Puritan and Transcendental attitudes. Consider, for example, the consequence of her adultery. It creates two relationships that control her future conduct. She is bound to Dimmesdale with ties of guilt and secret passion. And she becomes the mother of little Pearl—the scarlet letter incarnate. Although Hester is willing to live and die for each of these people, in fact she cannot influence either. Both Dimmesdale and Pearl must work out for themselves the different consequences of adultery. For the Puritan minister the consequence is death. The scarlet letter becomes etched into his flesh until his weak body gives up the ghost. He torments himself with guilt and hypocrisy until he confesses and dies on the scaffold. For Pearl the consequence is freedom from all law and restraint. Conceived beyond the Puritan community, Pearl becomes the innocent child of the forest. She grows in natural beauty and independence, the virtues of Transcendentalism, until she is ready to escape across the ocean. Both Dimmesdale and Pearl finally leave Hester behind. She can neither die with the Puritan minister nor live, except briefly, with her liberated child. If the act of adultery has caused the death of the minister, and created the life of the girl, it has left Hester Prynne suspended between death and life—forced to witness the disintegration of her man and the development of her child without being able to change or join either. Halfway between the two people with whom she should have the most intimate ties, Hester knows the tragic meaning of lonely and helpless solitude.

Another measure of the conflict between Puritan and Transcendental can be found in the different attitudes toward nature. The Puritans described by Hawthorne look with fear upon the dark forest as a region inhabited by wild beasts, Indians, and devils. The wilderness represents the unconscious mind with all its threatening forces of irrational desire and secret passion. When the Puritan minister travels into the woods, he is tempted to commit adultery. In another Hawthorne story a typical young Puritan is attracted deeper into the forest until he leaves his faith behind and joins the black communion of the Devil. In the wilderness the Puritan learns that his moral code was only a disguised whisper from the Devil. All apparent virtue is then revealed as a counterfeit display of evil. The worst fear of the Puritan is the prospect of watching the clear rules of the superego succumb to the confusion of the unconscious.

The Transcendentalists, however, were ready to welcome the irrational celebration of nature. In *The Scarlet Letter* it is young Pearl who feels completely at home in the forest. When questioned by the Puritan authorities about her origin, Pearl replies that she "had been plucked by her mother off the bush of wild roses." Even the fox and the wolf in the forest recognize "a kindred wildness in the human child." When

Pearl walks among the dark trees, she is accompanied by a ray of sunlight. Small wonder that Pearl is able to transcend the cares of the Puritan community. "I have no Heavenly Father!" says Pearl impulsively. She is not bound by the commandments of the superego. Pearl is free.

Where does Hester stand in relation to the dark woods of the unconscious? Hawthorne places her carefully between the town and the forest. She lives in a small cottage at the edge of the Puritan community. She is able to come and go in the town as well as the forest, but she cannot feel at home in either place. She has broken the moral code of the town, and she can never achieve the complete freedom or satisfaction of the forest. Her position between the Puritan community and the surrounding woods dramatizes once more the irresolvable conflict within her character.

Hester also stands in the middle of the debate between allegiance to the community and individualism. Despite his brief experience in the forest, Dimmesdale never loses his position as moral and religious leader of the Puritan community. All his individual desires are finally sacrificed to the demands of Puritan conscience. Hester's attempt to revive his independent spirit is doomed to failure. When the dying minister exposes the scarlet letter to the amazed crowd, his individual character disappears in the ritual of public confession. His young daughter, however, remains independent of all Puritan control. Despite the instruction urged by Governor Bellingham, and provided by Hester, Pearl remains the "elf-child" of the forest. Her instinctive hatred of Puritan society protects her independence. "No law," wrote Emerson, "can be sacred to me but that of my nature." Such is the self-reliant philosophy of young Pearl.

Hester can neither surrender her will totally to the community nor achieve complete independence. The scarlet letter is her passport into areas of lonely speculation. She entertains thoughts that might "undermine the foundations of the Puritan establishment," but she continues to live with compromises. She broods like Hamlet about the basic value of life and often yearns for death. "Was existence worth accepting, even to the happiest among them? As concerned her own individual existence, she had long ago decided in the negative, and dismissed the point as settled" (*Scarlet Letter*, p. 165). She feels the paralysis of will that accompanies tragic vision. Her native resolution is also sacrificed to the pale thoughts which possess her troubled mind. Unable to identify with the corrupt worlds in which they live, neither Shakespeare's tragic character nor Hawthorne's can rest content with alienation. Both desire to know if their solitude will end with the grave. "What dreams may come," Hamlet wants to know, "when we have shuffled off this mortal coil?" And Hester with her last words to Dimmesdale asks the same question: "Thou lookest far into eternity, with those bright dying eyes! Then tell me what thou seest?" Neither character is quite willing to accept the common religious answer provided by his or her community. Hamlet, who knows how a dead king "may go a progress through the guts of a beggar," doubts that angels will ever sing him to his rest. And Hester, who "had wandered, without rule or guidance, in a moral wilderness," doubts that eternal damnation is the certain punishment for her adultery. But neither character is able to find a replacement for the orthodox answer that has become unacceptable. Hamlet constantly probes the meaning of death. The mocking grin of Yorick's skull tells him everything and nothing. Hester likewise is unable to resolve her doubts. She cannot see beyond the "dark labyrinth of mind." Both tragic characters have broken from the certainties of the past; they are individuals released from any collective myth, and therefore neither has a predictable or hopeful future.

Hawthorne found himself in a similar position. The religion of his ancestors, by the time he wrote *The Scarlet Letter,* had long ceased to provide credible answers. His contemporaries were already celebrating the triumph of individual will and natural inspiration. But Hawthorne could find little satisfaction in the new freedom. Like Hester he was uncertain about sexual morality; he lived between the town and the forest, between attraction to the public world and the solitude of his own imagination. He knew too much about guilt and passion to enjoy the optimism of his contemporaries. Among the contradictions of the past and present, like Shakespeare, he found the substance for his tragic art.

After his last meeting with Herman Melville, Hawthorne summed up the religious uncertainty of his old friend: "He can neither believe, nor be comfortable in his unbelief; and he is too honest and courageous not to try to do one or the other."[21] The summary also reveals much about Hawthorne. With little faith in the religion of his Puritan ancestors, and with less sympathy for the naive substitute offered by his contemporaries, Hawthorne was caught between the past he largely repudiated and a very indifferent future. Reluctantly, often with pious complaints to the contrary, he continued on his psychological and imaginative journey into the depths of passion and guilt. Following the path of his own fictional character, Hawthorne "wandered without a clew in the dark labyrinth of mind: now turned aside by an insurmountable precipice; now starting back from a deep chasm. There was wild and ghastly scenery all around . . . and a home and comfort nowhere." After *The Scarlet Letter* Hawthorne wrote three further romances and attempted to write three more. The frustration and decline of Hawthorne's late years is a familiar story. It follows predictably from the irresolvable conflicts in the tragic drama of Hester Prynne. Only *The Scarlet Letter,* among all of Hawthorne's writing, stands fully at the religious crossroads of the American renaissance.

On his final Atlantic passage Hawthorne told a friend that he would like "to sail on and on forever, and never touch the shore again." With his creative talent splitting apart, and his country on the verge of civil war, it is hardly surprising that Hawthorne saw "a home and comfort nowhere." Only one of his contemporaries possessed the necessary genius and the courage of the imagination to "sail on and on." The most daring and successful adventure of the American renaissance was the voyage of Herman Melville.

7

THE SACRED HUNT
Herman Melville

In America, observed de Tocqueville in 1831, "religious insanity is
very common." The proliferation of new Christian sects in the nineteenth century led to a babel of competing and conflicting prophecies.
To all appearances Herman Melville took almost no part in the frenetic
religious activity of his age. While his contemporaries were preparing
for the coming millennium, forming missionary societies to convert
the world, finding gold tablets left by the angel Moroni, transforming
revivalism into frontier vaudeville, and splintering the remnants of the
Puritan faith into a confusion of different claims, Melville was hard at
work transforming his own experience into narrative fiction. While his
contemporaries were busy advocating moral reform, temperance, the
abolition of slavery, communal living, salvation through camp meetings,
free love, graham crackers, and Christ, Melville was exploring the religious
depths of his own mind. Although Melville had almost no influence upon
the spiritual imagination of his fellow Americans in the middle of the
nineteenth century, it now seems clear in retrospect that Melville's
art is the most complete drama of religious speculation recorded by any
heir to the Puritan vision.

Melville charted his own voyage from "Luther's day . . . to Darwin's
year." He recorded the tides and storms of religious yearning and defiance. Melville traveled in his own mind to the "wondrous depths,
where strange shapes of the unwarped primal world glided to and fro
before his passive eyes." And most important of all, he dared to "draw
out Leviathan with a hook." The voyages of Melville, literal and imaginary, extended American thought into new reaches of psychological,
anthropological, and religious vision.

146

The shadow of Calvinism fell strongly upon the young mind of Herman Melville. He was subject, like Hawthorne, to the dogmas and piety of his mother's Puritan faith. He was required to attend church services at the old North Church in Albany, which his mother officially joined when the grief and ordeal of early widowhood strengthened the narrowness of her orthodox convictions. The theology of the Dutch Reformed Church, with the doctrine of original sin very much in prominence, had remained substantially unaltered since the Synod of Dort in 1619. "Therefore all men," Melville was taught, "are conceived in sin, and are by nature children of wrath, incapable of any saving good, prone to evil, dead in sin, and in bondage thereto." It is not surprising that Melville later praised Hawthorne for that "great power of blackness in him" that derives its force from "that Calvinistic sense of Innate Depravity and Original Sin."

The early exposure to Calvinism left Melville, like Hawthorne, with more than a vision of potential evil; it left him with an abiding distrust and contempt for the ministers of orthodox dogma. Melville's suspicion of clergymen and missionaries was later confirmed when he witnessed how the attempt to bring Christianity to the natives of the South Pacific actually brought "disease, vice, and premature death." When Melville satirized the missionaries in his early novels, he provoked a minor outburst of indignant criticism. The scandal, no doubt, intensified his anticlerical feelings; it also helped to sell additional copies of his first books.

Melville's famous substitute for Harvard and Yale was half a decade of sailing before the mast. He worked his way across five oceans on a merchant ship, three whaling ships, and a man-of-war. Emerson and Hawthorne had received a formal education in language and literature that was unavailable to Melville, but he received a firsthand education in the extraordinary dangers of nature that no other American writer could equal. Only six years after Emerson published his essay about the transcendental pleasures of the natural world, Melville was living for a few weeks among cannibals in the Typee Valley of the Marquesas Islands. His vision of nature in the South Pacific—"the universal cannibalism of the sea"—canceled any hope of his ever accepting the optimistic conclusions reached by men like Emerson. Any Transcendental faith in the benevolence of nature could only seem to Melville to be the result of innocence, naiveté, or wishful thinking. Melville was traveling in the South Pacific at the same time as Charles Darwin, and they were both fascinated by the constant warfare among all forms of life. For both men it was an education in primitive history. The shock and dismay reported in Darwin's *Journal of Researches* . . .

during the Voyage of HMS Beagle around the World was finally muted into the scientific objectivity of his later *Origin of Species.* But Melville could not reach the calm waters of scientific detachment. His moral and religious sensibility remained outraged by the realization that unending combat is the fundamental law of existence. The religion of his childhood had promised a natural world, however fallen it might be, that could still reflect the intelligence of a sovereign and just Creator. But in the South Pacific, among the uncatalogued creatures of the deep, Melville saw the face of chaos. During a moment of anguished reflection in *Moby-Dick,* the doomed captain of the whaling ship witnesses "the horrible vulturism of earth" and questions the ultimate cause: "And all the time, lo! that smiling sky, and this unsounded sea! Look! see yon Albicore! who put it into him to chase and fang that flying-fish? Where do murderers go, man!"[1] The voyage from "Luther's day" to "Darwin's year" left Melville with more questions than he could answer.

If all creatures are destined to prey upon one another in their fight for survival, then hunting and killing are chief among the primitive shaping forces of the human imagination. Anthropologists have long studied how ancient patterns of hunting led to rituals of slaughter and then to religions of animal and human sacrifice. Fear and veneration of the hunted animal, often endowed with the qualities of a totem beast, are at the root of the religious imagination. The invention of primitive gods followed the worship of sacred animals. Although the study of anthropology was just beginning to mount its first assault on the parochial limits of the Christian myth at the time of Melville's death, he anticipated many of the results. The years spent on a whaling ship, hunting and killing the great beast of the ocean, awakened in Melville's imagination the "strange shapes of the unwarped primal world." Witnessing the killing of the whale, followed by the "cutting-in" or stripping of the blubber, and then the "trying-out" or boiling the flesh into oil, Melville knew the whole process of animal slaughter. Although he lacked the scientific background and temperament to order his perceptions with the systematic logic of Charles Darwin, his imaginative record of experience retained such an integrity of fact and detail that even Sir James Frazer later praised the accuracy of Melville's description. In telling the full truth about whale hunting, Melville was able to dramatize some of the oldest rituals of his tribe.

What does the hunting of whales have to do with the religious imagination? It is probably true that few of the seventeen thousand men working aboard the American whaling fleet in the middle of the last century would have been aware of much connection. For them whaling was merely a dangerous and sometimes profitable industry. In the days before petroleum the whale oil was needed to keep the lamps of America burning. But Melville saw the whale hunter as the modern descendant of Job and Perseus and Saint George. Who dares to draw out Leviathan with a hook? Who has the power to slay dragons? Who endures the storm of angry gods and vindicates the heroic will of man? Melville saw that hunting the dangerous beast is the primitive activity that shaped the human imagination into rituals of fear and reverence. He also saw that hunting is a male display of potency and the necessary will to dominate nature. When the ritual of sacrifice is consummated aboard the whaling ship with the cutting-in and trying-out of the animal carcass, Melville describes the hellish scene as the visual equivalent of Ahab's mad religious passion: "Then the rushing Pequod, freighted with savages, and laden with fire, and burning a corpse, and plunging into that blackness of darkness, seemed the material counterpart of her monomaniac commander's soul" (*Moby-Dick,* p. 354). When Ahab dares to slay the sacred animal or totem beast, he asserts the potency of his own proud will; he tests the power of blasphemy. When Ahab fails to kill Moby-Dick, he proves the fatality of the ultimate hunt.

Melville opens "the great flood-gates of the wonder-world" to witness the mythic beasts of the primitive imagination: the ocean serpents, the dragons, the great leviathans. Just as Hawthorne used the image of the dark forest to represent the depths of the unconscious mind, Melville uses the ocean with its uncatalogued wonders. To voyage in pursuit of the whale is therefore to hunt what Melville calls "the image of the ungraspable phantom of life." The image of the hunted animal has been transformed into a mysterious and haunting presence in the unconscious mind. Melville's narrator confesses that he is unable to explain how this transformation has taken place: "How all this came to be—what the White Whale was to them, or how to their unconscious understandings, also, in some dim, unsuspected way, he might have seemed the gliding great demon of the seas of life,—all this to explain, would be to dive deeper than Ishmael can go" (*Moby-Dick,* p. 162). But this disclaimer of knowledge comes only after a descent into the unconscious, fifty years before Freud, that is unsurpassed in its intuitive boldness.

When the hunted animal is transformed into a psychological image— "the ungraspable phantom"—it assumes qualities of divine power that suggest the mystery and wrath of Jehovah. Some critics of Melville's novel have objected to the association of divine qualities with the brute animal. Critics like Lawrance Thompson, anchored in the Christian tradition, can only accuse Melville of blasphemy. From their point of view it seems wicked or absurd to endow a sperm whale with any of the attributes of God. But Melville understood how the image of the hunted beast is associated in the primitive mind with fabulous and divine powers. He suspected that all gods are the created myths of the human imagination in contact with the wonders and terrors of nature.

When the image of the hunted animal has been transformed into a "phantom" in the mind of the hunter, the quest for the mysterious prey threatens to draw the hunter into a labyrinth where he is lost or into a vortex where he is drowned. Either symbol suggests the ultimate danger of the psychological quest. Long before the whale hunters in *Moby-Dick* are buried beneath the great shroud of the sea, Melville warns of the danger and futility of hunting the psychological image: "But in pursuit of those far mysteries we dream of, or in tormented chase of that demon phantom that, some time or other, swims before all human hearts, . . . they either lead us on in barren mazes or midway leave us whelmed" (*Moby-Dick*, p. 204).

Why should frustration and death await the man who goes in pursuit of "far mysteries" or "that demon phantom"? (What other terms could Melville use to hint at his mixture of psychological and religious truth?) Insofar as the image of the hunted animal has been endowed with sacred qualities, the hunt has become blasphemous, and the hunter is destroyed because he dares to overreach himself. The totem animal cannot be killed. The hunter is appropriately lost in vengeance and pride. But there is a more important reason why the hunt is ultimately self-destructive. When the image of the hunted animal is transformed into a "phantom" in the hunter's mind, it is mixed with the hunter's idealized picture of himself. "In our own hearts," Melville wrote, "we fashion our own gods," and Melville knew that the heart is a mirror of private wishes and fears—the "phantom" is not only the hunted animal, it is also a reflection of self. That is why Melville announced at the beginning of *Moby-Dick* that the story of Narcissus is "the key to it all." The Greek youth is drowned in the attempt to reach his own image: "And still deeper the meaning of that story of Narcissus, who because he could not grasp the tormenting, mild image he saw in the fountain, plunged into it and was drowned. But that same image, we ourselves see in all rivers and oceans. It is the image of the ungraspable phantom of life; and this is the key to it all" (*Moby-Dick*, p. 14). While the Greek youth gazes into the fountain, or Captain Ahab stares into the ocean, the hunter and the hunted are mirror images, and to launch any attack on the "phantom" is therefore self-destructive. When Narcissus reaches into the water, when Ahab hurls himself out of the whaleboat, the hunter and the hunted are finally one.

The life and death of Ernest Hemingway offer a modern example. When asked why he felt driven to fish and hunt, Hemingway replied, half in jest, that he must hunt and shoot wild animals in order to keep from killing himself. In the final years of his life he suffered from the feeling that he was being hunted down. He knew the helpless despair of Captain Ahab who felt near the end of the hunt that forces beyond his control were driving him on to certain death: "We are turned round and round in this world, like yonder windlass, and Fate is the hand-spike." The psychological identity of hunter and hunted was finally dramatized when Hemingway turned the rifle toward himself.

Captain Ahab never quite understands that he is hunting a reflection of himself, but Melville shows the reader how Ahab grows to resemble the image of "eternal malice" that he pursues. Not only does Ahab's irrational hatred increase to match the supposed vindictiveness of the hunted animal; even his ship with its bulwarks "garnished like one continuous jaw" is a mirror image of its prey. "He who fights with monsters," Nietzsche later wrote, "should be careful lest he thereby become a monster." Mirror images are found throughout *Moby-Dick* because the correspondence of hunter and hunted is a basic psychological truth. It is also the underlying principle of Melville's symbolism. When the officers of the *Pequod* look at the gold doubloon nailed to the mast, each man sees his own reflection. When Ahab stares into the ocean, he is searching in his own mind for the "ungraspable phantom." What he sees is also the image of the totem beast—"the glorified White Whale as he so divinely swam." And true to the story of Narcissus, Ahab plunges to his death in the pursuit of his own likeness. Once Ahab has created a god in his own image, he can finally become, however unwittingly, his own sacrificial victim.

Despite Melville's attempt to display the similarity of Captain Ahab and the dangerous animal that he pursues, some readers may feel that the difference between man and beast is more important. And despite Melville's effort to present Moby Dick as a "grand god," some may feel that the incarnation of divine power in a sperm whale is unlikely and absurd. The equation of hunted animal, self-reflection, and sacred image would seem more plausible if the hunted object were another human being. Because animal sacrifice preceded human sacrifice in the evolution of the religious imagination, it is more difficult to recapture its psychological significance. And because the sacrificial animal at the center of the Christian myth is a human being—the lamb of God is Christ—more primitive alternatives may now be regarded as not only inexplicable but also blasphemous.

Although Melville does refer occasionally in *Moby-Dick* to the hunting down of human animals—"Cannibals?" says Ishmael, "who is not a cannibal?"—it is only in a later book, *The Confidence-Man,* that the goal of hunting becomes the murder of other human beings. The colonel who hunts Indians in *The Confidence-Man* is in many ways a duplicate of the whale-hunting captain in *Moby-Dick.* Both men are committed irrevocably to the fatal quest. With only one or two minor changes, the following description of Colonel John Moredock could also be applied to Captain Ahab:

> At last, taking counsel with the elements, he comes to his resolution. . . . He makes a vow, the hate of which is a vortex from whose suction scarce the remotest chip of the guilty race may reasonably feel secure. . . . He commits himself to the forest primeval; there, so long as life shall be his, to act upon a calm, cloistered scheme of strategical, implacable, and lonesome vengeance.[2]

The image of the vortex at the end of the hunt suggests the ultimate plunge into the unconscious depths. Perhaps it would have been better for Melville to use the metaphor of the labyrinth (it is difficult to imagine a vortex in the "forest primeval"), but even the careless mixing of metaphors is evidence of the interchangeability of Moredock and Ahab in Melville's imagination. In the very next paragraph, still remembering the analogies of *Moby-Dick,* Melville compares the "Indian-hater" to a swordfish and a "deep-sea denizen." Colonel Moredock is a religious hero in the tradition of Ahab, because he too is committed to a lonesome vengeance against the image of eternal malice. But the killing of Indians, rather than sperm whales, brings us closer to the primitive ritual of human sacrifice at the heart of the Christian myth. It is not surprising that Melville describes the quest of the Indian-hater in theological terms. Colonel John Moredock pours on the altar of his own "devout sentiment" the blood and wine of his sacrificial victims.

Because the hunter and the hunted are now both human beings, their function as psychological mirror images is more credible. Melville even describes how the hunter of Indians and his detested prey can momentarily exchange roles: "The Indian-hater is suddenly seized with a sort of calenture; hurries openly towards the first smoke, though he knows it is an Indian's, announces himself as a lost hunter, [and] gives the savage his rifle" (*The Confidence-Man,* p. 131). The desire to kill is thus deeply related to the wish to be killed. When the Indian-hater gives the rifle into the hands of his deadly enemy, the action is tantamount to suicide. By why should anyone wish to become a sacrificial victim? The question, of course, is central to the religion predicated on the imitation of Christ. Why should anyone eat and drink the body and blood of the slain god, if not to share vicariously in his martyrdom? The pathway to Calvary is a psychological inversion of the sacred hunt. Instead of attempting to kill the image of the beast or man, the martyr is willing to be killed. But if the hunted object is a self-image in either event, then the martyr and the hunter are inseparable. That is why Melville describes "moody stricken Ahab . . . with a crucifixion in his face." The fierce hunter of Moby Dick half-realizes in advance that his attempt to kill the "demon phantom" will mean his own death. Some of the best passages of the novel dramatize Ahab's anguished presentiment of the fatality of his quest. Colonel John Moredock also knows that his deliberate attempt to kill Indians demands the renunciation of this world, a solemn leavetaking from all his kin, and the desperate equivalent of "death-bed adieus." And Melville knew that Jesus required his "fishers of men" to forsake the world and all its possessions, to "lose their lives," if they expected to follow his example of sacrifice.

In the early days of Christianity there was some competition between the atonement made possible by Christ's martyrdom and the promise of earthly power offered by Mithras, an attractive Persian god who was known as a legendary hunter. Although the Christian myth came to dominate the imagination of the West, it could never fully suppress the complementary impulse of proud defiance. Is it better to kill or to be killed? Is it better to hunt down the enemy in the forest and ocean, or to turn the other cheek to all tormentors? Captain Ahab and Colonel Moredock both take the path of implacable vengeance. But in their choice they are still forced by the correspondence of hunter and hunted to embody both sides of the argument. The religions of submission and defiance spring from twin motives in man's psychological experience of the sacred hunt. Moredock hunts and kills Indians with the "devout sentiment" of a religious hero, and Ahab "with a crucifixion in his face" throws his life away in the vain attempt to slay the white whale.

How clearly did Melville understand the rituals of animal and human sacrifice that are dramatized in his books? Was his anticipation of modern psychology and anthropology sufficient for him to see the Christian religion in the larger context of hunting and sacrificial death? It is true that Melville saw with Darwin the murderous instinct of all living things. "Consider, once more," Melville wrote, "the universal cannibalism of the sea; all whose creatures prey upon each other, carrying on eternal war since the world began." It is also true that Melville knew enough about the origins of religious myth to have at least a partial understanding of the primitive deification of animals. He knew, for example, that the Hindu god Vishnu had been incarnated as a whale. He also knew that white animals, the White Dog of the Iroquois or the White Elephant of Pegu, have been singled out for special worship. But where did Melville discover the fatality of hunting the totem beast? Or the psychological correspondence of hunter and hunted as mirror images? Or the dependence of the religious hunt upon human sacrifice? Is it adequate to say, as one critic of Melville has done, that "his imagination ran before the anthropologists"? It is tempting to invoke "the aboriginal myth-making fancy" that might be responsible for directing his imagination. Or to praise the power of his intuition that opens to him the memory of primitive experience stored in the "collective unconscious." But such "explanations" simply confess our inability to explain how the shaping forces and obsessive symbols of the human imagination are passed down through generations.

All that can be said for sure is that Melville's imagination was stimulated by his experience of the whole ritual of animal sacrifice at the heart of the whaling industry, and by his wide reading of history and legend, which ranged from the stories of leviathan in the Old Testament to the most recent accounts of hunting and killing the great whales. But it is doubtful that either his experience or his scholarship could allow Melville to look at the primitive roots of Christianity with sufficient detachment to be able to see its place in the evolution of religious myths. Although he probed the symbols of his primitive vision with unremitting curiosity, he could not rest content with the implication that all gods are the projected fears and desires of the human imagination. Although he saw the indifference of nature, the "colorless, all-color of atheism," he could not personally excuse or forgive the God of his fathers for the vision of chaos. Melville's writing is a long record of the struggle with religious yearning and doubt. "He can neither believe," Hawthorne observed of Melville, "nor be comfortable in his unbelief; and he is too honest and courageous not to try to do one or the other." Such religious uncertainty was not uncommon in the century which began with the defiant individualism of Byron and concluded with the negative voice of Nietzsche. But in the middle of the century Melville brought together his unusual experience and his deep imagination to create a drama of his religious speculation that is without parallel in its scope and intensity.

ISHMAEL'S VIEW OF RELIGIOUS HISTORY

Ahab's blasphemous hunt for the sacred beast provides the intensity of Melville's great book, but it is the speculative, brooding, ironic imagination of Ishmael that gives *Moby-Dick* its extraordinary scope. Ishmael is sometimes a particular character in the story, but more often he tends to become the omniscient voice of the author. Ishmael not only goes on the hunt after the "grand hooded phantom," he also records for us his impressions of all the other hunters. Even before the pursuit of Moby Dick begins, Ishmael is the tolerant and at times reluctant witness of other religious ceremonies. In this way Melville is able to place Ahab's fatal quest within a larger context of nineteenth-century religious alternatives. Ishmael observes the range of experience from "Luther's day" to "Darwin's year," and Ahab's defiant quest is only one, although the most dramatic, of the religious possibilities.

1. Puritan. The first religious ceremony encountered by Ishmael involves a Negro congregation listening to an old-fashioned Puritan sermon—"the preacher's text was about the blackness of darkness, and the weeping and wailing and teeth-gnashing there." Melville knew that for some time the appeal of Puritan dogma in America had been drifting down the social scale. While the upper classes in New England moved steadily through more liberal versions of Christianity in the direction of Unitarianism, fundamental Puritan attitudes found a receptive audience among the poor and uneducated. That is one reason why revivalism in the nineteenth century tended to be a frontier activity; the extraordinary campaign of the Baptists and the Methodists was most successful in the South and West. The centers of learning and power in the East had long since abandoned their original religious piety in exchange for a tolerant respectability. But a rude parody of Calvinism could still be witnessed at Methodist camp meetings, at Baptist revivals, and especially in Negro churches of either sect. When Ishmael stumbles into the church, he imagines at once that the congregation is already in Hell—"It seemed the great Black Parliament sitting in Tophet"—and Ishmael does not waste any time in making his exit. With ironic sarcasm he sums up this first religious encounter as "wretched entertainment at the sign of 'The Trap!'"

Ever since the dogmas of Calvin had been imposed upon him in childhood, Melville had been impatient with the "wailing and teeth-gnashing" of Puritan rhetoric. Still he was ready to honor the "power of blackness" in Hawthorne as well as himself. What he objected to was not the knowledge of evil inherent in Calvinism—Melville always recognized the need for some concept of original sin—it was the cruel exploitation of fear that disturbed him. Thus Ishmael describes the minister as a "black Angel of Doom . . . beating a book in a pulpit," a minister attempting to frighten his audience with the vision of God's wrath. Melville's contempt for the spectacle is hardly disguised in Ishmael's sarcastic commentary. Although Ishmael will present himself, with considerable irony, as "a good Christian; born and bred in the bosom of the infallible Presbyterian Church," his immediate reaction to the Puritan rhetoric is disdain and repugnance. Melville's own distaste for the Calvinism of his childhood is evident in Ishmael's hasty rejection of "The Trap" with its "wretched entertainment."

2. *Pagan.* Melville escaped the religion of his childhood when he went away to sea. He lived for a short time among the pagan natives in the South Pacific, and there he saw how the simple virtues of Polynesia were being destroyed by an invasion of Christian missionaries. Although his observations had been dramatized more than once in his earlier novels, Melville drew upon them again in the early chapters of *Moby-Dick.* After Ishmael retreats from the Negro church, he next meets an extraordinary representative of pagan culture. Melville seems to enjoy the irony of presenting Queequeg, a pagan harpooner, as more Christian in spirit than those who call themselves Christians. Although he may spend a Sunday evening in New Bedford attempting to sell a shrunken head, Queequeg later demonstrates a loving commitment to his fellow man that is unsurpassed by any other character in the book. Ishmael is comically frightened of Queequeg at first, but it is not long before Ishmael concludes that it is better to "sleep with a sober cannibal than a drunken Christian." If Queequeg is at all representative of the virtues of his people, then any missionary effort in Polynesia is unnecessary and foolish—Queequeg's character needs no improvement. He is fearful, however, that contact with Christianity has already made him unfit to ascend "the pure and undefiled throne of thirty pagan Kings." Melville's implication that Christianity is something that corrupts human character, while the noble savage in contrast is innocent and pure, may have disturbed some members of his contemporary audience. But the contrast had been commonplace among the philosophers of the Enlightenment, especially Voltaire and Rousseau, who had relished the opportunity more than seventy years before to advertise the virtue of South Sea pagans at the expense of orthodox Christians.

The inverted contrast of pagan and Christian not only allows Melville to satirize the hypocrisy of modern Christianity—"I'll try a pagan friend," says Ishmael, "since Christian kindness has proved but hollow courtesy"—this lesson in comparative religion also allows him to see the relative absurdity of all religious ceremony. Ishmael concludes that "Presbyterians and Pagans alike . . . are all somehow dreadfully cracked about the head, and sadly need mending." Ishmael reaches his cynical conclusion after he has joined together with Queequeg in the worship of his pagan god. Queequeg has a small wooden idol named Yojo who must be honored once a day with an offering of burnt biscuit. Ishmael's skeptical tolerance of Yojo—"a rather good sort of god, who perhaps meant well enough upon the whole, but in all cases did not succeed in his benevolent designs"—matches his own suspicion that the God of the Christians is at least mildly incompetent. When Ishmael sees Queequeg bow down before Yojo, he does not think that the pagan religious ceremony is any more or less absurd than the rituals of Christian worship. When Ishmael joins Queequeg, he reasons in a comic fashion that it is his Christian duty to violate the first and second of the Ten Commandments. With an untroubled conscience he bows down before Yojo, and kisses the nose of the wooden idol. His friendship with Queequeg is more important than the rituals and dogmas of Presbyterian or pagan.

Ishmael begins to argue religion with Queequeg only when it comes to the strict observance of Ramadan. When the pagan harpooneer observes an entire day of fasting and meditation, Ishmael believes that he is violating the "obvious laws of Hygiene and common sense." Ishmael's usual tolerance then gives way to critical protest: "I labored to show Queequeg that all these Lents, Ramadans, and prolonged ham-squattings in cold, cheerless rooms were stark nonsense" (*Moby-Dick,* p. 81). Melville allows Ishmael to dismiss casually the Christian season of penitence along with the pagan ritual of fasting as if both were equally meaningless. Ishmael then continues his critical protest by suggesting that religious attitudes may be little more than symptoms of ill health. Whatever is "bad for the health," Ishmael argues, is also "useless for the soul." He therefore dismisses with cynical delight the whole Puritan vision of damnation—"hell is an idea first born on an undigested apple-dumpling; and since then perpetuated through the hereditary dyspepsias nurtured by Ramadans." Ishmael's lecture to Queequeg on the history of religion—"beginning with the rise and progress of the primitive religions, and coming down to the various religions of the present time"—is obviously designed to convert belief into skepticism. The sources of Melville's own disillusionment are evident in Ishmael's cynical argument. Melville not only witnessed for himself the contrast of pagan and Christian religions in the South Pacific; he also read widely in the literature of comparative mythology. Of special importance to him was the old and infamous *Dictionary* by Pierre Bayle. There he found a reasoned and skeptical exposure of the primitive origins of the Calvinism of his own childhood. He also found some strong hints about the psychopathology of religious behavior. Armed with the wide vision of anthropology, Melville could have Ishmael reduce the pagan and Christian religions alike to the insignificance of being classed among "the various religions of the present time" which can all be traced back to "primitive" superstition. And equipped with some knowledge of the psycho-physical determinants of religious belief, Melville could have Ishmael dismiss the idea of Hell as a symptom of bad health. Melville was thus able to dramatize the attack on Christianity from two modern directions.

3. Christian Obedience. Early in the novel Ishmael makes a visit to the Christian whaling chapel in New Bedford where he listens to Father Mapple preach a dramatic sermon on the proper obedience that man owes to God. Using the story of Jonah for his text, Father Mapple stresses the sin and terror and futility of rebelling against a sovereign Power. The sermon follows the conventional Puritan model: first the intensification of fear evoked by images of torment and destruction— the ship is battered with a terrible storm until Jonah is thrown overboard where he descends into the belly of the whale; and second, the offering of hope that comes when Jonah repents and is saved. Ishmael makes no comment upon this Christian sermon. He leaves with Father Mapple still kneeling in the pulpit, and returns immediately to the Spouter-Inn where he joins Queequeg in kneeling down before his wooden idol and offering Yojo some burnt biscuit.

The sermon preached by Father Mapple is sometimes interpreted by critics as a moral against which to measure the rest of *Moby-Dick.* Is not Captain Ahab a sinner who rebels against God, fails to repent, and therefore is hurled to damnation? Yes and no. To measure Captain Ahab merely from the Christian viewpoint of Father Mapple is just as inadequate as to judge Hester Prynne only in terms of Puritan morality. Both Hester and Ahab take part in a sinful rebellion that calls into question the very laws by which they are condemned. Hester endows her act of natural passion with a "consecration of its own." Ahab commits himself to the fatal hunt with "a crucifixion in his face." Ahab is not just rebelling against the image of divine power; he is questioning its very nature and existence. He does not know if the white whale is "agent" or "principal." He does not know if there is anything behind the mask of nature. Ahab's determination to "strike through the mask" is more than an example of religious disobedience; it is a dramatic attempt to stab at the very heart of divine power. Ahab wants to put God on trial. If the nature and existence of God are the ontological goals of Ahab's quest, then what authority remains to measure Ahab's conduct? "Who's to doom," Ahab rightly says, "when the judge himself is dragged to the bar?" The conventional moral of disobedience preached by Father Mapple is therefore not adequate to measure Ahab's metaphysical quest. Melville admits as much when he later has Ishmael announce that "in landlessness alone resides the highest truth." The pulpit of the whaling chapel may resemble the prow of a ship, but the days of Father Mapple as a sailor and harpooneer are definitely in the past. The minister and his theology are left behind when the "flood-gates of the wonder-world" are opened, and the voyage begins in pursuit of Moby Dick.

If the words of Father Mapple about disobedience are not adequate to describe the "morally intolerable truth" of Captain Ahab, the minister's call for repentance and salvation is likewise unsatisfactory. If it is better "to perish in that howling infinite," as Melville's narrator strongly implies, then what has happened to the value of repentance? It would violate the integrity of Ahab's quest if he were to submit his will to the very power that he seeks to arraign. Repentance would only make sense to Ahab if he could believe in a just God capable of granting eternal grace. But Ahab has no such belief, and the promise of Christian salvation is dramatized elsewhere in the novel as a false hope. There is a large painting on the wall just behind Father Mapple which depicts a scene of heavenly intervention. The painting shows "a gallant ship beating against a terrible storm. . . . But high above the flying scud and dark-rolling clouds, there floated a little isle of sunlight, from which beamed forth an angel's face. . . . 'Ah, noble ship,' the angel seemed to say, 'beat on, beat on. . . . The sun is breaking through; the clouds are rolling off—serenest azure is at hand'" (*Moby-Dick*, p. 43). The saccharine tone of the description may indicate Melville's hint at the unreality of angels and their reassuring messages. In any event no angel appears when the voyage of the *Pequod* reaches its moment of extreme danger. The first mate of the ship does believe in the chance of divine rescue, but when destruction is imminent, and Starbuck calls, "My God, stand by me now!"—where is the angel with the promise of heavenly light? Starbuck is lost with the rest, pagan and Christian alike, beneath "the great shroud of the sea."

Melville expected no less for himself. The chance for immortality preached in the religion of his childhood had turned in his mind into an impossible wish. Hawthorne recorded one of his last conversations with Melville—he "began to reason of Providence and futurity, and of everything that lies beyond human ken, and informed me that he had 'pretty much made up his mind to be annihilated'; but still he does not seem to rest in that anticipation."[3] Father Mapple claims in his Christian sermon that even in the belly of the whale the sinner may repent and be saved. Melville did not share that belief, but he continued to fight against the prospect of annihilation. Melville, like Captain Ahab, could not stop challenging the "heartless voids and immensities of the universe."

4. Transcendental. Ishmael's experience of different religions before the voyage of the *Pequod* is broad but rather superficial. He stumbles by accident into the Negro church; he bows down before Queequeg's wooden idol; he visits the whaling chapel and listens to the sermon of Father Mapple; but in each case Ishmael remains essentially uncommitted. The friendship of Queequeg is important to Ishmael, but not the religious beliefs of the pagan harpooneer. It is only during the long voyage that the spiritual imagination of Ishmael is deeply aroused. His favorite place on the ship is at the masthead, where he is able to gaze hypnotically at the broad expanse of the ocean and let his mind drift in reverie with the currents of wind and water. His consciousness is altered by this hypnotic enjoyment in a manner that recalls Emerson's description of a mystical experience in *Nature.* Emerson felt that his power of vision was able to transcend all limits—"I become a transparent eyeball; I am nothing; I see all." He felt his own identity blend with the spirit of a divine Being: "The currents of the Universal Being circulate through me; I am part or parcel of God." Ishmael describes how a similar experience may occur to any "sunken-eyed young Platonist" allowed to stand watch at the masthead of a whaling ship:

> . . . lulled into such an opium-like listlessness of vacant, unconscious reverie is this absent-minded youth by the blending cadence of waves with thoughts, that at last he loses his identity; takes the mystic ocean at his feet for the visible image of that deep, blue, bottomless soul, pervading mankind and nature. . . .
> There is no life in thee, now, except that rocking life imparted by a gently rolling ship; by her, borrowed from the sea; by the sea, from the inscrutable tides of God. [*Moby-Dick,* p. 140]

Melville's description of the mystical experience is more successful than Emerson's because the image of the sea may graphically represent the tides of nature, man, and God. The vantage point of the masthead also provides a realistic setting for the mystical vision. Melville therefore avoids the grotesque abstraction of Emerson's "transparent eyeball." Both accounts, however, dramatize the loss of individual identity followed by an assumption of divine presence. Both dramatize the paradox at the heart of Christian mysticism: "For whosoever will save his life shall lose it: and whosoever will lose his life for my sake shall find it." Melville, however, understood more than Emerson about the deceptive nature and the possible danger of the mystical experience.

Although Ishmael enjoys his moments of reverie at the masthead, he does not attribute the full mystical experience to himself. Instead he refers to "young Platonists" who are more susceptible to the visions of Transcendentalism. Melville was familiar with the Platonic tradition which had nourished the ideas of Emerson. He also knew the philosophical writing that supported the romantic movement, especially the work of Coleridge, De Quincey, and Carlyle. Melville recognized that a mystical reverie, like an opium dream, may delude an individual into believing that he has become "part or parcel of God" (Emerson), or united with "the inscrutable tides of God" (Ishmael). Melville, however, remained skeptical of the experience. Wasn't the "sunken-eyed young Platonist," he wondered, losing contact with the natural world as he moves further into his dream of the supernatural? Wasn't the feeling of god-like vision merely an extraordinary form of self-deception? Wasn't the individual, who experienced the symbolic death of his own identity, apt to awaken in danger of losing his actual life?

Melville has Ishmael conclude his description of the Transcendental experience with a strong warning:

> But while this sleep, this dream is on ye, move your foot or hand an inch; slip your hold at all; and your identity comes back in horror. Over Descartian vortices you hover. And perhaps, at midday, in the fairest weather, with one half-throttled shriek you drop through that transparent air into the summer sea, no more to rise for ever. Heed it well, ye Pantheists! [*Moby-Dick*, p. 140]

What Melville's warning lacks in subtlety, it makes up for with its sharp focus on the danger of the mystical reverie. Melville was writing in the middle of the nineteenth century when prophets on both sides, Transcendental and Christian, were advocating the mystical reception of divine power from nature and God. Emerson failed to recognize how the surrender of individual will to the Universal Being could be suicidal. Nor did the various Christian sects, still believing in the chance of salvation, see the danger of blind confidence in the supernatural. But Ishmael remains above his young Platonist, and Melville remains above Ishmael. While others were lost in one mystical religion or another, Melville was saved by his skepticism.

5. *Skeptic.* Ishmael describes himself as "neither believer nor infidel, but . . . a man who regards them both with equal eye." The balance of Ishmael's detached vision is best illustrated in his commentary on the whiteness of the whale. Although he admits to being appalled by the blank color of Moby Dick, Ishmael retains his calm detachment with a careful analysis of the many symbolic meanings of the color white. Melville displays some of his anthropological knowledge when he has Ishmael discuss examples of the worship of animals as wide-ranging as the sacred White Dog of the Iroquois and the White Elephant of Siam. Melville hints at the origins of divine power when he describes how the human imagination responds to basic symbols. He explains how the legendary White Steed of the prairies might appear to the eyes of old trappers and hunters as an "archangelical apparition." Even to the bravest Indian, Melville reports, the White Steed was "the object of trembling reverence and awe." How did the white horse come to be regarded as a divine creature? "Nor can it be questioned," Melville asserts, "that it was his spiritual whiteness chiefly, which so clothed him with divineness."

After describing how a number of white animals have been worshipped, Melville next has Ishmael explain how their whiteness may also inspire fear and terror. Why should the same color which has so many positive associations also have the power to evoke fear? Ishmael has some difficulty in providing an answer. There is "an elusive something," he says, "in the innermost idea of this hue." He refers to "the supernaturalism of this hue," and claims that "it calls up a peculiar apparition to the soul." This hardly sounds like much of an explanation, but the semireligious vocabulary—words like "supernaturalism" and "soul"—actually functions as part of Melville's theory of symbolism. He wonders if symbols do not have the power to release a primitive experience of "transcendent horrors" stored in the deepest levels of human memory. The age of the terror and the depth of its repression would then help to explain why the person confronting the symbol does not know exactly what it is that he fears—he is paralyzed by a "certain nameless terror." That is why Ishmael talks about "an elusive something . . . to analyse it, would seem impossible . . . this phantom more terrible than all . . . the fear of that hideous whiteness" (*Moby-Dick*, pp. 164-68).

Melville's theory of symbolism anticipates by more than half a century Jung's concept of the "collective unconscious." Both Melville and Jung assert that some memory of primitive experience is inherited by each generation. Melville cites the example of a young colt born and raised in a peaceful valley of Vermont. Even when the animal has not experienced any immediate danger, he may still display the instinct of fear common to his species. Melville thus concludes that fear is an inherited phenomenon, and that a particular symbol may provoke the instinctive response. Melville knows that many will doubt his argument; he therefore defends himself in advance: "But in a matter like this, subtlety appeals to subtlety, and without imagination no man can follow another into these halls. And though, doubtless, some at least of the imaginative impressions about to be presented may have been shared by most men, yet few perhaps were entirely conscious of them at the time, and therefore may not be able to recall them now" (*Moby-Dick*, p. 167).

When Melville does not find a psychological term to explain how a symbol may reach to the hidden level of the mind, he often uses religious words to hint at the same process. Therefore he claims that a symbol is a "mystic sign" that may reveal "knowledge of the demonism in the world." The demons, of course, are the ancient fears that haunt the human imagination. "Though in many of its aspects," writes Melville, "this visible world seems formed in love, the invisible spheres were formed in fright." Melville thus anticipates the modern theory of repression. If experiences of terror are typically repressed, then the unconscious part of the human mind was truly "formed in fright."

What are the archetypal fears which might be summoned from the unconscious by the color white? Melville suggests three possible answers. First, the sight of an albino animal may inspire fear because of its abnormality. The odd lack of color shocks and repels the viewer. At the same time, however, the viewer may feel awe and wonder at the unusual whiteness. Melville sees the mixture of fear and reverence—the primal response to the sacred animal—as twin sources of the religious imagination. The hunt for the great albino whale is thus a ritual of terror and worship.

The second ancient terror connected with the color white is the fear of death. The vision of whiteness "stabs us from behind with the thought of annihilation." The biblical image of Death riding a pale horse is cited by Melville as the "king of terrors." "It cannot well be doubted," writes Melville, "that the one visible quality in the aspect of the dead which most appals the gazer, is the marble pallor lingering there. . . . And from that pallor of the dead, we borrow the expressive hue of the shroud in which we wrap them" (*Moby-Dick,* p. 166). The spirits of the dead are described as phantoms in a "snowy mantle," and Melville even imagines the ghosts "rising in a milk-white fog." When the primitive imagination wants to escape the haunting confrontation with death, the pale ghosts are transformed into the whiteness of angels. But the negative aspects of the color white are allowed to predominate in *Moby-Dick.* The great shroud of the sea will roll over all the men, with the exception of Ishmael, who have dared to follow Captain Ahab in his quest for the white whale. Only Ishmael understands the full dimensions of whiteness. At the end of the book the swirling vortex of the ocean will subside to a "creamy pool" where Ishmael alone will float unharmed.

The third archetypal fear associated with symbolic whiteness is the terror of being lost in a blank universe. Melville believes that this fear is the worst of all, because for the religious imagination it is the equivalent of atheism: "Whiteness is not so much a color as the visible absence of color, and at the same time the concrete of all colors; is it for these reasons that there is such a dumb blankness, full of meaning, in a wide landscape of snows—a colorless, all-color of atheism from which we shrink?" (*Moby-Dick,* p. 169). The image of a snow-filled landscape as an example of blank nature is also used by Robert Frost in "Desert Places." Both Melville and Frost use the image to dramatize the fear of meaninglessness: "A blanker whiteness of benighted snow/ With no expression, nothing to express." And both stress the analogy of the natural emptiness with the "desert places" of the mind.

It is Ishmael who is most fully aware of the meaninglessness. At times Captain Ahab may wonder if there is anything behind the mask of nature, but he generally remains convinced that the white whale is a significant symbol. Captain Ahab is a man of faith, even though his faith is inverted and blasphemous. It is only Ishmael who realizes that the whiteness may stand for everything and nothing—the "colorless, all-color of atheism." That is why Ishmael is able to observe so many different religious positions—pagan, Christian, and Transcendental—and not become truly committed to any one of them. Ishmael, like his namesake in the Bible, is condemned to wander as a perpetual orphan. Detached, skeptical, ironic, indifferent, ready for everything and nothing,

Ishmael anticipates the anti-heroes so prevalent in modern literature. Like the title character in Camus's *The Stranger,* Ishmael is tempted to resign himself to the "benign indifference of the universe." Like the central figure in Eliot's *The Waste Land,* Ishmael listens to the fire sermon, fears death by water, and has looked "into the heart of light, the silence." He is "neither believer nor infidel." His mind is open to all the colors of the spectrum despite his suspicion that all are "subtile deceits." Ishmael just misses the fate of "the wretched infidel [who] gazes himself blind at the monumental white shroud that wraps all the prospect around him." Although he is on the verge of suicide at the beginning of the novel, he does not despair before the vision of a blank world. At the end of the book Ishmael is still drifting in the midst of the "colorless, all-color of atheism."

Ishmael's skepticism and irony tend to undermine the significance of the many religious positions that he observes. His rejection of the Puritan rhetoric heard briefly at the Negro church is a scornful disclaimer— "wretched entertainment at the sign of 'The Trap.'" His worship of Queequeg's pagan idol is merely a humorous burlesque. His response to the Christian sermon preached by Father Mapple is remarkably noncommittal. His account of Transcendentalism includes a critical warning. And his analysis of the symbolic value of whiteness renders the many colors of the religious spectrum invisible among the "heartless voids and immensities of the universe." If Ishmael's skeptical mind tends to question the value of all he observes, his own character is not exempt from the pervasive irony. He is not just amused by pagans and Puritans; he is also able to smile at his own insignificance. A self-deprecating mockery accompanies his narration throughout most of the novel. The full extent of his cynicism and irony is revealed in the following confession: "There are certain queer times and occasions in this strange mixed affair we call life when a man takes this whole universe for a vast practical joke, though the wit thereof he but dimly discerns, and more than suspects that the joke is at nobody's expense but his own" (*Moby-Dick,* p. 195).

Ishmael's words struck an odd note in the middle of the nineteenth century. Although Melville's contemporaries were seldom able to agree which of the many rival voices of prophecy and millennial expectation to follow, they were typically convinced that life was serious and significant. Few were ready to take "this whole universe for a vast practical joke." Ishmael's view, however, anticipates the twentieth-century awareness of radical absurdity. The clichés of modern literature from the early poetry of Eliot to the recent plays of Beckett echo the themes of chaos, alienation, and religious loss. Melville later expanded

Ishmael's ironic commentary about the world as a "vast practical joke" into a whole novel which dramatizes a voyage on April Fools Day. *The Confidence-Man,* with its many cynical and satiric questions, was suitably ignored by Melville's contemporaries, but its affinity with the skeptical temperament of much twentieth-century literature has been lately appreciated.

CONSEQUENCES OF THE VOYAGE

During the whaling voyage Ishmael also describes how some members of the crew have cause to change their religious views. Queequeg, for example, begins the voyage with a confident faith in the benevolent power of his pagan deity. But after he suffers a painful injury from the jaw of a shark, Queequeg declares bitterly that "de god wat made shark must be one dam Ingin." His disillusionment is significant, because it was Queequeg at the beginning of the novel who demonstrated the most faith in the virtues of friendship and charity. He is betrayed, like Captain Ahab, by the very cannibalism of nature. Ahab's leg was severed by the crooked jaw of Moby Dick; Queequeg almost loses his hand to the "murderous jaw" of the shark; both men are awakened to a fatalistic conviction of the "eternal malice" at the heart of nature. Both experience "the universal cannibalism of the sea" that Melville and Darwin observed on their voyages through the South Pacific.

Another character on the whaling voyage is granted an even closer view of the "heartless" and "indifferent" God at the depths of creation. Ahab's cabin boy, young Pip, is left to float on the open sea after he jumps overboard in fear during the chase of the whale. Temporarily abandoned on that "heartless immensity," Pip loses his reason, but gains an extraordinary vision of God at work in the very act of creation. Pip's body is rescued alive from the water, but his soul never recovers from his experience of the "wondrous depths, where strange shapes of the unwarped primal world glided to and fro before his passive eyes." What does Pip see in the depths of the unconscious mind? What "horrors of the half known life" are revealed to him? Nowhere else does Melville dramatize the psychological and religious meanings of the symbolic ocean with greater boldness. Pip sees "the joyous, heartless, ever-juvenile eternities." He sees "the multitudinous, God-omnipresent, coral insects, that out of the firmament of waters heaved the colossal orbs." And ultimately Pip sees "God's foot upon the treadle of the loom." Pip's initiation into the wondrous depths of the mind, where Creation goes on eternally, renders him insane as far as his shipmates are concerned. He is considered mad because his vision of Creation has uncovered the deep irrational powers. But there is small consolation in his vision. The "eternities" he witnesses are "heartless." The divine forces at work on the foundations of the universe are like coral insects building their reefs under the ocean. The evolution of life is shown to be relentlessly natural. God is a mechanical energy at work on the "treadle of the loom." There is no place for human wishes, hopes, or dreams in this process of creation. Young Pip is therefore left to feel "indifferent as his God."

Pip's symbolic descent beneath the ocean foreshadows the actual fate of almost all his shipmates. Captain Ahab persuades his crew to swear their allegiance to his vengeful quest, and consequently they lose their lives in the mad attempt to hunt and kill Moby Dick. Ishmael also joins in the oath, and says that "Ahab's quenchless feud seemed mine," but Ishmael's wide-ranging irony and skepticism preclude his allegiance to any particular religious commitment. While Ahab fixes all his intensity upon the pursuit of a single image, Ishmael drifts from one religious encounter to another until they all blend into "the colorless all-color of atheism." Ishmael's participation in Ahab's quest is therefore kept to the minimum required for his role as narrator. Even that role is occasionally abandoned as Melville shifts into an omniscient point of view. Many events in the second half of the novel are not directly witnessed by Ishmael, and thus it is impossible to know just what he might think of them. Does he feel, for example, that Ahab's quest is blasphemous, heroic, or perhaps both? How does Melville want the reader to respond? Such questions may be approached by judging the implicit difference between the concentrating mind of Ahab, who focuses the power of his strong will upon one symbol, and the expanding mind of Ishmael, who understands that whiteness is everything and nothing.

Should Melville be identified with the religious views of either Ahab or Ishmael? To what extent does their creator share the proud defiance of one character or the cynical indifference of the other? There is no shortage of evidence in support of either claim, nor is there any critical agreement on the revolutionary nature of Melville's religious vision. Dramatizing pride and defiance as heroic virtues was not at all uncommon in the century that began with the romantic individualism of Byron. But using a narrative voice that is self-deprecating and ironic was a bold anticipation of the anti-heroic attitude that dominates so much of twentieth-century literature. And Melville alone was able to combine the two different voices in one novel. Thus we hear the proud rhetoric of Ahab, who resembles King Lear in his defiance of the cruel

gods. And we hear the ironic questions of Ishmael as he looks into the
blank face of nature. Whether Melville himself "quarreled with God"
is less important than Melville's historical awareness of how the rebellion against divine power came at a strategic moment in the development of the modern imagination. Melville understood how the tragic
vision of Shakespeare was a turning point against the Christian assumptions of medieval Europe. At the height of the American renaissance,
the best work of Herman Melville represents a similar turning point.

Melville was reading Shakespeare when the plans for *Moby-Dick* were
beginning to come together in his mind. His famous comparison of Hawthorne and Shakespeare appeared in the *Literary World* during the
summer of 1850. In the essay Melville explains what he valued most
in the imagination of Shakespeare:

> It is those deep far-away things in him; those occasional flashings-
> forth of the intuitive Truth in him; those short, quick probings at
> the very axis of reality:—these are the things that make Shakespeare,
> Shakespeare. Through the mouths of the dark characters of Hamlet,
> Timon, Lear, and Iago, he craftily says, or sometimes insinuates
> the things, which we feel to be so terrifically true, that it were
> all but madness for any good man, in his own proper character, to
> utter, or even hint of them.

After Pip has experienced a glimpse of the dark intuitive truth at the
very axis of reality, and his shipmates believe that he is mad, it is only
Captain Ahab who understands and befriends the small Negro boy. Ahab
has been branded himself with the forked lightning of truth. Throughout the novel Ahab dares to speak the words that good men like Starbuck are even afraid to hear. And to some in the novel Ahab's truth
is close to madness. Melville's tragic character is worthy of his Shakespearean predecessors. Captain Ahab matches the Prince of Denmark in
his brooding interrogation of the unknown power behind the mask of
nature; he resembles Timon of Athens in his vengeance against the
"universal cannibalism" of life; he is like King Lear in his proud
defiance of the cruel gods; and he also imitates Iago and Macbeth
in the ruthless thrust of a powerful and destructive individualism.
Like many of the strong personalities of Renaissance drama, Captain
Ahab questions the assumptions of Christian theology and challenges
the very authority of divine power.

THE REVOLUTION OF FAUST

Among the characters of Renaissance tragedy who challenge the authority of a sovereign God, the most important is the proud rebel who
makes a bargain with Mephistopheles. In Marlowe's play Doctor Faustus
is willing to exchange his soul for three things: he wants additional
knowledge, pleasure, and power. He refuses to believe that any knowledge should be forbidden. After reaching the limits of science and
philosophy, he still wants to know more about the secrets of nature
and God. He also refuses to believe that any pleasure should be regarded
as sinful. After tasting the available delights on earth, he still yearns to
kiss the immortal Helen of Troy. And he refuses to believe that a strong
ambition for power is morally wrong. Scoffing at the idea that only the
meek shall inherit Heaven, Faustus aspires to rival God in power. In all
three ways Faustus replaces the assumptions of a Christian past with the
new ambitions of the Renaissance. He transforms the value of pride from
a cardinal sin into the chief virtue of individualism.

The transformation, however, is not complete. At the end of Marlowe's play the tragic protagonist does exit through the mouth of Hell.
Before his ultimate damnation Faustus sees a vision of Christian mercy—
"See, see where Christ's blood streams in the firmament!"—but it is too
late, he thinks, to repent and be saved. In the gospel according to Father
Mapple, there is always time to repent. Even from the belly of the whale
the voice of a repentant sinner may be heard by a sovereign and merciful God. But in the closing decade of the sixteenth century Marlowe
saw that it was already too late for a full acceptance of the Christian
Gospel. The rebellion of Doctor Faustus dramatizes fundamental questions about the value of knowledge, pleasure, and power. It challenges
the moral law in the case of pride. The revolution against the authority
of God is then irreversible. Although the tragic character of Faustus—
the Promethean hero of Renaissance drama—is punished for stealing
the heavenly fire, the secrets of knowledge, pleasure, and power will
not be abandoned. The roots of the Enlightenment may all be traced
to secular advances made during the Renaissance.

The Puritans in England and America made extraordinary efforts to
halt and reverse the secular progress of the Renaissance. They fought
in England against the plays of Marlowe and Shakespeare, and the
theaters were closed in 1642 when the Puritans gained the political
advantage. In the colonies of New England the political force of the

Puritans was more effective, and for almost a century the prohibition against drama was maintained. Although men like Cotton Mather and Jonathan Edwards were very aggressive in their reading of history and philosophy, they remained almost totally unaware of the Renaissance playwrights. The secular imagination of America was overshadowed for so long by the cloud of Puritan repression, it was not until the middle of the nineteenth century that a rebirth of tragic literature produced the dramatic novels of Hawthorne and Melville.

Early in the nineteenth century when the story of Faustus was revived in Germany and England by Goethe and Byron, the Christian judgment at the end of the story was altered or removed. Melville knew the work of Goethe and Byron, and the creation of Ahab does owe much to the romantic individualism of the nineteenth century, but Ahab is still a tragic character who recalls the heroes of the Renaissance stage. Melville was so influenced by his recent study of Shakespeare that the deck of the whaling ship is often turned into a stage, and the narrative form of *Moby-Dick* is altered so that Ahab may speak in soliloquy. As a tragic protagonist Ahab not only resembles the "dark characters" of Shakespeare; he also shares most of the attributes of Marlowe's Faustus.

What does it mean in psychological terms to make a pact with the Devil? When Faustus bargains with Mephistopheles, when Ahab follows the advice of Fedallah, what is happening in their minds? Is not the myth of the Devil the imaginative projection of the fear that is associated with desires that have long been repressed in the unconscious? The pact with the Devil then would represent a way of overcoming that fear, at least temporarily, and thus releasing the hidden desires. That is what happens when Faustus strives for the knowledge, pleasure, and power that were long prohibited to obedient Christians. But the sudden release of the old desires may trigger such a torment of guilt that the individual is apt to collapse in fear and anguish. That is what occurs at the end of Marlowe's play. When Captain Ahab makes his pact with the Devil, he also liberates his blasphemous instincts. He is then free to worship the dark side of his own nature. Hatred, vengeance, pride, all become his virtues. But the indulgence of repressed instinct is once again accompanied by suffering and anguish. Ahab sees his own guilt reflected in the eyes of Starbuck. Near the height of his pride, he feels some remorse, and one tear of sorrow and regret does fall into the ocean. Then he is ready to follow the Devil into the jaws of Hell.

Why should the pact with the Devil imply a challenge to the authority of divine power? In religious terms, of course, the Devil is defined as God's enemy, and the warfare is understood to be permanent. But what is the psychological meaning? If the Devil is the fearful projection of the repressed instincts that haunt the inferno of the mind, and a pact with the Devil is a method for releasing those instincts, then the psychological opponent of the Devil is that part of the mind that would normally control the hidden desires. The force of discipline in the psyche is the conscience or superego which develops when the commands of parental authority—"Do not do this or that!"—are gradually internalized. But man's invention of the voice of God is also an extension of the same process. The authority of God is a projection in supernatural terms of the conscience still issuing the command "Thou shalt not!" If any attempt to release the instincts of pleasure and ambition is a direct challenge to the authority of the superego, it follows that a pact with the Devil is a challenge to the laws of God. That is why the insubordination of Faustus represents both a psychological and a religious revolution. When Ahab baptizes his harpoon in the name of the Devil, he is dramatizing his vengeful instinct, and at the same time he is intensifying his willful attack on the authority of God.

When Ahab's attempt to kill Moby Dick is seen in the context of the Renaissance challenge to the Christian faith, the historical significance of his quest is more apparent. He is putting God on trial because he feels that the existing moral and religious laws are fundamentally unjust. In Nietzsche's awkward phrase the heroes of the Faust tradition are demanding a "transvaluation of values." The most complete development of the Faust story comes at the end of the nineteenth century in the philosophy of Nietzsche's "superman." While rejecting the Christian virtues of humility and obedience as examples of a "slave morality," Nietzsche recommends the Renaissance values of willful ambition and secular pride. The victory of the hero in the Faust tradition ultimately implies the "death of God" because the full liberation of repressed desires means the effective breakdown of the psychological restraints—both natural and supernatural. There is nothing left at the end to check the pride of Ahab except the limits of his own mortality. With a devil's curse—"From hell's heart I stab at thee"—he strikes through the mask of nature. With the venom of his strongest instinct—"For hate's sake I spit my last breath at thee"—he repudiates the image of divine power.

The rivalry of God and Faust may also be understood in terms of a contest between father and son. The image of God is often described as a "heavenly Father" because the superego which projects the image has been created and reinforced by the example of parental authority. Doctor Faustus therefore behaves like a disobedient son, and Captain Ahab does likewise. When the yardarms of the whaling ship glow with energy from an electrical storm, Ahab identifies the flame as his "fiery father," and then announces dramatically that the "right worship" of the spirit of fire is "defiance." The heroes in the Faust tradition are all defiant because the pact with the Devil liberates their repressed instincts, and the target of their defiance is a father figure because the instincts must fight to overcome the restraint imposed by parental commands.

If the story of Faustus symbolizes a rebellion against the image of the Father, the conflict may be interpreted as a form of oedipal rivalry, and the motivating energy is therefore sexual. Doctor Faustus uses Mephistopheles to supply him with Helen of Troy. In Goethe's drama Faust uses the help of the Devil to seduce Gretchen. In Byron's poem the phantom of Astarte, whom Manfred loved and destroyed, is summoned from the dead. Helen of Troy is the classical example of the woman who belongs to someone else. Gretchen is a devout young girl who belongs to her heavenly Father. Astarte is Manfred's twin sister, and the oedipal rivalry is acted out in terms of incest. How does Captain Ahab fit into this tradition? There are no women on the fatal hunt for Moby Dick, and in any event Ahab has been symbolically castrated before the voyage begins. Nevertheless the hunt for the sacred animal is typically interpreted by anthropologists as an attempt to demonstrate sexual power. A ritual of hunting is often part of the tribal recognition of a boy's initiation into manhood. But Captain Ahab is certainly not a young hunter acting out a ritual of initiation. He has spent forty years at war with "the horrors of the deep." He is also a husband and a father. Ahab does not follow the other examples of the Faust story and seduce a beautiful woman that some father, natural or supernatural, may already possess. But he does act out a symbolic drama of oedipal rivalry. With all that remains of the frustration and fury of his doomed passion, Ahab throws his harpoon at Moby Dick. The end of his terrible hunt is the attempt to kill the image of divine power that once challenged his manhood.

Why is Captain Ahab unable to kill Moby Dick? Why should so many heroes in the Faust tradition be doomed to failure? Is there something about the very nature of oedipal rivalry that renders the conflict irresolvable? After the father has been killed, after the woman has been seduced, the Faust hero in Mozart's opera is finally driven into Hell by the statue of the dead father. The reappearance of the father at the end suggests the indestructibility of the image of parental authority. Captain Ahab may hurl defiance at the symbol of his "fiery father," but his rebellion is in vain. From the Christian viewpoint any man who attempts to rival the power of God is doomed to failure because the limited nature of man is no match for the strength of divine power. Doctor Faustus and Don Giovanni are both forced into the mouth of Hell. Captain Ahab and the unrepentant Jonah cannot avoid the open jaw of the whale. From the psychological viewpoint the rebellion against divine authority is not successful because the pact with the Devil not only liberates the repressed instincts of the ego and the id; it also awakens the fear and guilt connected with those impulses. The quest for power and pleasure therefore involves the cost of suffering and death. When Captain Ahab makes his first appearance before the crew of his whaling ship, he stands before them "in all the nameless regal overbearing dignity of some mighty woe." When he makes his last attempt to kill Moby Dick, Ahab loses his own life.

Versions of the Faust legend began to appear in myth and literature as early as the Greek story of Prometheus, but it was not until the Renaissance that a man who is challenging divine authority could be presented as a tragic hero. The rebellion of Doctor Faustus against the traditional values of the Christian faith represents a new confidence in secular pride. It is the same confidence that would later nourish the values of the Enlightenment and then develop in the nineteenth century into many forms of romantic individualism and self-reliance. Marlowe was fortunate to be writing at just the right time in England to contrast the limitations of the Christian faith with the secular energies being released by the Renaissance. A similar crossroads was reached in America in the middle of the nineteenth century. Melville was then able to dramatize the full religious conflict of supernatural and secular ideologies. He was able to contrast the orthodox beliefs held by Starbuck and Father Mapple with the irony and skepticism of Ishmael. Caught in the middle is Captain Ahab, who can no longer subordinate his own proud will to any supernatural power, nor reach the degree of indifference that allows Ishmael to drift superficially from one religion to another. He cannot be the obedient son like Starbuck; he cannot even be the outcast son like Ishmael; Ahab has no choice but to stand and challenge his "fiery father."

The full religious paradox of Captain Ahab's position is revealed in the famous description of him as "a grand, ungodly, god-like man." His rebellion against divine authority is "ungodly," but his assertion of jealous power recalls Jehovah in vengeance and tyranny. Although Ahab was "nominally included in the census of Christendom," Melville writes, "he was still an alien to it." Ahab can be temporarily softened by the appeals of Starbuck but not dissuaded from the end of his blasphemous quest. The pact with the Devil is irrevocable, the sermon of Father Mapple notwithstanding: Ahab knows the bitter moment of destruction cannot be postponed.

The three main characters of *Moby-Dick* represent three different stages in the history of the religious imagination: Starbuck would feel at home in a morality play of the late Middle Ages, Captain Ahab is the tragic hero of the American renaissance, and the narrator of Melville's book anticipates the anti-heroes of modern literature. The three characters represent a brief history of the relationship between man and God. At first the image of the supernatural Father commands faith and obedience—Starbuck never doubts the authority of God. But in the Renaissance the sovereignty of divine power is challenged by the strong assertion of human will—Ahab does not see any limit to his vengeance against the higher powers. "Talk not to me of blasphemy," says Ahab, "I'd strike the sun if it insulted me." In the aftermath of the rebellion all that remains are the disinherited sons, the orphans, the outcasts—Ishmael drifting on the open sea.

The historical progression is implied by Melville's treatment of the three religious positions. The Christian faith of Starbuck and Father Mapple is dramatized as a limited and untrustworthy guide to present realities. When Starbuck looks into the ocean, he must close his eyes to the essential facts of murder and chaos: "Tell me not of thy teeth-tiered sharks, and thy kidnapping cannibal ways. Let faith oust fact; let fancy oust memory; I look deep down and do believe" (*Moby-Dick*, p. 406). His religious faith is thus maintained at the cost of willful ignorance and blindness. The reluctance of Starbuck to acknowledge the voyage from "Luther's day" to "Darwin's year" is dramatized by Melville with a mixture of criticism and pity. The Christian sermon of Father Mapple cannot reveal the "highest truth" which Melville says resides in "landlessness alone." When Starbuck is threatened by destruction at sea, his faith in God is of no avail. His desperate call—"My God, stand by me now!"—is futile in the face of the imminent catastrophe.

The weakness of Starbuck is contrasted by Melville with the strength of Captain Ahab. In their early dialogue the superiority of Ahab is apparent. The caution expressed by Starbuck about the blasphemous nature of the hunt for Moby Dick is overpowered by the stronger passion of Ahab. Melville attempts at every turn to make Captain Ahab "a mighty pageant creature, formed for noble tragedies." His constant effort to inflate the character of Ahab is one indication of Melville's own resolve to present the religious challenge of the Renaissance hero without hesitation or compromise. The results, however, are mixed. Ahab certainly belongs among the few tragic figures of American literature, but there are moments when Melville's talent fails him, and the presentation of Ahab seems either boring or pretentious. In the following description Melville tries in vain to increase the stature of Ahab: "There was an infinity of firmest fortitude, a determinate, unsurrenderable wilfulness, in the fixed and fearless, forward dedication of that glance" (*Moby-Dick,* pp. 110–11). Melville is straining for heroic emphasis, but the forced alliteration only exposes the hollow exaggeration. The influence of Shakespearean drama upon Melville was not entirely beneficial. The presentation of Ahab at its worst is pseudo-Shakespearean rant. Melville knew that his Renaissance hero posed a direct challenge to the residual Christian piety of the mid-nineteenth century. Perhaps that is why Melville at times could not resist the temptation to exaggerate the "infinity of firmest fortitude" in the mere glance of his extraordinary character.

It was the high moment of the American renaissance when Melville was able to share his accomplishment with Hawthorne: "I have written a wicked book, and feel spotless as the lamb." The very creation of *Moby-Dick* was an act of boldness and rebellion worthy of the Faust tradition, but Melville did not feel the guilt typically associated with the Faust hero. Instead his letter to Hawthorne indicates the kind of ironic detachment that appears in the novel in the narrative voice of Ishmael. It is the skepticism of Ishmael that separates Melville from the narrow resolution of Ahab. It is also the homeless wandering of Ishmael that suggests the future for the religious speculation of Melville. Beyond the wreck of the *Pequod* will come the mock voyage of the Ship of Faith moving downstream on April Fools Day. And then after writing *The Confidence-Man* with its ironic satire of different forms of moral and religious delusion, Melville traveled to Jerusalem to see the holy places of Christianity. The caustic observations recorded in his journal are worthy of a yet more experienced Ishmael. "Is the desolation of the land," Melville asked himself while traveling through Judea, "the result of the fatal embrace of the Deity?"[4]

The vision of desolation follows naturally from the climax of *Moby-Dick.* The worst fears of Ahab are realized when the whale approaches the ship with "his whole aspect" showing "retribution, swift vengeance, [and] eternal malice." Where else in literature is there a more powerful revelation of the heartless will that rules the created world? Not until Yeats's vision of the Second Coming—"what rough beast, its hour come round at last,/Slouches towards Bethlehem to be born?"— does there appear an indictment of divine force in the same degree of outrage and despair. The "god-bullied hull" of the *Pequod* with its crew of pagans and Christians alike is doomed to sink into the "yawning gulf" of the Pacific. When the bird of heaven, "with archangelic shrieks," is caught in the flag of Ahab, the pact with the Devil is complete, and the ship with all its captives is ready to "sink to hell." Once more the story of Faust has reached its inevitable conclusion. But this time the contest of human and divine authority results in a scene of almost total desolation. All the races and religions on board the *Pequod* are carried down beneath the "great shroud of the sea." Only Ishmael survives the wreckage of the sacred hunt—buoyed up by a coffin, he drifts round and round on the creamy pool left by the vortex of the sinking ship. The "inscrutable tides of God" that he once described from the mast-head of the *Pequod* now become a "soft and dirge-like main." "And if thou gaze long into an abyss," Nietzsche wrote, "the abyss will also gaze into thee." The "great flood-gates of the wonder-world" have opened for Ishmael, but now the ocean is desolate, and the lone sur-vivor floats on the "colorless all-color of atheism." The outcast son of Abraham only survives to tell the story of how once upon a time a tragic hero led his crew against the crooked jaw of Moby Dick.

How many harpoons will the image of God hold until it sinks back into the depths of the unconscious sea? The vision of desolation at the end of *Moby-Dick* foreshadows the barren landscape of the religious imagination in the twentieth century. What remains after the shipwreck of the *Pequod?* Only "post-mortem effects," said D. H. Lawrence. The poetry of T. S. Eliot, the subject of the next and last chapter, is the best guide to the wasteland inherited by the descendants of Ishmael.

8

T. S. ELIOT AMONG THE INFIDELS

Imitations of Jeremiah have been popular in the American imagination
for more than three hundred years. The prophecy of sin and destruction
was repeated often by Puritan ministers during the second generation of
the Massachusetts Bay Colony. Winthrop's "city upon a hill" was
described as a wasteland of sin and corruption as early as 1660. The
warning of death and Hell was dramatized with such lurid intensity
in *The Day of Doom* that it remained the most celebrated poem in
the New World for more than a century. The ghost of Jeremiah, warning against the backsliding of Puritans and the approaching wrath of
God, was still heard in New England until just before the American
Revolution. Then the optimistic voice of the Enlightenment, expressed
by men like Franklin and Jefferson, gradually replaced the old rhetoric
of fear and punishment. The new optimism was expanded in the nineteenth century by the Transcendentalists who exchanged the vision of
supernatural torment for the inspiration of harmony in nature. After the
Civil War, however, the disintegration of American culture seemed to
betray the hopes of both Jefferson and Emerson. The Enlightenment vision
of democratic equality was ignored by the new aristocrats of an uncon-
trolled capitalism, and the Transcendental dream of a natural paradise
was mocked by the growth of big industry and congested cities. Even
as passionate a Transcendentalist as Whitman was disillusioned enough
to describe America in 1871 as a "dry and flat Sahara" broken only by
"cities, crowded with petty grotesques, malformations, phantoms, playing
meaningless antics." The rhetoric of Jeremiah had to be revived to
describe a new landscape of spiritual emptiness. But the Old Testament

vision of a purgatorial journey "through a land of deserts . . . through a land of drought, and of the shadow of death" did not achieve its full dramatization in American poetry until T. S. Eliot published *The Waste Land* in 1922. His picture of spiritual drought—the "empty cisterns and exhausted wells"—echoes the voice of God heard by the Jewish prophet: "For my people have committed two evils; they have forsaken me the fountain of living waters, and hewed them out cisterns, broken cisterns, that can hold no water" (Jeremiah 2:13). Eliot's description of cities falling into ruin is also foreshadowed by the warning delivered to Israel: "The young lions roared upon him, and yelled, and they made his land waste: his cities are burned without inhabitant" (Jeremiah 2:15). *The Waste Land* is a dramatization of a living Hell written for a new century of infidels.

Who was this modern Jeremiah? Why did T. S. Eliot so often assume the voice of a prophet calling in the wilderness? Few poets have ever achieved his notorious position as a public critic and moralist. Starting his career as a philosopher and poet, Eliot expanded his activities to include a wide range of drama, poetry, and criticism. But all his talents were focused upon a coherent warning against the spiritual despair of the twentieth century. In many of his poems, plays, and essays, Eliot complained about "the disintegration of Christendom, the decay of a common belief and a common culture." The descendants of Melville's Ishmael, Eliot was convinced, were still floating on the "colorless all-color of atheism." The scorn of Jeremiah was not reserved for the outcast children of Abraham. "In the present ubiquity of ignorance," Eliot protested, "one cannot but suspect that many who call themselves Christians do not understand what the word means."[1]

Eliot's ancestors came to America when the rhetoric of Jeremiah was enjoying its first popularity in the New World. Andrew Eliot emigrated to Massachusetts just in time to be among the first readers of *The Day of Doom.* He later served as a juror at the Salem witch trials. A few years after the hanging of the witches, Andrew Eliot did publicly regret, unlike Judge Hathorne, his share in the whole sorry persecution. The contrast between the juror's confession of error and the judge's stubborn moral righteousness was reversed among their famous descendants. While Nathaniel Hawthorne in the nineteenth century probed the error and guilt of dogmatism, T. S. Eliot believed in the twentieth century that the "spirit of excessive tolerance is to be deprecated."

Although T. S. Eliot came to embrace a form of Christianity more inclusive than the rigid Puritanism of his first American ancestors, many of his habits of mind still resembled those of the early Puritans.

His preoccupation with sin and his dread of vulgarity were as sharp and nagging as the conscience of Cotton Mather. His trust in moments of divine grace and his concern to have intellect and emotion act in harmony were as important to Eliot as they had been to Jonathan Edwards. Moral anxiety, theological speculation, eschatological vision, all characterize Eliot's religious imagination. No other poet and critic has done so much to recall the modern intellect to the spiritual concerns of the seventeenth century. Whether recommending the prose of Bishop Andrewes or the poetry of John Donne, Eliot wanted to remind his audience of a time when passion and intelligence could work together in their commitment to a Christian God. Since the middle of the seventeenth century, Eliot believed, the Anglo-American imagination had suffered from a disastrous split between feeling and intellect. While the mind was committed to a scientific and rational analysis of the material universe, only the emotions were left to support a sentimental and debased religion. Eliot blamed this "dissociation of sensibility" for the disintegration he perceived in both theology and art. "The chief clue," he wrote in 1933, "to the understanding of most contemporary Anglo-Saxon literature is to be found in the decay of Protestantism."[2]

Eliot knew that his own family in the nineteenth century had been in the vanguard of the destructive movement. His grandfather, the Reverend William Eliot, had belonged to the generation of students at Harvard just between Emerson and Thoreau. After his graduation from the divinity school in 1834, he organized the first Unitarian church in St. Louis and later founded Washington University. Two of his four sons in turn became Unitarian ministers. Although the Reverend William Eliot died a year before the birth of his most famous grandson, the poet's childhood was richly endowed with the family memories of his influence and authority: "The standard of conduct was that which my grandfather had set; our moral judgments, our decisions between duty and self-indulgence, were taken as if, like Moses, he had brought down the tables of the Law, any deviation from which would be sinful."[3] T. S. Eliot spent his early years in St. Louis and Boston encouraged by the intellectual tradition of his family and vaguely unsatisfied with their rigid Unitarianism. Years later Eliot complained: "I was brought up outside the Christian Fold, in Unitarianism; and in the form of Unitarianism in which I was instructed, things were either black or white. The Son and the Holy Ghost were not believed in."[4] Undoubtedly the Reverend William Eliot would have been amazed to hear that his faith was "outside the Christian Fold," but T. S. Eliot had long since decided that any religion without the Son and the Holy Ghost could not rightly be called "Christian."

Eliot was hardly the first to rebel against what Emerson had labeled "corpse-cold Unitarianism." But Eliot was neither willing to follow Emerson into the mystical vapors of Transcendentalism nor able to follow a philosopher like Irving Babbitt all the way into secular humanism. Eliot felt the need for a community of faith supported by traditional ritual and dogma. In 1927 he formally entered the Anglo-Catholic communion. In the same year he received British citizenship. His official acceptance of the English church and state reversed the long history of the Eliot family in the New World. The descendant of Puritans and Unitarians had unwound the thread of history until he could reach back to a vital Christian faith untroubled by provincial schism or secular compromise. The transformation of a young man from the best Unitarian family in St. Louis into a self-avowed "classicist in literature, royalist in politics, and anglo-catholic in religion" was more than just a unique and remarkable odyssey of the religious imagination; it revealed at every step of the conversion the secular alternatives, the landscape of anxiety, and the spiritual contradictions of the century.

When Eliot came to Harvard in 1906, he could not fail to notice that his opinions already differed from the majority of his fellow students. He wanted to receive a full classical education at a time when the study of Greek and Latin had already come under attack as impracticable. He wanted to study philosophy and literature while the majority of students were preparing for careers in business, law, and medicine. He learned Italian in order to read Dante, and he even learned some Sanskrit in order to read the scriptures of Buddhism. Contemporary American culture seemed to him hopelessly materialistic, utilitarian, and shallow. In his early satirical verse Eliot described the readers of the *Boston Evening Transcript* as mindless scarecrows tossed about "in the wind like a field of ripe corn." What disturbed Eliot the most about his native country was the strident individualism and the shallow optimism that dominated popular American culture at the turn of the century. He deplored the economic mythology of Horatio Alger and the political chauvinism of Theodore Roosevelt. Eliot discovered some escape from the philistines by studying literature and philosophy at Harvard, but when the offer of a graduate scholarship enabled him to travel and study abroad, he did not return to America for more than eighteen years.

Eliot's dissatisfaction with his countrymen followed a long tradition of complaint in American literature. More than fifty years earlier Melville had satirized in *The Confidence-Man* the hypocrisy and greed of American business ethics, the gullibility of faithful men, and the naiveté of American humanitarian ideals. After the Civil War the satire continued, with Mark Twain repeatedly indicting the rude vanity and crass materialism of his fellow Americans. But Eliot could neither share the tragic skepticism of Melville nor the bitter cynicism of Mark Twain. He felt that both belonged to the Devil's party: Melville by describing the individualism of Captain Ahab as heroic, and Twain by surrendering to a ruthless naturalism without scope for the dignity of man or the power of God. Eliot believed that the romantic tendencies of Melville's art should be resisted. He saw how the glorification of Captain Ahab's defiance could lead to the anti-Christian sentiment of Nietzsche's "superman." And beyond the philosophy of Nietzsche he saw the specter of Nazi Germany. Even as a young man Eliot believed that any display of radical individualism was a sign of pride. His creative theory outlined in "Tradition and the Individual Talent" warned against the romantic exploitation of personality. The artist must be understood within the whole tradition of his art, and humility—"the only wisdom we can hope to acquire"—is the chief virtue recommended for both man and artist. Eliot was therefore suspicious of all heroic pretense. Twice he witnessed his century trapped in a world war of aggression and pride. His own art would be deliberately anti-romantic and anti-heroic. The ironic "Love Song of J. Alfred Prufrock" is an early example.

VISIONS OF HELL

Eliot began "Prufrock" as a graduate student at Harvard, and completed the poem during his visit to Germany in 1911. A few years later the poem became Eliot's first significant publication. It is a poem of adolescent desire and frustration despite the self-conscious aging of the dramatic persona. It is also a poem of metaphysical yearning and despair set within a modern context of indifference and triviality. The poem is deliberately anti-romantic. The expectation of romance—"Let us go then, you and I,/When the evening is spread out against the sky" —is quickly choked and dissipated in images of ether, fog, and smoke. It is soon clear that the hesitant protagonist of the poem will not be able to approach any woman with his "overwhelming question." His mind is too filled in advance with their possible criticism—"How his hair is growing thin!" Or their probable indifference—"That is not what I meant at all." Even the romantic fantasy of the mermaids proves unsatisfactory when the pathetic and lonely Prufrock admits near the end of the poem, "I do not think that they will sing to me."

The poem is also deliberately anti-heroic. Prufrock's initial question, "Do I dare/Disturb the universe?" is later replaced with the ridiculous "Do I dare to eat a peach?" The timid protagonist of the poem must finally abandon all pretense of heroic accomplishment, and admit instead "I am not Prince Hamlet, nor was meant to be."

The epigraph to the poem, borrowed from Dante's *Inferno,* indicates that Prufrock is trapped in a contemporary Hell. Although the poem echoes the words of Ecclesiastes and also includes references to Lazarus and John the Baptist, its religious significance chiefly rests in the dramatization of a living inferno. Prufrock suffers from vague desires, both romantic and metaphysical, that he can neither satisfy nor forget. He is trapped in an endless cycle of routine unfulfillment. He is surrounded by characters and objects presented as trivial, indifferent, and futile. The poem projects much of Eliot's adolescent dissatisfaction with a contemporary world that would neither allay his shy and painful self-consciousness nor respect his spiritual unrest. Eliot was able to cope with his personal hell of anxiety and frustration because he was learning how to transmute his awkwardness among the philistines into sophisticated poetry. He mastered the disguise of irony, the dramatic persona of Prufrock, and the techniques of experimental, modern, symbolic verse. But most important of all, he began to understand the wisdom of Dante—Hell is invented by a man with literary imagination and the deep wounds of moral insight. In time he would also dramatize a modern Purgatory and finally at least a few hints of Paradise. But first he would expand his vision of contemporary Hell into the full length of *The Waste Land.*

The lonely anguish of Prufrock is acted out against the background of meaningless social routine. His inhibited desires are never revealed to the bored women who "come and go/Talking of Michelangelo." His romantic aspirations are mocked by the trivial context of "tea and cakes and ices." Eliot's dramatic persona is trapped in a mild and polite underworld of frustrated passion. Despite the technical innovations of the poem, Eliot was still portraying the kind of Hell that Browning or Swinburne or even Oscar Wilde could have imagined. The indifferent women in the poem belong to the genteel decadence of the nineties; they are not the sirens and nymphs of a real underworld. Even the frustrated desire of Prufrock appears rather artificial, more pretense than passion. Only in *The Waste Land* does Eliot dramatize the woman who "drew her long black hair out tight" and the intense "burning, burning, burning" of sterile lust. It is finally in *The Waste Land* that Eliot manages to compress the "immense panorama of futility and anarchy which is contemporary history" into a poem that often reflects the passion and terror of Dante's inferno.

No poem in the twentieth century has attracted as much critical attention as *The Waste Land*. It has been acclaimed as a "modern epic" and denounced as a "gigantic hoax." It has been celebrated as a "master work of the twentieth century imagination" and blamed for the "disintegration of modern literature." Moreover it has been dissected and analyzed by a swarm of critics ready and willing to track down obscure sources and allusions. Eliot himself added the first footnotes to his poem, and the mills of scholarship have been grinding ever since. But the chief purpose here is to see the poem as a metaphysical drama, and to understand its place in the development of Eliot's religious imagination.

"His despair, his disillusion," Eliot wrote in an essay on Pascal, are "essential moments in the progress of the intellectual soul. . . . They are the analogue of the drought, the dark night, which is an essential stage in the progress of the Christian mystic."[5] Eliot was fascinated by Pascal's conversion from "worldly knowledge" to a consuming interest in "mystical experience." The dry, sterile thunder in *The Waste Land,* the landscape of fear and anguish, the shifting scenes of futility and impotence, all represent the stage of despair and disillusionment in the striving of the religious imagination. The pathway of the saint begins among the dry rocks of the desert where the emptiness of human vanity and the fearful shadows of mortality are traditionally exchanged for the signs of a divine power. In Eliot's poem the desert echoes with the sound of Jehovah speaking to the Old Testament prophets. Awareness of death is the first ordeal of the spirit in the desert. "I will show you fear in a handful of dust," says a powerful voice in "The Burial of the Dead," the opening section of *The Waste Land*. The fear of death is counteracted with the hope for resurrection. After crossing the landscape of drought and despair, the religious traveler expects to come to the miracle of life-giving water. Eliot takes us in his poem through a complex wasteland, a mixture of the ancient and the modern, scenes of anguish from the Old Testament and glimpses of terrible boredom and futility amid the chaos of the present world. Near the end of the poem we do come to the bank of the sacred river in Buddhist scripture. The voice of divine power does speak in the thunder. But the poem ends without a clear spiritual resolution. While the dramatic persona in the final scene turns his back upon the desert landscape, "the arid plain behind me," his attempt to bring order out of chaos is fragmentary and inconclusive. The steep ascent of Purgatory will necessarily be the subject of another poem.

Eliot was both amused and frustrated to discover *The Waste Land* praised for many of the wrong reasons. The poem was hailed as an exposé of a disillusioned generation. The hero of F. Scott Fitzgerald's first novel in 1920 announced that his generation had emerged from World War I to find "all Gods dead, all wars fought, all faiths in man shaken." Eliot's poem was received by many critics a few years later as a vivid display of the meaninglessness experienced by the postwar generation. The superficial label from Gertrude Stein—"You are all a lost generation"—soon became the empty currency of literary criticism. Interpreters of *The Waste Land* overlooked the purpose of the experience in the desert. Ignoring what Eliot called "an essential stage in the progress of the Christian mystic," the vision of chaos in *The Waste Land* was accepted uncritically as if it were an end in itself. Eliot was so annoyed by the smug indulgence of meaninglessness that he voiced a strong counterattack: "When I wrote a poem called *The Waste Land* some of the more approving critics said that I had expressed the 'disillusionment of a generation,' which is nonsense. I may have expressed for them their own illusion of being disillusioned, but that did not form part of my intention."[6] But still the critics insisted on interpreting *The Waste Land* merely as a "criticism of the contemporary world," and Eliot finally overreacted by dismissing his own poem as "just a piece of rhythmical grumbling."

The misunderstanding between Eliot and his critics was due in part to the debased currency of literary and social criticism—expectations of a religious void were automatically reinforced by the many clichés of emptiness and chaos. At times Eliot felt that the gap between himself and those ready to welcome the decay of religious vision was impossibly great. "The acrimony which accompanies much debate," he wrote in 1933, "is a symptom of differences so large that there is nothing to argue about."[7] But some of the misunderstanding was due merely to the disconnected structure of *The Waste Land*. The experimental style of the poem no doubt guaranteed its immediate notoriety, but it also delayed a coherent interpretation. The critical disagreement was also increased by references in the poem to so many different religions, cultures, and literatures. When Eliot put together quotations from Saint Augustine's *Confessions* and Buddha's "Fire Sermon," and then reported in a footnote that "the collocation of these two representatives of eastern and western asceticism . . . is not an accident," he provoked a number of critics into feeling that no excuse could justify the unclear and arbitrary poetic method. And still more readers were frustrated by the anthropological theories supporting the coherence of the poem. Many resented the recommended detour to Frazer's *Golden Bough* and Weston's *From Ritual to Romance*. What right did a poet have to make such demands upon his audience? When berated with the difficulty of his poem, Eliot merely adopted the disguise of Old Possum and smiled with mock concern.

The metaphysical drama of *The Waste Land* is Eliot's tribute to the imagination of Dante. The poem represents a tormented progress through Hell and at least an approach to the vision of Purgatory. Quotations from Dante's *Inferno* are interspersed throughout *The Waste Land*. At times the anguish of sin is represented by Eliot in the desert landscape of the Old Testament prophets. At times the setting is a modern city with crowds of anxious people. But in either context the dramatic personae stand in need of spiritual rebirth. They desperately yearn for a sign from the heavens, the distant sound of God's thunder, and the blessing of rain.

The spiritual condition of the characters in *The Waste Land* is measured by their separation from the cycles of nature. The life-bringing rains should come in the spring; the season of rebirth should be the high point of the religious calendar; but in *The Waste Land* the characters are uprooted and cannot anticipate the spring with any confidence or joy. April is therefore "the cruellest month." A voice at the beginning of the poem announces that spring rain will only awaken painful memory and unfulfilled desire among the inhabitants of a modern wasteland. No escape from the paralysis of fear and indifference seems possible. Voices of prophecy are heard throughout the poem. "I will show you fear in a handful of dust," says a voice with Old Testament authority. "Fear death by water," says a common fortune teller in modern London. But the nightmare journey continues and the fear is unrelieved.

Eliot dramatizes the plight of the wasteland by retelling the ancient legend of the Fisher King. The significance of the legend is explored in both Frazer's *The Golden Bough* and Weston's *From Ritual to Romance*. Among the ancient cultures of the eastern Mediterranean, the celebration of rebirth included the fishing of a symbolic deity from the flooded rivers. The resurrection of the god in the season of spring rains would symbolize the promise of fertility to the land. But if the king was unable to fish the god from the river, his country would remain dry and sterile. Such is the prevailing circumstance of *The Waste Land*. The legend of the Fisher King is an ancient story of religious and sexual initiation. The unsuccessful king is both unregenerate and impotent. His land is denied the symbol of grace, the rain will not fall, and his people are condemned to a living hell of unfulfilled desire. In Eliot's poem the dramatic personae are tormented with the sound of "dry sterile thunder without rain," and their scenes of passion are mechanical and barren.

Eliot read enough anthropology to understand how the ancient fertility rites which celebrate the natural rebirth of the land in the spring are a necessary prologue to the religious myth of resurrection. The ancient story of the Fisher King is connected in Miss Weston's book with the Christian legend of the Holy Grail which spread through Europe in the Middle Ages. Both are a test of religious and sexual power. In the legend of the Holy Grail, the medieval knight journeys on a symbolic quest to find two things: the sacred cup which Christ used at the Last Supper, and the lance which pierced Christ's side at the Crucifixion. Without the grail the knight is cut off from the sacrament of Communion, and without the lance the knight is sexually impotent. In *The Waste Land* the search for the Holy Grail becomes a nightmare journey among the dry rocks of the desert and the falling ruins of contemporary Europe. In the fifth section of the poem Eliot establishes a parallel between the ordeal of the disciples shortly after the Crucifixion and the hardships of the knight on the quest. On the road to Emmaus the disciples are unable to recognize the Christ who has returned to them. In many of the Grail legends the knight fails to realize how close he may be to grace and power. Even the curse of sterility can traditionally be lifted from the Fisher King if an innocent child approaches with the right question. In all three circumstances the despair and disillusionment may be cured by renewed faith in the signs of resurrection. But the disciples are filled with doubt, the medieval knight is misled by pride, and the Fisher King has upset the cycle of natural procreation. The spiritual drought will last until the soul is emptied of the worldly desire and vanity which prevail in the wasteland.

At the end of Eliot's poem the Fisher King is sitting on the shore with the arid plain behind him. In the twilight of his ruined land, between the time of death and rebirth, the last dramatic persona of *The Waste Land* is attempting to patch together the fragments of his disconnected life. He assembles quotations in different languages, the chaos is not vanquished, but all the quotations at least point indirectly to the expectation of divine peace beyond the burning fires of Purgatory. There is no simple optimism at the end of *The Waste Land,* but the heart of despair has been confronted, and the hell of negative passion has been endured. Eliot is ready to follow Dante into another world.

VISIONS OF PURGATORY

The spiritual progress from Hell to Purgatory is dramatized in "Ash Wednesday." In this poem of transition Eliot describes "the time of tension between dying and birth." The speaker of the poem is still among "the rocks/In the last desert," but his prayers invoke the "Blessed sister, holy mother, spirit of the fountain, spirit of the garden." Spiritual movement is symbolized in the poem by the gradual ascent of a winding staircase. A similar progress is found in Dante and in the work of St. John of the Cross which Eliot had just been reading. When he borrowed the image of climbing stairs to suggest the purgatorial ascent, Eliot knew as well as the Spanish mystic that any desired escape from the "dark night of the soul" could not be accomplished merely by a determined struggle against disbelief. "The soul cannot be possessed of the divine union," wrote St. John of the Cross, "until it has divested itself of the love of created beings." What is required then is a paradoxical mixture of discipline and resignation. Thus a voice in Eliot's poem says again and again: "Teach us to care and not to care/Teach us to sit still." The individual spirit must be purged of all selfish desire before accepting the words of Dante—"Our peace in His will."

Eliot started to write "Ash Wednesday" in the same year that he formally became a member of the Anglican Communion. When he acknowledged his faith in the dogmas and rituals of his adopted church, Eliot was mindful of reversing the journey from England to Massachusetts which his Puritan ancestors had made almost three hundred years before. But he was more interested in rejecting the progress of his contemporaries. In his essay on "Religion and Literature," Eliot complained about the "gradual secularization of literature." He knew how peculiar his own religious voice must sound among modern writers "who have never heard the Christian Faith spoken of as anything but an anachronism."[8] Eliot did not underestimate the distance he was creating between himself and his secular contemporaries. At a time when the triumphs of science were creating an unprecedented belief in natural philosophy, Eliot was determined to stress "the primacy of the supernatural over the natural life." At a time when the comparative study of religion tended to erode the special claims of any one faith,

Eliot was prepared to accept the Anglican dogmas because "the Christian scheme seemed to me the only one which would work."[9]

Eliot's public admission of his religious faith, and the growing orthodoxy of his criticism and poetry, provoked a storm of negative comment from his secular audience. He was labeled a pseudo-believer, and his acceptance of Anglican dogma was ridiculed as a matter of "swallowing camels." Even his good friend and fellow poet Ezra Proud made fun of him for "talking a lot of cod about a dead god." Among liberal critics Eliot was accused of having surrendered his intellectual birthright—"He is a man who has abdicated." When he wrote that Baudelaire was "essentially a Christian, born out of his due time," Eliot was also describing the pain and loneliness of his own plight. What his detractors could not understand was how Eliot could write some of the most advanced poetry of the twentieth century and still affirm the rituals and dogma of an obsolete church. Did Eliot not know that historical scholarship had questioned the authenticity of Holy Scripture? Did he not know that anthropologists had uncovered the roots of his religion in primitive fears and tribal rituals? Did he not know that psychoanalysts had described the connection of religious energy and sexual repression? Did Eliot not know that contemporary philosophy in the form of logical positivism had denied the supernatural premise of his faith? or that modern ethics in the form of existentialism had repudiated the "moral absolutism" which he affirmed? How could Eliot still maintain a religion which had been doubted and diluted beyond repair? How could he adopt a faith which had fallen victim to rational skepticism, debilitating compromise, and modern indifference? And so his critics expressed their disbelief. But neither blind to the objections, nor unaware of the alternatives, Eliot kept on his journey through the desert.

After the publication of *The Waste Land* in 1922, Eliot accepted the editorship of the *Criterion*. For almost two decades he used his position as editor to carry on a public campaign as a self-appointed guardian of literary taste and cultural standards. His many occasional essays published during the same years also added weight to his public reputation. Even sympathetic critics began to call Eliot a "literary dictator." His judgments covered a wide range of subjects from the religious philosophy of Pascal to the experimental poetry of Ezra Pound. Although the virtues of objectivity and impersonality were praised by Eliot as characteristics of true poetry, his own poems emerged as thinly disguised biographical dramas. The insecurity and anxiety of the poet were hardly concealed behind the dramatic masks of Prufrock and the Fisher King. And the same was true of Eliot's prose writing. Although he adopted the critical disguise of objective judge and dispassionate commentator, his personal taste and bias were still apparent.

A consistent point of view, however paradoxical, does emerge from the many different essays which Eliot wrote during the twenties and thirties. He warned repeatedly against the rootlessness of modern culture, although he himself had moved from St. Louis to Boston to England. He often spoke against the shallowness and hypocrisy of "an age of unsettled beliefs," although his own poetry had ironically added to the celebration of the wasteland. He frequently emphasized the value and need for tradition, although his own verse continued to be very innovative and experimental. And he advocated the significance of religious dogma, although he knew that most church doctrine had been riddled with liberal skepticism. The public, which had been intrigued by the sophisticated form of *The Waste Land,* was slow to comprehend the reactionary thrust of Eliot's views. Some critics, who had praised the early poetry as a revelation of chaos, now felt betrayed by Eliot's apparent move in the direction of conservative beliefs and religious dogmatism. When Eliot announced in 1928 that he considered himself to be a "classicist in literature, royalist in politics, and anglo-catholic in religion," their worst suspicions were confirmed.

In the next decade Eliot responded to his critics with books and essays designed to analyze and evaluate religious alternatives. In 1933 he published *After Strange Gods: A Primer of Modern Heresy.* It was denounced by an outraged critic as "one of the narrowest and most bigoted critical books of modern times."[10] In 1936 he published *Essays Ancient & Modern* which included both "Religion and Literature" and "Catholicism and International Order." It was suggested by another unfriendly critic that Eliot had condemned himself "to an unreal position." In 1939 he wrote *The Idea of a Christian Society.* And the critical abuse continued. Despite Eliot's many attempts to explain his position, it was said of him in bitter complaint that he did "not propose to have commerce with the world."

In all his writing during this period Eliot emphasized two themes: the importance of tradition and the primacy of the supernatural. Neither was surprising, considering that Eliot had long been interested in both the history of literature and the records of Christian mysticism. But the two subjects came together in the religious imagination of Eliot in a unique and powerful way.

When Eliot used the word "tradition," he was neither indulging in nostalgia for the past nor implying that the present was necessarily inferior. And he certainly was not advocating a simple repetition of history. Eliot used the word "tradition" to indicate the whole record of the imagination in achieving formal expression of basic human desires in both literature and religion. He saw imagination as the creative force which gives order to experience by transforming a chaos of emotions into the patterns of art and the rituals of faith. For the creative process to continue, Eliot felt, the imagination must be in contact with the living record of its past achievements. The literary artist must be educated in the history of his craft. Eliot therefore never doubted the value of a classical education. And for the religious imagination to remain alive, Eliot thought, it must be nourished by the rituals and liturgy of a long established church. Eliot was thus skeptical of any attempt to fabricate a new set of religious images. He dismissed *A Vision* by W. B. Yeats as an example of desperate mythmaking, neither rooted in historical experience nor sanctioned by a living faith. Without the support of tradition, Eliot believed, authentic literature and religion were impossible. When Eliot complained about the ignorance of his contemporaries—"There never was a time so completely parochial, so shut off from the past"—he was expressing his fear that the modern imagination had become uprooted and was dying.

The importance of tradition was united in Eliot's writing with the essential role of the supernatural. No other poet of the twentieth century knew the spiritual dryness of the wasteland so well, and yet still believed in the power of divine inspiration. "The supernatural," Eliot wrote, "is the greatest reality here and now."[11] For Eliot the history of the imagination was not just the evolution of human consciousness; it was a continuing dialogue between the supernatural and the natural. That is why his theory of history gives first priority to the idea of incarnation. And it also helps to explain why so many of his poems resemble prayers. Eliot believed in the Gospel According to St. John—"In the beginning was the Word, and the Word was with God, and the Word was God." Literature and religion therefore both have the same origin, and it is the task of the poet to find the pattern of words to give form to his continuing experience of the divine. In Eliot's poem "Ash Wednesday" the form is a prayer of intercession. In his later series of poems, *Four Quartets,* the doctrine of incarnation from the beginning of the Gospel According to St. John is turned into a metaphysical drama about the intersection of time and eternity. The development of Eliot's poetry into religious drama separated him further from those contemporaries whom he accused of vainly ignoring the supernatural. "Human wisdom," he insisted, "cannot be separated from divine wisdom without tending to become merely worldly wisdom, as vain as folly itself."[12] He warned repeatedly against the growing secularization of modern writing—"the greater part of our current reading matter is written for us by people who have no real belief in a supernatural order"—because he was convinced that when the tradition of the supernatural Word is neglected, religion and literature will vanish together. "I do not believe," he wrote in 1948, "that the culture of Europe could survive the complete disappearance of the Christian Faith."[13]

Eliot did not recognize the findings of anthropology or psychoanalysis to be incompatible with the claims of traditional religion. He read widely in the literature of anthropology which appeared early in the century. The influence of Frazer's *The Golden Bough* is evident in much of Eliot's poetry—it is of central importance to *The Waste Land*. But Eliot's belief in the Christian myth was not disturbed by his knowledge of its many antecedents among the primitive cultures of the eastern Mediterranean. Instead he accepted the various rituals and legends uncovered by the anthropologists as examples of primitive efforts to give literary and religious shape to the incarnation of the divine Word. While the discoveries of anthropologists were received by others as proof that all religions were merely human inventions, Eliot maintained that the very roots of the human imagination were nourished by contact with a supernatural order. "Man is man because he can recognize supernatural realities, not because he can invent them." The anthropologists might describe any number of legends and rituals as analogous to the Christian myth; Eliot would simply accept them all as evidence of a spiritual dialogue between man and God. *The Waste Land* could therefore bring together references to the various primitive gods in *The Golden Bough,* as well as Jehovah and Buddha, and still be a very Christian poem.

Eliot responded to the claims of psychoanalysis in a similar manner. As a young man he was fascinated by the recent studies of schizophrenia. The divided personality of J. Alfred Prufrock may be a reflection of Eliot's interest in the state of mind in which all desire is repressed or inhibited and sexual energy is released in the fantasies of wishful thinking. Prufrock daydreams about mermaids, but he is intimidated by the women who come and go in the poem. Eliot also knew the major writings of Freud and Jung. Although at times he dismissed their theories with amusement and scorn, he did admit that "psychology has very great utility. . . . It can revive and has already to some extent revived, truths long since known to Christianity, but mostly forgotten and ignored."[14] Eliot could not accept Freud's conclusion that all images in the unconscious mind represent fears and desires first known and then suppressed by individual consciousness. Eliot believed instead that images stored in the depths of the psyche were a composite record of literature and religion. His view was similar to the "collective unconscious" proposed by Jung or the idea of "Spiritus Mundi" suggested by Yeats. But Eliot would go further than either of them in attributing the source of images in the unconscious mind to possible divine intervention. Jung declared with caution that "an archetypal image of the Deity . . . is the most we can assert psychologically about God," but Eliot did not doubt the supernatural origin of such images. The theory of incarnation was central to his understanding of psychology as well as theology. He therefore accepted the findings of psychoanalysis, especially the interpretation of dreams, as a useful way of recovering the "truths long since known to Christianity."

While Eliot was interested in the spiritual content of the unconscious mind, he rejected the theories of Freud and Jung that attempted to explain the creation of religious myth in terms of sexual energy. Freud's summary of religion as "the universal obsessional neurosis" and Jung's assertion that "the gods *are* libido" were both dismissed by Eliot as examples of spiritual blindness. The scientific claims of anthropology and psychology hardly seemed to impress Eliot. He retained a poet's interest in the images of the unconscious mind, and a Christian's interest in the roots of the spiritual imagination, but the actual process of mythmaking—how energy is transformed into symbols—he preferred to leave as a divine mystery.

Eliot knew that scientific materialism was the chief enemy of his religious convictions. He saw only two possibilities: either history is viewed as an incarnation of supernatural power, or it is accepted merely as natural evolution. "There are two and only two finally tenable hypotheses about life: the Catholic and the materialistic." This formula had the advantage of eliminating all the middle positions, from Transcendentalism to Unitarianism, which Eliot felt were impossible and foolish compromises. If the Word of God had not been received by the prophets of the Old Testament, Eliot believed, it surely could not be found among the vain prophets of the nineteenth century. By insisting that only two choices were possible, Eliot was able to dramatize the conflict of faith and materialism in stark all-or-nothing terms. By separating the philosophy of science he was able to attack it with greater strength. "A purely 'scientific' philosophy," Eliot wrote, "ends by denying what we know to be true." Eliot was highly suspicious of the rational claims made by scientific materialism. He scoffed at "that deceitful goddess of Reason who was only born some hundred and fifty years ago." Although he and Bertrand Russell enjoyed a long relationship of mutual respect, the rational skepticism expressed in Russell's "A Free Man's Worship" seemed wholly inadequate to Eliot. Thirty years after its publication Eliot still felt obliged to ridicule "the heroic satisfaction of the free man's worship of nothing." Eliot seldom missed an opportunity to blame his contemporaries for their uncritical faith in scientific progress. He scorned the ignorance and self-satisfaction of a materialistic age "when all dogma is in doubt except the dogmas of science." It is not surprising that as a young student Eliot failed to pass his examinations in physics. He was never able to understand how Russell could live confidently in a universe without divine sanction. Why didn't Russell experience, Eliot wondered, "the misery of man without God?"

When writing on the growth of Pascal's religious philosophy, Eliot attempted to explain the sequence of feeling and thought which culminates in faith: "The Christian thinker . . . finds the world to be inexplicable by any non-religious theory: among religions he finds Christianity, and Catholic Christianity, to account most satisfactorily for the world and especially the moral world within; and thus . . . he finds himself inexorably committed to the dogma of the Incarnation."[15] Eliot was disturbed but not shaken by the fact that a philosopher of science like Bertrand Russell found this sequence of thought to be incredible and the conclusion preposterous. In order to guarantee the traditional education necessary for the survival of a religious culture in an age of scientific materialism, Eliot called for a renewal of interest in classical study, and a "revival and expansion of monastic teaching orders." Eliot, of course, was not sanguine about the prospects, but he did console himself with the thought that Christianity was never meant to triumph completely in an imperfect world. The doctrine of original sin became more important to him as a convenient way of accounting for a world that remained unreceptive to his religious dogmas.

Although the philosophical views of Eliot were again and again denounced as reactionary, he continued to reach a growing audience. His essays and speeches were applauded, debated, and criticized, but never ignored. His poems became required assignments in thousands of university classes. Adding footnotes to *The Waste Land* became a major academic industry. And in 1934 Eliot began a new career as a dramatist with the London premierè of *The Rock,* a religious pageant-play commissioned by a group of English churches. The performance of *Murder in the Cathedral* the following year established Eliot as an important dramatic writer. Four more plays, including *The Cocktail Party* which achieved a fair commercial success, confirmed Eliot's talent as a playwright. His growing reputation brought him such honors as the Order of Merit and the Nobel Prize for Literature. Eliot was prepared to accept the role of a literary elder statesman—the public mask had long been part of his repertoire—and he used every opportunity to advance his views on poetry, culture, and religion.

Eliot's spiritual journey is summarized in a series of poems which appeared between 1935 and 1942. The poet returns imaginatively in *Four Quartets* to particular settings that have had special significance for him: the shore of the Mississippi where he spent his childhood, the coast of New England which he enjoyed as a college student, the English town where his ancestors once lived, and one further English setting which Eliot recognized as a place of meditation and prayer. In each setting the poetic speaker reflects upon the paradox of having to live in time and yet still desiring to have knowledge of eternity. Scattered throughout *Four Quartets* are brief pictures of a timeless state:

> the moment in and out of time,
> The distraction fit, lost in a shaft of sunlight,
> The wild thyme unseen, or the winter lightning
> Or the waterfall, or music heard so deeply
> That it is not heard at all, but you are the music
> While the music lasts.

Only brief hints of eternity are possible here amid "the waste sad time/Stretching before and after," and the poet often explains how difficult it is to find words for his imperfect vision. *Four Quartets* often reads like an apology for metaphysics. But Eliot does succeed in dramatizing the different stages of his spiritual development. The desert of *The Waste Land* is recalled by references to "dead water and dead sand" or "the parched eviscerate soil." The purgatorial journey of "Ash Wednesday" is recalled with echoes of St. John of the Cross—"We must be still and still moving . . ./Through the dark cold and the empty desolation." The prose writing of Eliot is recalled by "the conscious impotence of rage/At human folly." And the goal of the religious quest is suggested by the hints of Paradise which Eliot presents with images from Dante:

> All manner of thing shall be well
> When the tongues of flame are in-folded
> Into the crowned knot of fire
> And the fire and the rose are one.

No other poem in the twentieth century includes a more complete vision of "the still point of the turning world" or a better account of the difficulties inherent in the discipline of the religious imagination.

HISTORY REVISITED

In 1937 Eliot visited the small village in England which his ancestors left in the seventeenth century to come to America. He was intrigued by the paradox of time. How could it be, he wondered, that he was moving back into a strange but familiar past? Could time be circular? "In my beginning is my end." Could it be that his spiritual journey was a retreat in time to the roots of his own religious imagination? In the final poem of *Four Quartets* the circle is completed: "And the end of all our exploring/Will be to arrive where we started/And know the place for the first time." Eliot, however, went all the way back to an Anglo-Catholic vision that even his Puritan ancestors in the seventeenth century had considered substantially outdated. Nevertheless he had more in common with those ancestors, who brought their radical Christianity to the New World, than with any of their descendants. The poetry of Eliot dramatizes what Yeats would call an unwinding of the gyre, a reversal of history back through stages of decay and compromise until it reaches a coherent vision of the source, or to use the language of Eliot, until it approaches the moment of incarnation.

Eliot would have felt at home among the first generation of Puritans in the Massachusetts Bay Colony. They came from the England of Bishop Andrewes and John Donne. They knew the temptations of the wilderness, the banishing of heretics, and the politics of righteousness. Eliot shared many of their spiritual aspirations, and he shared their moral awareness of the sin inherent in human nature. But the first generation of Puritans in America enjoyed the challenge of a fresh beginning. Eliot had no experience to compare with the vision announced by Governor Winthrop of building the City of God in the wilderness. Instead Eliot was forced to acknowledge the decline of any authentic Protestant faith in America. Both the Unitarianism of his childhood and the liberal Christianity held by some of his contemporaries seemed to Eliot to repudiate the covenant with God affirmed by the early Puritans.

The dark warnings of Jeremiah, which Eliot echoed in *The Waste Land,* had been dramatized forcefully in the sermons of Cotton Mather and the poetry of Michael Wigglesworth. But in the second and third generations of the Puritan experience in America the views of the religious leaders still held almost a monopoly on the intellectual and spiritual life of the Massachusetts Bay Colony. Cotton Mather was alarmed by independent tendencies beginning to be evident at Harvard College, but the ties between religion, civil politics, and education were still very much intact. When the Puritan leaders preached against spiritual backsliding, the citizens of the colony were not only expected to be in regular attendance at church, they were also required to support the churches with their taxes. But in the twentieth century Eliot had to confront the full spectacle of disintegration. He saw on all sides "an age of unsettled beliefs and enfeebled tradition." His essay entitled "The Idea of a Christian Society" was a protest against a century in which the surviving churches found themselves largely excluded from the intellectual control of either government or education. "I believe that the choice before us," he wrote in 1939, "is between the formation of a new Christian culture, and the acceptance of a pagan one." Cotton Mather may have accused his congregation of not listening well enough to the truth of his sermons, but Eliot had to acknowledge that the majority of his contemporaries would never respond at all to the dogmas of his religion. And his intellectual critics, Eliot believed, were often among the worst of the infidels. "The whole of modern literature," Eliot complained, "is corrupted by what I call Secularism."[16]

Despite Eliot's deep concern about "the misery of man without God," he did not care much for evangelical crusades. He doubted the value of faith that was not the result of slow and painful discipline, and he felt distaste for any exaggerated public display. He was highly suspicious of the extreme behavior generated by the Great Awakening in the eighteenth century, and he could never fully appreciate the theological genius of Jonathan Edwards. Nevertheless it is probable that Eliot had more in common with the last of the great Puritans than he generally cared to admit. Eliot preferred to find his models among the Christian poets and philosophers of the Middle Ages, but he was often very close to Edwards both in dogma and sensibility. Both writers were apt to dramatize the experience of grace with images of "a white light" and "the heart of light." Eliot also agreed with Edwards about the central importance of the doctrine of original sin. The world to both of them was a wilderness or a wasteland only at rare intervals redeemed by supernatural light. Edwards did possess a command of rational argument beyond any power of analysis evident in the critical essays of Eliot. But a dramatic sense of humor and a constant awareness of irony were available to Eliot which helped his work to achieve a richness and complexity seldom found in the intense but

narrow vision of Edwards. Both authors extended the tradition of
Christian writing, and both gave to their centuries the most complete
description of the trial, frustration, and coherence of the religious
imagination.

Beyond the death of Edwards in 1758, Eliot saw nothing in the
religious history of America but a series of broken covenants. He did
not care at all for the goals of the Enlightenment. Eliot denounced
the rise of natural science as a symptom of materialism, and he ridiculed the "deceitful goddess of Reason." He reserved special scorn
for the practical morality of Benjamin Franklin. Eliot believed that
man should empty himself of pride and vanity in order to prepare
for the gift of divine grace. He was therefore convinced that all the
busy work recommended by Franklin amounted to little more than a
vain distraction from a genuine religious life. Success in any worldly
pursuit was a poor substitute for eternal salvation. "All amibitons of an
earthly paradise," Eliot wrote, "are informed by low ideals." The worship of material progress in any age struck Eliot as proof of spiritual
decay and indifference. The Boston of Cotton Mather which Franklin
experienced as a young boy left him with the lasting impression that
religious dogmatism was an unnecessary evil. Tolerance and skepticism
therefore became two of his important virtues. The Boston of the
fading genteel tradition which Eliot experienced as a young student
left him with the impression that a culture without religious dogma
is undesirable and meaningless. He therefore rejected skepticism as
superficial, and suggested that "the virtue of tolerance is greatly over-
estimated." Although Franklin and Eliot belong at opposite ends of
the religious spectrum, there were a few similarities. In the sly humor
of Franklin's personality there was more than a hint of "Old Possum."
In the methodical industry of Eliot's life there was more than a touch
of "Poor Richard." And both men lived to give some definition to the
phrase "elder statesman."

The political ideals of the Enlightenment were also regarded by Eliot
with considerable disdain. With his conviction of original sin, Eliot
could not share Jefferson's optimism about the essential goodness
of human nature. With his belief in authority and hierarchy, Eliot
was not convinced that democracy was either possible or desirable.
After he became a British citizen in 1927, Eliot described himself as
a "royalist in politics." When other writers of his generation supported
the battle in Spain against fascism, Eliot proclaimed the neutrality of
his artistic conscience. Politics caught his interest only when he saw
a chance to recommend educational reforms that might protect the

heritage of literature and religion. Franklin and Jefferson both founded universities designed to be free of any religious bias. Eliot, however, lamented the overwhelming tide of secular education. "There is no great university," he protested, "in which the religious foundation is now anything but vestigial."[17]

Eliot blamed the Enlightenment for increasing the momentum of the secular forces digging away at the roots of Christianity. The ideals of Franklin and Jefferson seemed to him shallow and dangerous. Beneath the rhetoric of scientific materialism and political democracy, Eliot saw a moral and religious emptiness. The progress of experimental science, he feared, would question the basis of all religious belief until mere rational skepticism might prevail. The leveling force of democracy would erode the standards necessary for culture and religion. The ideals of Franklin and Jefferson were at best, Eliot thought, a naive expression of scientific and democratic humanism. To writers in his own century who looked upon humanism as a possible alternative to religion; Eliot replied, "The humanistic point of view is auxiliary to and dependent upon the religious point of view." In a less charitable mood Eliot described the humanism of his contemporaries as "a by-product of Protestant theology in its last agonies." Eliot could never forgive Franklin and Jefferson for smiling with a cheerful faith in human nature all the time they were digging the grave of Christianity.

The resurgence of a mystical philosophy among the Transcendentalists in the nineteenth century also failed to impress Eliot. He found the religion of Emerson and Thoreau especially distasteful. Eliot looked upon the mysticism of Emerson with the cold disdain that a classicist might be expected to feel for the eccentric ravings of the romantic imagination. From a Christian point of view it seemed to Eliot that the philosophy of Emerson was either heretical, unintelligible, or both. Eliot was greatly annoyed by the casual manner in which Emerson discounted the rituals of the historical church and the dogmas of Holy Scripture. Moments of visionary insight, Eliot believed, must be rooted in a life of prayer, discipline, and humility. But Emerson had been willing to empty the churches in order to have individuals seek their inspiration at once in a mystical union with nature. Eliot simply doubted the authenticity of such an independent faith. Was not the visionary mysticism of Emerson a pleasant and vain delusion? Was not his self-reliance a sign of egotism and pride? Eliot could not believe that Transcendentalism was anything more than a dangerous heresy which stood without a valid religious basis or a sound moral perspective.

What disturbed Eliot the most about the philosophy of Transcendentalism was its unquestioned belief in radical individualism. He did not share Emerson's faith in the inherent goodness of human nature. Quite to the contrary, Eliot saw the life of each individual as a battlefield of memory and desire where the past and the future come together in a constant trial of virtue and sin. No person should confront the trial, Eliot thought, merely by trusting to the integrity of his own instincts. The desires of an individual in a world marred by original sin could never be entirely pure or innocent. Eliot therefore believed that an established church was necessary to guide the discipline of individual men and bring them into a communion which might transcend the waywardness of personal will. The conservative political and religious views held by Eliot were based firmly upon a traditional Christian vision of original sin. Eliot thus considered the philosophy of Transcendentalism to be a mixture of shallow optimism and dangerous self-delusion. Worst of all was Emerson's doctrine of self-reliance, which Eliot saw as proof that Transcendentalism was nothing but a poor excuse for the display of individual pride.

Eliot was convinced that Emerson should be held partly responsible for the drift in America away from established Christianity in the nineteenth century. The Unitarian religion practiced by the Eliot family in Boston and St. Louis was an inadequate substitute, Eliot felt, for the historical Christian faith. But the liberal tide had been encouraged even further by Emerson when he left the Unitarian ministry because he believed that it was not sufficiently progressive. The negative and destructive character of liberalism was sharply described by Eliot in the next century: "In religion, Liberalism may be characterised as a progressive discarding of elements in historical Christianity which appear superfluous or obsolete. . . . It loses force after a series of rejections, and with nothing to destroy is left with nothing to uphold and with nowhere to go."[18] Unable to find spiritual nourishment in the religion of his childhood, Eliot turned back to the roots of Christianity among the primitive cultures of the eastern Mediterranean, and followed the development of religious vision to the full expression of Dante and Aquinas. The establishment of the Anglican church in the sixteenth and seventeenth centuries seemed to Eliot the best structure for preserving the essential rituals and dogmas of the historical faith. Since the middle of the seventeenth century, however, Eliot felt that the liberal and destructive forces had been gaining momentum. The philosophers of the Enlightenment on both sides of the Atlantic had advanced the ideals of science and democracy at the expense of dogmatic religion. And in America in the nineteenth century men like Emerson and Thoreau continued the fight against historical Christianity until there was nothing left for Eliot to inherit but empty churches and a compromised faith. New congregations, of course, were still being recruited among the uneducated, but Eliot could not find a spiritual home in the country which had been liberated by the progressive humanism of Franklin and the self-reliance gospel of Emerson.

Eliot did find something to praise in the writing of Nathaniel Hawthorne. Although he blamed Hawthorne for an "indifference to religious dogma," he still acknowledged Hawthorne's "exceptional awareness of spiritual reality" and his "profound sensitiveness to good and evil." Eliot also recognized Hawthorne as a "genuine artist," whose observation of moral conflict in *The Scarlet Letter* would enjoy "the permanence of art." But Eliot saw clearly enough that *The Scarlet Letter* was a criticism of "the Puritan morality" as well as "the Transcendentalist morality." If Hawthorne could focus a skeptical light on both sides of the dramatic conflict, what could there be left for him to affirm beyond the power of art and the truth of psychological analysis? That was not enough for Eliot. Hawthorne possessed the ability of a novelist to probe the motives of his characters until reaching the depths of fear and desire, and then he was able to dramatize the full ambiguity of psychological conflict without imposing any moral judgment. Eliot was no stranger to the depths of Hell, but he was not content with a dispassionate record of psychological conduct. The heart of darkness had meaning to him only in a religious context. The suffering of Hell was always connected in Eliot's mind with the discipline of Purgatory and the hope for Paradise. The imagination of Eliot could not separate itself from the Christian myth with the same ironic detachment that was characteristic of Hawthorne. The author of *The Scarlet Letter* revealed the skepticism of a tragic artist; the author of *The Waste Land* and *Four Quartets* displayed the traditional concern of a Christian moralist. It is not surprising that Eliot found little to celebrate in the tragic literature of the American renaissance.

Eliot found even less to admire in the novels of Herman Melville. The rediscovery of Melville in this century happened to coincide with the growth of Eliot's reputation as a literary critic, but the two events were unfolding simultaneously in opposite directions. While the power of Melville as an unconventional novelist was being celebrated, Eliot was writing essays on the religious vision of Dante and Pascal. While the voyage of Captain Ahab was being praised as a classic expression of American individualism, Eliot was revealing the dead end of lonely pride in *The Waste Land*. Many of the critics who were ready to applaud the attack upon supernatural power launched by Melville were naturally dismayed by Eliot's criticism of mere secular values.

Melville and Eliot both turned against the religious training of their early years, but they proceeded in different directions. Melville rejected the dogmas of the Puritan religion because of doubts awakened by his tormented skepticism, and Eliot turned away from the mild Unitarianism of his youth in order to affirm the doctrines of a more historical Christian faith. Neither Melville nor Eliot was able to feel in harmony with his contemporaries: Melville anticipated the atheism of the next century, and Eliot looked back to the Christian coherence of Europe in the Middle Ages. Despite the metaphysical scope of *Moby-Dick* Eliot could not appreciate the religious drama of Melville's writing. He condemned Melville's display of heroic pride at the expense of Christian piety. Eliot could not feel much sympathy for the tragic individualism of Captain Ahab. Nor could he feel any admiration for Ahab's grand assault against the very incarnation of divine power. Eliot might have described the rhetoric of Ahab as blasphemy, if he had been able to take any of Ahab's speeches with much seriousness. Instead Eliot merely dismissed Melville's religious vision as limited and naive.

As a young sailor in the South Pacific Melville had observed how the natives were corrupted by the Christian missionaries, and for the rest of his life he remained skeptical of evangelical piety. As a young student on both sides of the Atlantic Eliot witnessed the decline of Christian culture, and he became more convinced that neither religion nor literature could survive without the ritual and dogma of an established church. Melville was an inveterate wanderer who extended the boundaries of the American imagination with his relentless quest. Eliot, however, wanted to return to a time when the adventure of a religious life was neither an expression of individualism nor an excuse for the assertion of pride.

How could Eliot resist the tide which for more than two hundred years had been carrying the American religious imagination away from the orthodox design of the early Puritans? How could Eliot repeal the progress of Franklin and Jefferson, undo the work of Emerson, and ignore the skeptical vision of Hawthorne and Melville? How could Eliot live in "an age of unsettled beliefs and enfeebled tradition" and still affirm the Christianity shared by his ancestors in the seventeenth century? Is it fair to dismiss Eliot as an anachronism? Or does the religious imagination of America somehow come full circle in this century? Is it accurate to call Eliot one of the last great Christian writers to win recognition in a world of infidels? Or does the poetry and drama and criticism of Eliot foreshadow a popular resurrection of confidence in the supernatural? Whether the majority of the American people in the twentieth century have been moving toward the achievement of the secular goals of the Enlightenment, or moving backward in the direction of Christianity, cannot be answered with any certainty. Obviously there have been large numbers of people in all recent periods of American history who understand the skeptical arguments, and perhaps even greater numbers who remain opposed or indifferent.

In the first hundred years of the Puritan experience in the New World, the leading writers all helped to define the relationship between man and God within the theological design inherited from John Calvin. In the following two hundred years the major authors considered in this study all departed from the basic assumptions of Christianity in order to advance their vision of scientific materialism, democratic humanism, transcendental individualism, or the skeptical insights of tragic literature. Only in the twentieth century did Eliot return to the dogmas of traditional Christianity. He knew that he was "born out of his due time." Occasionally he complained about living "in a period of debility like our own," and wondered aloud if either literature or religion would survive in "the dark ages before us." But all the time he continued to dramatize his vision in poems and plays and a wide variety of essays. He understood how the previous two hundred years had moved in a secular direction, and he did not have many illusions about stopping or reversing the trend. Still he believed in shaping his art according to the dictates of his religious conscience. He thus revealed the horror and boredom of a contemporary Hell to an audience who no longer believed in damnation. He dramatized the suffering and discipline of Purgatory to readers who had forgotten that either had any religious meaning. And he wrote poetry about his own fitful awareness of Paradise for an audience largely unconcerned with any definition of supernatural grace. "There sprung up a whole literary generation," wrote R. P. Blackmur in 1951, "whose only knowledge of Christianity was what they got by reading Eliot."

Eliot knew that he was a Christian writer, often praised for the wrong reasons, in a world of infidels. The prophecies of spiritual decline voiced by the first imitators of Jeremiah in the Puritan colonies were brought to fulfillment by Eliot in his dramatic picture of men and women who burn with fear and lust in the barren desert of the twentieth century. The final gift of Christianity was the knowledge of its failure. The ancestors of Eliot who joined the great Puritan migration to the New World would have recognized the shade of Jeremiah in the vision of judgment which Eliot created for his own time. But the wilderness of America had disappeared, and the dream of a New Jerusalem had disappeared as well. The loyal descendant of the early Puritans was ready to mix again with the dust of the Old World. Always mindful of his symbolic role, Eliot requested that his ashes be placed in the church of the small village in Somersetshire which his ancestors left in the seventeenth century to come to America. His end was our beginning.

NOTES

1: SOVEREIGN IN AMERICA

1. William Bradford, *Of Plymouth Plantation, 1620-1647,* ed. S. E. Morison (New York, 1952), pp. 61-62.
2. John Winthrop, *A Model of Christian Charity* (1630), in Perry Miller and T. H. Johnson, eds., *The Puritans: A Sourcebook of their Writings,* 2 vols. (New York, 1963), 1: 199.
3. Bradford, p. 316.
4. "Sinners in the Hands of an Angry God," *Jonathan Edwards: Representative Selections,* ed. C. H. Faust and T. H. Johnson (New York, 1935), p. 164.
5. "Personal Narrative," ed. Samuel Hopkins, *The Life and Character of the Late Reverend Mr. Jonathan Edwards* (Boston, 1765), reprinted in *Jonathan Edwards: A Profile,* ed. David Levin (New York, 1969), p. 26.
6. Michael Wigglesworth, *The Day of Doom* (1662), in Miller and Johnson.
7. "Personal Narrative," pp. 30-31.

2: JEREMIAH IN NEW ENGLAND

1. John Winthrop, *A Model of Christian Charity* (1630), in Perry Miller and T. H. Johnson, eds., *The Puritans: A Sourcebook of their Writings,* 2 vols. (New York, 1963), 1: 199.
2. See Williston Walker, *Creeds and Platforms of Congregationalism* (New York, 1893), pp. 367-439.
3. Cotton Mather, *Magnalia Christi Americana,* 2 vols. (Hartford, 1820), 1: 59.
4. William Bradford, *Of Plymouth Plantation,* ed. S. E. Morison (New York, 1952), p. 334.
5. Edmund S. Morgan, *The Puritan Dilemma: The Story of John Winthrop* (Boston, 1958), p. 96.
6. Sydney E. Ahlstrom, *A Religious History of the American People* (New Haven, 1972), p. 147.
7. *The Diary of Cotton Mather,* 2 vols., ed. W. C. Ford, in *Massachusetts Historical Society Collections,* 7th series (Boston, 1911-1912) 8: 472.
8. Ibid., p. 639.

9. Ibid., 7: 307.
10. Ibid., 8: 484.
11. Ibid., p. 3.
12. Ibid., 7: 475.
13. Cotton Mather, "Return of Several Ministers," in Increase Mather, *Cases of Conscience Concerning Evil Spirits* (London, 1693).
14. *Diary of Cotton Mather,* 8: 663.

3: THE GREAT AWAKENING

1. Letter to Benjamin Colman, May 30, 1735, *The Works of Jonathan Edwards* 4 *(The Great Awakening)*: 104, ed. C. C. Goen (New Haven, 1972).
2. Quoted in Sydney E. Ahlstrom, *A Religious History of the American People* (New Haven, 1972), p. 302.
3. *The Autobiography of Benjamin Franklin,* ed. L. W. Labaree, R. L. Ketcham, H. C. Boatfield, and H. H. Fineman (New Haven, 1964), p. 175.
4. William Cooper, preface to Edwards's *The Distinguishing Marks of a Work of the Spirit of God* (Boston, 1741), in Goen, 4 *(The Great Awakening)*: 217.
5. "The Spiritual Travels of Nathan Cole," *Some Aspects of the Religious Life of New England,* ed. G. L. Walker (Boston, 1897), pp. 91–92.
6. George Whitefield, *The Seventh Journal* (London, 1741).
7. *Boston Evening Post,* July 5, 1742.
8. See the *Boston Weekly Post-Boy,* March 28, 1743, and the *Boston Evening Post,* April 11, 1743.
9. Charles Chauncy, *Enthusiasm Described and Caution'd Against* (Boston, 1742), p. 4.
10. Richard D. Mosier, *The American Temper* (Berkeley, 1952), p. 76.
11. Eugene E. White, "Decline of the Great Awakening in New England: 1741 to 1746," *New England Quarterly* 24 (no. 1): 35–52.
12. Clinton Rossiter, *Seedtime of the Republic* (New York, 1953), p. 57.
13. Perry Miller, "Jonathan Edwards and the Great Awakening," in Daniel Aaron, ed., *American Crisis: Fourteen Crucial Episodes in American History* (New York, 1952), p. 6.
14. Increase Mather, *The Mystery of Christ Opened and Applyed* (Boston, 1686), p. 145.
15. Charles Chauncy, *The New Creature Describ'd, and Consider'd as the Sure Characteristick of a Man's Being in Christ* (Boston, 1741), p. 20.
16. "Sinners in the Hands of an Angry God," *Jonathan Edwards: Representative Selections,* ed. C. H. Faust and T. H. Johnson (New York, 1935), pp. 164–65.
17. John Hancock, *The Examiner, or Gilbert against Tennent* (Boston, 1743), p. 2.
18. Samuel Hopkins, *The Life and Character of the Late Reverend Mr. Jonathan Edwards* (Boston, 1765), reprinted in *Jonathan Edwards: A Profile,* ed. David Levin (New York, 1969), p. 2.
19. Edwin S. Gaustad, *The Great Awakening in New England* (New York, 1965), p. 138.
20. Sidney Mead, *Church History* 23:4:314.
21. George Bancroft, quoted in Edward M. Griffin, *Jonathan Edwards* (Minneapolis, 1971), p. 5.
22. See Perry Miller, *Jonathan Edwards* (New York, 1949), pp. 71–99, and Peter Gay, *A Loss of Mastery: Puritan Historians in Colonial America* (Berkeley, 1966), pp. 88–117.

23.   See Vernon L. Parrington, *Main Currents in American Thought,* 3 vols., 1 *(The Colonial Mind, 1620-1800):* 148–62, (New York, 1927), and Alan Heimert, *Religion and the American Mind: From the Great Awakening to the Revolution* (Cambridge, Mass., 1966), pp. 2–20.

24.   "Personal Narrative," ed. Samuel Hopkins, *The Life and Character of the Late Reverend Mr. Jonathan Edwards* (Boston, 1765), reprinted in Levin, p. 26.

25.   Levin, pp. 30–31.

26.   Ibid., p. 27.

27.   Ibid., pp. 27–28.

28.   Miller, *Jonathan Edwards,* p. 193.

29.   John E. Smith, ed., *The Works of Jonathan Edwards,* 2: *(Religious Affections)* 12 (New Haven, 1959).

30.   Anne Bradstreet, "To My Dear Children" (1672), *The Works of Anne Bradstreet,* ed. Jeannine Hensley (Cambridge, Mass., 1967), p. 243.

31.   Miller, *Jonathan Edwards,* p. 305.

32.   Smith, ed., *Works of Jonathan Edwards* 2: 44.

33.   James Carse, *Jonathan Edwards and the Visibility of God* (New York, 1967), p. 161.

4: THE ECLIPSE OF GOD

1.   Augustine, *The City of God against the Pagans,* book 8, section. 1.

2.   "Whether the British Government Inclines More to Absolute Monarchy, or to a Republic," *The Philosophical Works of David Hume,* ed. T. H. Green and T. H. Grose, 4 vols. (1882), 3: 125.

3.   *The Autobiography of Benjamin Franklin,* ed. L. W. Labaree, R. L. Ketcham, H. C. Boatfield, and H. H. Fineman (New Haven, 1964), p. 146.

4.   Hume, 4: 108.

5.   Peter Gay, *Deism: An Anthology* (Princeton, 1968), p. 21.

6.   Bacon, *The Great Instauration,* in *Works,* ed. J. Spedding, R. L. Ellis, and D. D. Heath, 14 vols. (1857–74), 4: 8.

7.   Bacon, *The New Organon,* in *Works,* 4: 79.

8.   Descartes, "Discours sur la méthode," *Oeuvres,* ed. C. Adam and P. Tannery, 12 vols. (1897–1910), 4: 9.

9.   Ibid., p. 63.

10.   *The Encyclopédie of Diderot and d'Alembert: Selected Articles,* ed. John Lough (1954), p. 73.

11.   Hobbes, *Elements of Philosophy: The First Section, Concerning Body* (1656). The tribute to Galileo is in the dedication.

12.   Quoted in G. S. Brett, *A History of Psychology,* 3 vols. (London, 1921), 2: 257.

13.   Locke, *Essay Concerning Human Understanding,* book 2, chapter 1, section 2.

14.   *Voltaire's Notebooks,* ed. Theodore Besterman (1952), p. 45.

15.   Locke, *Reasonableness of Christianity,* in *Works,* 6: 135.

16.   *Newton's Philosophy of Nature,* ed. H. S. Thayer (New York, 1953), p. 42.

17.   Quoted by Joseph Campbell, *The Masks of God: Creative Mythology* (New York, 1968), p. 596.

18.   Increase Mather, *An Essay for The Recording of Illustrious Providences,* p. 109.

19.   Cotton Mather, *The Wonderful Works of God Commemorated* (Boston, 1690), p. 25.

20.   Quoted by Perry Miller, *The New England Mind: The Seventeenth Century* (New York, 1939; reissued Cambridge, Mass., 1954), p. 212.

21.   Cotton Mather, *Biblia Americana* (manuscript in Massachusetts Historical Society), Genesis 1.

22. Cotton Mather, *Reasonable Religion* (Boston, 1700), p. 40.
23. John Toland, *Christianity Not Mysterious* (London, 1696), p. 127.
24. Cotton Mather, *The Christian Philosopher* (Boston, 1721), p. 304.
25. Jonathan Edwards, "History of the Works of Redemption," *The Works of President Edwards,* 4 vols. (1857), 1: 467.
26. John Trenchard, *The Natural History of Superstition* (London, 1709), p. 9.
27. Pierre Bayle, "Cainites," *Dictionnaire historique et critique,* 3 vols. (Rotterdam, 1697), 2: 721.
28. Hume, 4: 108.
29. Condorcet, *Sketch for a Historical Picture of the Progress of the Human Mind,* tr. June Barraclough, in *The Enlightenment,* ed. Leonard Marsak (New York, 1972), p. 139.
30. Ibid., p. 137.
31. Paul Henri Thiry, Baron d'Holbach, *La Contagion sacrée* (Paris, 1797), p. 1.
32. D'Holbach, *Le Bon Sens, ou Idées naturelles opposées aux idées surnaturelles* (London, 1772), p. 7.
33. Voltaire, *Examen important de Milord Bolingbroke,* in *Oeuvres complètes,* ed. Louis Moland, 52 vols. (1877-85), 26: 298.
34. Franklin, *Autobiography,* p. 17.
35. Ibid., p. 71.
36. Ibid., p. 64.
37. Ibid., p. 113.
38. Ibid., p. 114.
39. Ibid., p. 96.
40. Ibid., pp. 114-15.
41. Ibid., pp. 145-46.
42. Ibid., p. 147.
43. D. H. Lawrence, *Studies in Classic American Literature* (New York, 1964), pp. 18-19.
44. Benjamin Franklin, *Complete Works,* 10 vols. (New York, 1887), 8: 484.
45. *The Diary of Cotton Mather,* 2 vols., ed. W. C. Ford, in *Massachusetts Historical Society Collections,* 7th series (Boston, 1911-12) 8: 366.
46. Franklin, *Autobiography,* p. 152.
47. Ibid., p. 43.
48. Lawrence, p. 10.
49. "Personal Narrative," ed. Samuel Hopkins, *The Life and Character of the Late Reverend Mr. Jonathan Edwards* (Boston, 1765), reprinted in *Jonathan Edwards: A Profile,* ed. David Levin (New York, 1969), p. 28.
50. See *The Works of John Adams,* 10 vols. (Boston, 1856), 1: 661.
51. John Winthrop, "A Model of Christian Charity," *The Puritans: A Sourcebook of their Writings,* ed. Perry Miller and T. H. Johnson, 2 vols. (New York, 1963), 1: 195.
52. "The First Anniversary," *John Donne's Poetry,* ed. A. L. Clements (Norton Critical Edition, New York, 1966), p. 73.
53. William Ellery Channing, "The Essence of the Christian Religion," *The Perfect Life* (1873), in S. E. Ahlstrom, ed., *Theology in America: The Major Protestant Voices from Puritanism to Neo-orthodoxy* (Indianapolis, 1967), p. 208.
54. Jefferson's letter to Benjamin Waterhouse, June 26, 1822.
55. "A Bill for Establishing Religious Freedom," *The Papers of Thomas Jefferson,* ed. Julian P. Boyd, 2: 545-46.
56. Lucretius, *De rerum natura,* book 1, lines 146-48.
57. Immanuel Kant, "Beantwortung der Frage: Was Ist Aufklärung?" *Immanuel Kant's Werke,* ed. Ernst Cassirer, 11 vols. (Berlin, 1912-22), 4: 174.
58. Virgil, *Georgics,* book 2, lines 490-92.

59. Jefferson to Waterhouse, June 26, 1822.
60. "Personal Narrative," p. 26.
61. Jefferson to Waterhouse, June 26, 1822.
62. Jefferson's letter to Horatio G. Spafford, January 10, 1816.
63. *Thomas Jefferson on Democracy,* ed. Saul K. Padover (New York, 1967), p. 121.
64. Jefferson to Waterhouse, June 26, 1822.
65. Jefferson's letter to Mrs. Abigail Adams, January 11, 1817.
66. Jefferson's letter to Roger C. Weightman, June 24, 1826.
67. Jefferson's letter to Martha Jefferson, March 28, 1787.

5: TRANSCENDENTAL PROPHET

1. *Nature* (1836), in *The Collected Works of Ralph Waldo Emerson,* ed. Alfred R. Ferguson et al. (Cambridge, Mass., 1971), 1: 18.
2. Ibid., p. 16.
3. Emerson's text is 2 Corinthians 4: 18.
4. Immanuel Kant, *Critique of Pure Reason* (1781), 30.
5. *The Republic,* trans. Benjamin Jowett, in *The Works of Plato,* ed. Irwin Edman (New York, 1928), p. 478.
6. See the *Christian Examiner* (January, 1832), 11: 373-80, and *Boston Quarterly Review* (October, 1838), 1: 500-14.
7. *Boston Daily Advertiser,* August 27, 1838.
8. Orestes A. Brownson, *The Convert; or, Leaves from My Experience* (New York, 1837; rpt. 1857), p. 122.
9. *Christian Examiner* (November, 1838), 25: 268.
10. Andrews Norton, "A Discourse on the Latest Form of Infidelity" (1839), in *The Transcendentalists,* ed. Perry Miller (Cambridge, Mass., 1950), p. 212.
11. The Divinity School Address (1838), in Ferguson, 1: 76.
12. Theodore Parker, "The Writings of Ralph Waldo Emerson," *Massachusetts Quarterly Review* 3 (March, 1850): 200-55.
13. *Nature* (1836), in Ferguson, 1: 10.
14. Edward T. Taylor, quoted in *The Writers' America,* ed. Marshall B. Davidson (New York, 1973), p. 124.
15. "Sermon for the Ordination of F. A. Farley at Providence" (1828), *The Works of William E. Channing* (Boston, 1880), pp. 291-302.
16. Orestes A. Brownson, *New Views* (1836) in Miller, p. 117.
17. *Dissertation Concerning the End for Which God Created the World* (1765), in *The Works of President Edwards,* 4 vols. (New York, 1879), 2: 255.
18. Sydney E. Ahlstrom, *A Religious History of the American People* (New Haven, 1972), p. 605.

6: PURITAN ROMANCE

1. *The Letters of John Keats,* ed. M. B. Forman (New York, 1952), p. 71.
2. "Hawthorne and His Mosses," *The Literary World,* August 17 and 24, 1850.
3. D. H. Lawrence, *Studies in Classic American Literature* (New York, 1923; rpt. 1964), p. 83.
4. See J. T. Frederick, *The Darkened Sky: Nineteenth Century Novelists and Religion* (1969), p. 29; Edward C. Wagenknecht, *Nathaniel Hawthorne: Man and Writer* (1961), p. 185; and Hubert Hoeltje, *Inward Sky: The Mind and Heart of Nathaniel Hawthorne* (1962), pp. 460-61.

5. Julian Hawthorne, "The Salem of Hawthorne," *Century Magazine* 28 (May, 1884): 6.
6. Jonathan Cilley, quoted in Wagenknecht, p. 85.
7. Quoted in Randall Stewart, *Nathaniel Hawthorne: A Biography* (1948), p. 11.
8. Letter to Nathaniel Hawthorne, April 16, 1851, in *The Letters of Herman Melville*, ed. M. R. Davis and W. H. Gilman (New Haven, 1960), pp. 124–25.
9. Freud, *Collected Papers*, trans. J. Riviere, 5 vols. (New York, 1948–50), 3: 131.
10. *The Scarlet Letter*, ed. William Charvat et al. (Ohio State University Press, 1962), p. 166. All subsequent page references in the text will be to this edition.
11. Vernon Loggins, *The Hawthornes: The Story of Seven Generations of an American Family* (New York, 1951), p. 40.
12. "Main Street" (1849), in *The Snow-Image and Uncollected Tales*, ed. William Charvat et al. (Ohio State University Press, 1974), p. 70.
13. "Alice Doane's Appeal" (1835), in *The Snow-Image and Uncollected Tales*, pp. 278–79.
14. "Main Street," p. 77.
15. "Hawthorne and His Mosses," *Literary World*, August 17 and 24, 1850.
16. *Journals of Ralph Waldo Emerson*, ed. E. W. Emerson and W. E. Forbes, 10 vols. (Boston, 1914), 10: 39–40.
17. Quoted in Wagenknecht, p. 122.
18. "Earth's Holocaust," *Mosses from an Old Manse*, ed. William Charvat et al. (Ohio State University Press, 1974), pp. 403–4.
19. "The Celestial Railroad," *Mosses from an Old Manse*, p. 198.
20. "Hawthorne and His Mosses."
21. *The English Notebooks of Nathaniel Hawthorne*, ed. Randall Stewart (New York, 1941), p. 433.

7: THE SACRED HUNT

1. *Moby-Dick*, ed. Harrison Hayford and Hershel Parker (Norton Critical Edition, New York, 1967), p. 445. Subsequent page references in the text will be to this edition.
2. *The Confidence-Man: His Masquerade*, ed. Hershel Parker (Norton Critical Edition, New York, 1971), p. 130. Subsequent page references in the text will be to this edition.
3. *The English Notebooks of Nathaniel Hawthorne*, ed. Randall Stewart (New York, 1941), p. 432.
4. *Herman Melville: Journal up the Straits, October 11, 1856–May 5, 1857* (New York, 1935), p. 92.

8: T. S. ELIOT AMONG THE INFIDELS

1. *The Idea of a Christian Society* (New York, 1940), p. 43.
2. *After Strange Gods* (New York, 1933), p. 41.
3. *American Literature and the American Language* (1953), appendix, p. 4.
4. Book review, *Criterion*, July, 1931.
5. "The *Pensées* of Pascal," *Essays Ancient & Modern* (London, 1936), p. 152.
6. Quoted in F. O. Matthiessen, *The Achievement of T. S. Eliot* (New York, 1935; revised 1958), p. 106.
7. *After Strange Gods*, p. 11.

8. "Religion and Literature," *Essays Ancient & Modern,* p. 100.
9. "Christianity and Communism," *Listener,* March 16, 1932.
10. Oscar Cargill, *Intellectual America* (New York, 1941), p. 268.
11. *Christian Register,* October 19, 1933.
12. "Catholicism and International Order," *Essays Ancient & Modern,* p. 118.
13. *Notes towards the Definition of Culture* (New York, 1949), p. 126.
14. *Listener,* March 30, 1932.
15. *"Pensées* of Pascal," p. 146.
16. "Religion and Literature," p. 108.
17. *To Criticize the Critic* (New York, 1965), p. 111.
18. *The Idea of a Christian Society* (New York, 1940), pp. 13–14.

INDEX